The importance of what we care about

The importance of what we care about

Philosophical essays

HARRY G. FRANKFURT

CAMBRIDGE
UNIVERSITY PRESS

CAMBRIDGE UNIVERSITY PRESS
Cambridge, New York, Melbourne, Madrid, Cape Town, Singapore,
São Paulo, Delhi, Dubai, Tokyo

Cambridge University Press
32 Avenue of the Americas, New York, NY 10013-2473, USA

www.cambridge.org
Information on this title: www.cambridge.org/9780521336116

First published 1998
15th printiing 2009

A catalog record for this publication is available from the British Library.

ISBN 978-0-521-33324-5 Hardback
ISBN 978-0-521-33611-6 Paperback

Contents

Preface

The essays collected here will have to speak for themselves, of course, and there is not much point in my undertaking now to summarize or to paraphrase what I think each of them says. It would, no doubt, be more appropriate for me to provide a succinct but comprehensive articulation of the general philosophical themes or ambitions (presuming that there are such) upon which the essays converge and by which, despite their having been conceived and composed separately over a period of twenty years, they are in some way unified. I am pretty sure that the convergence is there, given what I know of the personal preoccupations to which my philosophical work responds and of their ineluctability in my life. Unfortunately, however, this is not to say that I understand what I have been up to well enough to be able to give a perspicuous and straightforward account of it. Along with the fragmentary observations that I can offer here, then, I must express uneasy recognition that my prefatory thoughts are unlikely to be any sharper in their aim or firmer in their grasp than those in the essays themselves.

A number of the essays deal rather closely, in one way or another, with questions that pertain to the nature and conditions of moral responsibility. This emphasis may be a bit misleading. Morality, as I understand it, has to do particularly with how we ought to conduct ourselves in our relations with others. Some of the essays do touch upon that. But my philosophical attention has for the most part been guided less by an interest in questions about morality than by a concern with issues belonging more properly to metaphysics or to the philosophy of mind – for instance, how we are to conceptualize ourselves as persons, and what defines the identities we achieve.

I tend to think of these issues as depending heavily for their resolutions upon the provision of adequate accounts of freedom and of personal ideals and not especially upon the provision of a theory of obligations and rights. No doubt, moral philosophy does have a role to play in the attempt to understand such matters, but its role is in my opinion a more limited one than is often supposed. For the most part, the ideals to which a person freely devotes his life are not exclusively or even primarily moral ideals. I have made a few stabs, in the title essay of the collection

vii

and in some of those that were written subsequent to it, toward the development of a theory of ideals. This is, surprisingly and unfortunately, a rather neglected subject, about which I wish I had more to say.

So far as freedom is concerned, it is of course true that freedom is commonly understood to be a necessary condition of moral responsibility. Moreover, the nature of freedom is often investigated, as in several efforts of my own, in the light of that particular connection. On the other hand, I do not think that it is mainly for the sake of moral responsibility that we care as much as we do about being free. Nor am I convinced that it is possible to illuminate what it means for us to be free only if we begin by construing freedom specifically as a condition that being morally responsible requires.

The considerations my essays recommend and address in connection with these matters are primarily structural rather than historical. Understanding what a person is, either as an entity of a certain generic type or as an individual, differs from understanding how he came to be that way. Inquiries of both kinds are important and interesting, and in certain ways they are closely related. Each of us is indisputably a creature of history. Without the past, we should be nothing; and it is only by appreciating that he is through and through the product of historical contingencies – biological, social, and personal – that a person can recognize and make sense of his own nature. Still, it is not inquiry into what has produced us but the endeavor to identify and to make sense of what we have become that is the more authentically philosophical enterprise. This insistence on trying to see things clearly for what they are, rather than in terms of other things, is, incidentally, what most readily connects the themes of my essays on bullshit and on egalitarianism to the rest.

In general, the approach I take in trying to understand what we are is to consider the structure and constitution of the self. My emphasis in this is mainly on the will. Reason has usually been regarded as the most distinctive feature of human nature and the most sharply definitive. I believe, however, that volition pertains more closely than reason to our experience of ourselves and to the problems in our lives that concern us with the greatest urgency. Thus it is the more personal and the more intimate faculty, and it may even be the more comprehensive as well. The inner organization of the will and what that implies for us are, in any case, the subjects I have mainly attempted to explore.

In the seventeenth century, mechanism became established as the dominant worldview of our culture. It has since that time come to seem obvious that either references to final causes are entirely illicit or they are no more than convenient ways of speaking designed to avoid clumsier (albeit more strictly accurate) formulations in terms of efficient causation. In the eighteenth century, the notion of an efficient cause was itself eviscerated by a devastating critique of the idea of inherent power. These compelling philosophical developments have made it difficult to give a good account of the difference between being active and being passive. For if things are understood as having neither purposes nor powers, in what way is it possible to comprehend them as being active at all? Nonetheless, the role of the active-passive distinction in human life is pervasive and deep. The difference between passivity and activity is at the heart of the fact that we exist as selves and agents and not merely as locales in which certain events happen to occur.

While I have not undertaken to analyze this distinction as such, various modes of it figure in the several discussions of necessity and of the will that convey another thematic preoccupation of my essays. It seems to me that discovering what we are is fundamentally, though perhaps only among other things, a matter of discovering what we must be. And it is thereby, to the extent that a person is defined by his will, a matter of discovering what we cannot avoid willing or cannot bring ourselves to will. The notion that necessity does not inevitably undermine autonomy is familiar and widely accepted. But necessity is not only compatible with autonomy; it is in certain respects essential to it. There must be limits to our freedom if we are to have sufficient personal reality to exercise genuine autonomy at all. What has no boundaries has no shape. By the same token, a person can have no essential nature or identity as an agent unless he is bound with respect to that very feature of himself — namely, the will — whose shape most closely coincides with and reveals what he is. Several of my essays, including the final one, which has not previously been published, are concerned with attempts to shed some light on the creation of, and on the importance to us of, these necessities.

Sources

The final essay in this collection is published here for the first time. The others previously appeared elsewhere in the order in which they are presented here by chapter number. Minor stylistic changes have been made in some of the reprinted material.

1. *Journal of Philosophy*, LXVI, no. 23 (December 4, 1969).
2. *Journal of Philosophy*, LXVIII, no. 1 (January 14, 1971).
3. *Essays on Freedom of Action*, ed. Ted Honderich (London: Routledge & Kegan Paul, 1973).
4. *Proceedings of the Aristotelian Society*, supplementary volume (1975).
5. "Identification and Externality" was originally published in *The Identities of Persons*, edited by Amelie Rorty (University of California Press, 1977). Copyright © 1976 The Regents of the University of California. Reprinted by permission.
6. *American Philosophical Quarterly*, 15 (1978).
7. *Synthese*, vol. 53, no. 2 (1982), pp. 257–72. Copyright © 1982 by D. Reidel Publishing Company. Reprinted by permission.
8. *How Many Questions? Essays in Honor of Sidney Morgenbesser*, ed. L. S. Cauman, Isaac Levi, Charles D. Parsons, Robert Schwartz (Indianapolis: Hackett Publishing Co., 1983).
9. *Philosophy and Phenomenological Research*, XLV, no. 1 (1984).
10. *Raritan*, VI, no. 2 (1986).
11. *Ethics* vol. 98, no. 1 (October, 1987).
12. *Responsibility, Character, and the Emotions: New Essays in Moral Psychology*, ed. Ferdinand David Schoeman (New York: Cambridge University Press, 1987). Copyright © 1987 by Cambridge University Press. Reprinted by permission.

I

Alternate possibilities and moral responsibility

A dominant role in nearly all recent inquiries into the free-will problem has been played by a principle which I shall call "the principle of alternate possibilities." This principle states that a person is morally responsible for what he has done only if he could have done otherwise. Its exact meaning is a subject of controversy, particularly concerning whether someone who accepts it is thereby committed to believing that moral responsibility and determinism are incompatible. Practically no one, however, seems inclined to deny or even to question that the principle of alternate possibilities (construed in some way or other) is true. It has generally seemed so overwhelmingly plausible that some philosophers have even characterized it as an *a priori* truth. People whose accounts of free will or of moral responsibility are radically at odds evidently find in it a firm and convenient common ground upon which they can profitably take their opposing stands.

But the principle of alternate possibilities is false. A person may well be morally responsible for what he has done even though he could not have done otherwise. The principle's plausibility is an illusion, which can be made to vanish by bringing the relevant moral phenomena into sharper focus.

I

In seeking illustrations of the principle of alternate possibilities, it is most natural to think of situations in which the same circumstances both bring it about that a person does something and make it impossible for him to avoid doing it. These include, for example, situations in which a person is coerced into doing something, or in which he is impelled to act by a hypnotic suggestion, or in which some inner compulsion drives him to do what he does. In situations of these kinds there are circumstances that make it impossible for the person to do otherwise, and these very circumstances also serve to bring it about that he does whatever it is that he does.

However, there may be circumstances that constitute sufficient conditions for a certain action to be performed by someone and that therefore make it impossible for the person to do otherwise, but that do not actually impel the person to act or in any way produce his action. A person may do something in circumstances that leave him no alternative to doing it, without these circumstances actually moving him or leading him to do it – without them playing any role, indeed, in bringing it about that he does what he does.

An examination of situations characterized by circumstances of this sort casts doubt, I believe, on the relevance to questions of moral responsibility of the fact that a person who has done something could not have done otherwise. I propose to develop some examples of this kind in the context of a discussion of coercion and to suggest that our moral intuitions concerning these examples tend to disconfirm the principle of alternate possibilities. Then I will discuss the principle in more general terms, explain what I think is wrong with it, and describe briefly and without argument how it might appropriately be revised.

II

It is generally agreed that a person who has been coerced to do something did not do it freely and is not morally responsible for having done it. Now the doctrine that coercion and moral responsibility are mutually exclusive may appear to be no more than a somewhat particularized version of the principle of alternate possibilities. It is natural enough to say of a person who has been coerced to do something that he could not have done otherwise. And it may easily seem that being coerced deprives a person of freedom and of moral responsibility simply because it is a special case of being unable to do otherwise. The principle of alternate possibilities may in this way derive some credibility from its association with the very plausible proposition that moral responsibility is excluded by coercion.

It is not right, however, that it should do so. The fact that a person was coerced to act as he did may entail both that he could not have done otherwise and that he bears no moral responsibility for his action. But his lack of moral responsibility is not entailed by his having been unable to do otherwise. The doctrine that coercion excludes moral responsibility is not correctly understood, in other words, as a particularized version of the principle of alternate possibilities.

Let us suppose that someone is threatened convincingly with a penalty he finds unacceptable and that he then does what is required of him by the issuer of the threat. We can imagine details that would make it reasonable for us to think that the person was coerced to perform the action in question, that he could not have done otherwise, and that he bears no moral responsibility for having done what he did. But just what is it about situations of this kind that warrants the judgment that the threatened person is not morally responsible for his act?

This question may be approached by considering situations of the following kind. Jones decides for reasons of his own to do something, then someone threatens him with a very harsh penalty (so harsh that any reasonable person would submit to the threat) unless he does precisely that, and Jones does it. Will we hold Jones morally responsible for what he has done? I think this will depend on the roles we think were played, in leading him to act, by his original decision and by the threat.

One possibility is that Jones$_1$ is not a reasonable man: he is, rather, a man who does what he has once decided to do no matter what happens next and no matter what the cost. In that case, the threat actually exerted no effective force upon him. He acted without any regard to it, very much as if he were not aware that it had been made. If this is indeed the way it was, the situation did not involve coercion at all. The threat did not lead Jones$_1$ to do what he did. Nor was it in fact sufficient to have prevented him from doing otherwise: if his earlier decision had been to do something else, the threat would not have deterred him in the slightest. It seems evident that in these circumstances the fact that Jones$_1$ was threatened in no way reduces the moral responsibility he would otherwise bear for his act. This example, however, is not a counterexample either to the doctrine that coercion excuses or to the principle of alternate possibilities. For we have supposed that Jones$_1$ is a man upon whom the threat had no coercive effect and, hence, that it did not actually deprive him of alternatives to doing what he did.

Another possibility is that Jones$_2$ was stampeded by the threat. Given that threat, he would have performed that action regardless of what decision he had already made. The threat upset him so profoundly, moreover, that he completely forgot his own earlier decision and did what was demanded of him entirely because he was terrified of the penalty with which he was threatened. In this case, it is not relevant to his having performed the action that he had already decided on his own to perform it. When the chips were down he thought of nothing but the threat, and fear alone led him to act. The fact that at an earlier time Jones$_2$ had decided for his own reasons to act in just that way may be relevant to an evaluation of his character; he may bear full moral responsibility for having made *that* decision. But he can hardly be said to be morally responsible for his action. For he performed the action simply as a result of the coercion to which he was subjected. His earlier decision played no role in bringing it about that he did what he did, and it would therefore be gratuitous to assign it a role in the moral evaluation of his action.

Now consider a third possibility. Jones$_3$ was neither stampeded by the threat nor indifferent to it. The threat impressed him, as it would impress any reasonable man, and he would have submitted to it wholeheartedly if he had not already made a decision that coincided with the one demanded of him. In fact, however, he performed the action in question on the basis of the decision he had made before the threat was issued. When he acted, he was not actually motivated by the threat but solely by the considerations that had originally commended the action to him. It was not the threat that led him to act, though it would have done so if he had not already provided himself with a sufficient motive for performing the action in question.

No doubt it will be very difficult for anyone to know, in a case like this one, exactly what happened. Did Jones$_3$ perform the action because of the threat, or were his reasons for acting simply those which had already persuaded him to do so? Or did he act on the basis of two motives, each of which was sufficient for his action? It is not impossible, however, that the situation should be clearer than situations of this kind usually are. And suppose it is apparent to us that Jones$_3$ acted on the basis of his own decision and not because of the threat. Then I think we would be justified in regarding his moral responsibility for what he did as unaffected by the threat even though, since he would in any case have submitted to the threat, he could not have avoided doing what he did. It would be entirely reasonable for us to make the same judgment concerning his moral responsibility that we would have made if we had not known of the threat. For the threat did not in fact influence his performance of the action. He did what he did just as if the threat had not been made at all.

III

The case of Jones$_3$ may appear at first glance to combine coercion and moral responsibility, and thus to provide a counterexample to the doctrine that coercion excuses. It is not really so certain that it does so, however, because it is unclear whether the example constitutes a genuine instance of coercion. Can we say of Jones$_3$ that he was coerced to do something, when he had already decided on his own to do it and when he did it entirely on the basis of that decision? Or would it be more correct to say that Jones$_3$ was not coerced to do what he did, even though he himself recognized that there was an irresistible force at work in virtue of which he had to do it? My own linguistic intuitions lead me toward the second alternative, but they are somewhat equivocal. Perhaps we can say either of these things, or perhaps we must add a qualifying explanation to whichever of them we say.

This murkiness, however, does not interfere with our drawing an important moral from an examination of the example. Suppose we decide to say that Jones₃ was *not* coerced. Our basis for saying this will clearly be that it is incorrect to regard a man as being coerced to do something unless he does it *because* of the coercive force exerted against him. The fact that an irresistible threat is made will not, then, entail that the person who receives it is coerced to do what he does. It will also be necessary that the threat is what actually accounts for his doing it. On the other hand, suppose we decide to say that Jones₃ *was* coerced. Then we will be bound to admit that being coerced does not exclude being morally responsible. And we will also surely be led to the view that coercion affects a person's moral responsibility only when the person acts as he does because he is coerced to do so – i.e., when the fact that he is coerced is what accounts for his action.

Whichever we decide to say, then, we will recognize that the doctrine that coercion excludes moral responsibility is not a particularized version of the principle of alternate possibilities. Situations in which a person who does something cannot do otherwise because he is subject to coercive power are either not instances of coercion at all, or they are situations in which the person may still be morally responsible for what he does if it is not because of the coercion that he does it. When we excuse a person who has been coerced, we do not excuse him because he was unable to do otherwise. Even though a person is subject to a coercive force that precludes his performing any action but one, he may nonetheless bear full moral responsibility for performing that action.

IV

To the extent that the principle of alternate possibilities derives its plausibility from association with the doctrine that coercion excludes moral responsibility, a clear understanding of the latter diminishes the appeal of the former. Indeed the case of Jones₃ may appear to do more than illuminate the relationship between the two doctrines. It may well seem to provide a decisive counterexample to the principle of alternate possibilities and thus to show that this principle is false. For the irresistibility of the threat to which Jones₃ is subjected might well be taken to mean that he cannot but perform the action he performs. And yet the threat, since Jones₃ performs the action without regard to it, does not reduce his moral responsibility for what he does.

The following objection will doubtless be raised against the suggestion that the case of Jones$_3$ is a counterexample to the principle of alternate possibilities. There is perhaps a sense in which Jones$_3$ cannot do otherwise than perform the action he performs, since he is a reasonable man and the threat he encounters is sufficient to move any reasonable man. But it is not this sense that is germane to the principle of alternate possibilities. His knowledge that he stands to suffer an intolerably harsh penalty does not mean that Jones$_3$, strictly speaking, *cannot* perform any action but the one he does perform. After all it is still open to him, and this is crucial, to defy the threat if he wishes to do so and to accept the penalty his action would bring down upon him. In the sense in which the principle of alternate possibilities employs the concept of "could have done otherwise," Jones$_3$'s inability to resist the threat does not mean that he cannot do otherwise than perform the action he performs. Hence the case of Jones$_3$ does not constitute an instance contrary to the principle.

I do not propose to consider in what sense the concept of "could have done otherwise" figures in the principle of alternate possibilities, nor will I attempt to measure the force of the objection I have just described.[1] For I believe that whatever force this objection may be thought to have can be deflected by altering the example in the following way.[2] Suppose someone – Black, let us say – wants Jones$_4$ to perform a certain action. Black is prepared to go to considerable lengths to get his way, but he prefers to avoid showing his hand unnecessarily. So he waits until Jones$_4$ is about to make up his mind what to do, and he does nothing unless it is clear to him (Black is an excellent judge of such things) that Jones$_4$ is going to decide to do something *other* than what he wants him to do. If it does become clear that Jones$_4$ is going to decide to do something else, Black takes effective steps to ensure that Jones$_4$ decides to do, and that he does do, what he wants him to do.[3] Whatever Jones$_4$'s initial preferences and inclinations, then, Black will have his way.

[1] The two main concepts employed in the principle of alternate possibilities are "morally responsible" and "could have done otherwise." To discuss the principle without analyzing either of these concepts may well seem like an attempt at piracy. The reader should take notice that my Jolly Roger is now unfurled.

[2] After thinking up the example that I am about to develop I learned that Robert Nozick, in lectures given several years ago, had formulated an example of the same general type and had proposed it as a counterexample to the principle of alternate possibilities.

[3] The assumption that Black can predict what Jones$_4$ will decide to do does not beg the question of determinism. We can imagine that Jones$_4$ has often confronted the alternatives – A and B – that he now confronts, and that his face has invariably twitched when he was about to decide to do A and never when he was about to decide to do B. Knowing this, and observing the twitch, Black would have a basis for prediction. This does, to be sure, suppose that there is some sort of causal relation between Jones$_4$'s state at the time of the twitch and his subsequent states. But any plausible view of

What steps will Black take, if he believes he must take steps, in order to ensure that Jones$_4$ decides and acts as he wishes? Anyone with a theory concerning what "could have done otherwise" means may answer this question for himself by describing whatever measures he would regard as sufficient to guarantee that, in the relevant sense, Jones$_4$ cannot do otherwise. Let Black pronounce a terrible threat, and in this way both force Jones$_4$ to perform the desired action and prevent him from performing a forbidden one. Let Black give Jones$_4$ a potion, or put him under hypnosis, and in some such way as these generate in Jones$_4$ an irresistible inner compulsion to perform the act Black wants performed and to avoid others. Or let Black manipulate the minute processes of Jones$_4$'s brain and nervous system in some more direct way, so that causal forces running in and out of his synapses and along the poor man's nerves determine that he chooses to act and that he does act in the one way and not in any other. Given any conditions under which it will be maintained that Jones$_4$ cannot do otherwise, in other words, let Black bring it about that those conditions prevail. The structure of the example is flexible enough, I think, to find a way around any charge of irrelevance by accommodating the doctrine on which the charge is based.[4]

Now suppose that Black never has to show his hand because Jones$_4$, for reasons of his own, decides to perform and does perform the very action Black wants him to perform. In that case, it seems clear, Jones$_4$ will bear precisely the same moral responsibility for what he does as he would have borne if Black had not been ready to take steps to ensure that he do it. It would be quite unreasonable to excuse Jones$_4$ for his action, or to withhold the praise to which it would normally entitle him, on the basis of the fact that he could not have done otherwise. This fact played no role at all in leading him to act as he did. He would have acted the same even if it had not been a fact. Indeed, everything happened just as it would have happened without Black's presence in the situation and without his readiness to intrude into it.

In this example there are sufficient conditions for Jones$_4$'s performing

decision or of action will allow that reaching a decision and performing an action both involve earlier and later phases, with causal relations between them, and such that the earlier phases are not themselves part of the decision or of the action. The example does not require that these earlier phases be deterministically related to still earlier events.

4 The example is also flexible enough to allow for the elimination of Black altogether. Anyone who thinks that the effectiveness of the example is undermined by its reliance on a human manipulator, who imposes his will on Jones$_4$, can substitute for Black a machine programmed to do what Black does. If this is still not good enough, forget both Black and the machine and suppose that their role is played by natural forces involving no will or design at all.

the action in question. What action he performs is not up to him. Of course it is in a way up to him whether he acts on his own or as a result of Black's intervention. That depends upon what action he himself is inclined to perform. But whether he finally acts on his own or as a result of Black's intervention, he performs the same action. He has no alternative but to do what Black wants him to do. If he does it on his own, however, his moral responsibility for doing it is not affected by the fact that Black was lurking in the background with sinister intent, since this intent never comes into play.

V

The fact that a person could not have avoided doing something is a sufficient condition of his having done it. But, as some of my examples show, this fact may play no role whatever in the explanation of why he did it. It may not figure at all among the circumstances that actually brought it about that he did what he did, so that his action is to be accounted for on another basis entirely. Even though the person was unable to do otherwise, that is to say, it may not be the case that he acted as he did *because* he could not have done otherwise. Now if someone had no alternative to performing a certain action but did not perform it because he was unable to do otherwise, then he would have performed exactly the same action even if he *could* have done otherwise. The circumstances that made it impossible for him to do otherwise could have been subtracted from the situation without affecting what happened or why it happened in any way. Whatever it was that actually led the person to do what he did, or that made him do it, would have led him to do it or made him do it even if it had been possible for him to do something else instead.

Thus it would have made no difference, so far as concerns his action or how he came to perform it, if the circumstances that made it impossible for him to avoid performing it had not prevailed. The fact that he could not have done otherwise clearly provides no basis for supposing that he *might* have done otherwise if he had been able to do so. When a fact is in this way irrelevant to the problem of accounting for a person's action it seems quite gratuitous to assign it any weight in the assessment of his moral responsibility. Why should the fact be considered in reaching a moral judgment concerning the person when it does not help in any way to understand either what made him act as he did or what, in other circumstances, he might have done?

This, then, is why the principle of alternate possibilities is mistaken. It asserts that a person bears no moral responsibility — that is, he is to be excused – for having performed an action, if there were circumstances that made it impossible for him to avoid performing it. But there may be circumstances that make it impossible for a person to avoid performing some action without those circumstances in any way bringing it about that he performs that action. It would surely be no good for the person to refer to circumstances of this sort in an effort to absolve himself of moral responsibility for performing the action in question. For those circumstances, by hypothesis, actually had nothing to do with his having done what he did. He would have done precisely the same thing, and he would have been led or made in precisely the same way to do it, even if they had not prevailed.

We often do, to be sure, excuse people for what they have done when they tell us (and we believe them) that they could not have done otherwise. But this is because we assume that what they tell us serves to explain why they did what they did. We take it for granted that they are not being disingenuous, as a person would be who cited as an excuse the fact that he could not have avoided doing what he did but who knew full well that it was not at all because of this that he did it.

What I have said may suggest that the principle of alternate possibilities should be revised so as to assert that a person is not morally responsible for what he has done if he did it because he could not have done otherwise. It may be noted that this revision of the principle does not seriously affect the arguments of those who have relied on the original principle in their efforts to maintain that moral responsibility and determinism are incompatible. For if it was causally determined that a person perform a certain action, then it will be true that the person performed it because of those causal determinants. And if the fact that it was causally determined that a person perform a certain action means that the person could not have done otherwise, as philosophers who argue for the incompatibility thesis characteristically suppose, then the fact that it was causally determined that a person perform a certain action will mean that the person performed it because he could not have done otherwise. The revised principle of alternate possibilities will entail, on this assumption concerning the meaning of "could have done otherwise," that a person is not morally responsible for what he has done if it was causally determined that he do it. I do not believe, however, that this revision of the principle is acceptable.

Suppose a person tells us that he did what he did because he was unable to do otherwise; or suppose he makes the similar statement that he did what he did because he had to do it. We do often accept statements like these (if we believe them) as valid excuses, and such statements may well seem at first glance to invoke the revised principle of alternate possibilities. But I think that when we accept such statements as valid excuses it is because we assume that we are being told more than the statements strictly and literally convey. We understand the person who offers the excuse to mean that he did what he did *only because* he was unable to do otherwise, or *only because* he had to do it. And we understand him to mean, more particularly, that when he did what he did it was not because that was what he really wanted to do. The principle of alternate possibilities should thus be replaced, in my opinion, by the following principle: a person is not morally responsible for what he has done if he did it only because he could not have done otherwise. This principle does not appear to conflict with the view that moral responsibility is compatible with determinism.

The following may all be true: there were circumstances that made it impossible for a person to avoid doing something; these circumstances actually played a role in bringing it about that he did it, so that it is correct to say that he did it because he could not have done otherwise; the person really wanted to do what he did; he did it because it was what he really wanted to do, so that it is not correct to say that he did what he did only because he could not have done otherwise. Under these conditions, the person may well be morally responsible for what he has done. On the other hand, he will not be morally responsible for what he has done if he did it only because he could not have done otherwise, even if what he did was something he really wanted to do.

2

Freedom of the will and the concept of a person

What philosophers have lately come to accept as analysis of the concept of a person is not actually analysis of *that* concept at all. Strawson, whose usage represents the current standard, identifies the concept of a person as "the concept of a type of entity such that *both* predicates ascribing states of consciousness *and* predicates ascribing corporeal characteristics . . . are equally applicable to a single individual of that single type."[1] But there are many entities besides persons that have both mental and physical properties. As it happens – though it seems extraordinary that this should be so – there is no common English word for the type of entity Strawson has in mind, a type that includes not only human beings but animals of various lesser species as well. Still, this hardly justifies the misappropriation of a valuable philosophical term.

Whether the members of some animal species are persons is surely not to be settled merely by determining whether it is correct to apply to them, in addition to predicates ascribing corporeal characteristics, predicates that ascribe states of consciousness. It does violence to our language to endorse the application of the term "person" to those numerous creatures which do have both psychological and material properties but which are manifestly not persons in any normal sense of the word. This misuse of language is doubtless innocent of any theoretical error. But although the offense is "merely verbal," it does significant harm. For it gratuitously diminishes our philosophical vocabulary, and it increases the likelihood that we will overlook the important area of inquiry with which the term "person" is most naturally associated. It might have been expected that no problem would be of more central and persistent concern to philosophers than that of understanding what we ourselves essentially are. Yet this problem is so generally neglected that it has been possible

---

1 P. F. Strawson, *Individuals* (London: Methuen, 1959), pp. 101–102. Ayer's usage of "person" is similar: "it is characteristic of persons in this sense that besides having various physical properties . . . they are also credited with various forms of consciousness" (A. J. Ayer, *The Concept of a Person* [New York: St. Martin's, 1963], p. 82). What concerns Strawson and Ayer is the problem of understanding the relation between mind and body, rather than the quite different problem of understanding what it is to be a creature that not only has a mind and a body but is also a person.

to make off with its very name almost without being noticed and, evidently, without evoking any widespread feeling of loss.

There is a sense in which the word "person" is merely the singular form of "people" and in which both terms connote no more than membership in a certain biological species. In those senses of the word which are of greater philosophical interest, however, the criteria for being a person do not serve primarily to distinguish the members of our own species from the members of other species. Rather, they are designed to capture those attributes which are the subject of our most humane concern with ourselves and the source of what we regard as most important and most problematical in our lives. Now these attributes would be of equal significance to us even if they were not in fact peculiar and common to the members of our own species. What interests us most in the human condition would not interest us less if it were also a feature of the condition of other creatures as well.

Our concept of ourselves as persons is not to be understood, therefore, as a concept of attributes that are necessarily species-specific. It is conceptually possible that members of novel or even of familiar non-human species should be persons; and it is also conceptually possible that some members of the human species are not persons. We do in fact assume, on the other hand, that no member of another species is a person. Accordingly, there is a presumption that what is essential to persons is a set of characteristics that we generally suppose — whether rightly or wrongly — to be uniquely human.

It is my view that one essential difference between persons and other creatures is to be found in the structure of a person's will. Human beings are not alone in having desires and motives, or in making choices. They share these things with the members of certain other species, some of whom even appear to engage in deliberation and to make decisions based upon prior thought. It seems to be peculiarly characteristic of humans, however, that they are able to form what I shall call "second-order desires" or "desires of the second order."

Besides wanting and choosing and being moved *to do* this or that, men may also want to have (or not to have) certain desires and motives. They are capable of wanting to be different, in their preferences and purposes, from what they are. Many animals appear to have the capacity for what I shall call "first-order desires" or "desires of the first order," which are simply desires to do or not to do one thing or another. No animal other than man, however, appears to have the capacity for reflective self-evaluation that is manifested in the formation of second-order desires.[2]

---

2   For the sake of simplicity, I shall deal only with what someone wants or desires, neglecting related phenomena such as choices and decisions. I propose to use the verbs

I

The concept designated by the verb "to want" is extraordinarily elusive. A statement of the form "*R* wants to *X*" – taken by itself, apart from a context that serves to amplify or to specify its meaning – conveys remarkably little information. Such a statement may be consistent, for example, with each of the following statements: (a) the prospect of doing *X* elicits no sensation or introspectible emotional response in *A;* (b) *A* is unaware that he wants to *X;* (c) *A* believes that he does not want to *X;* (d) *A* wants to refrain from *X*-ing; (e) *A* wants to *Y* and believes that it is impossible for him both to *Y* and to *X;* (f) *A* does not "really" want to *X;* (g) *A* would rather die than *X;* and so on. It is therefore hardly sufficient to formulate the distinction between first-order and second-order desires, as I have done, by suggesting merely that someone has a first-order desire when he wants to do or not to do such-and-such, and that he has a second-order desire when he wants to have or not to have a certain desire of the first order.

As I shall understand them, statements of the form "*A* wants to *X*" cover a rather broad range of possibilities.[3] They may be true even when statements like (a) through (g) are true: when *A* is unaware of any feelings concerning *X*-ing, when he is unaware that he wants to *X*, when he deceives himself about what he wants and believes falsely that he does not want to *X*, when he also has other desires that conflict with his desire to *X*, or when he is ambivalent. The desires in question may be conscious or unconscious, they need not be univocal, and *A* may be mistaken about them. There is a further source of uncertainty with regard to statements that identify someone's desires, however, and here it is important for my purposes to be less permissive.

Consider first those statements of the form "*A* wants to *X*" which identify first-order desires – that is, statements in which the term "to *X*" refers to an action. A statement of this kind does not, by itself, indicate the relative strength of *A*'s desire to *X*. It does not make it clear whether this desire is at all likely to play a decisive role in what *A* actually does or

"to want" and "to desire" interchangeably, although they are by no means perfect synonyms. My motive in forsaking the established nuances of these words arises from the fact that the verb "to want," which suits my purposes better so far as its meaning is concerned, does not lend itself so readily to the formation of nouns as does the verb "to desire." It is perhaps acceptable, albeit graceless, to speak in the plural of someone's "wants." But to speak in the singular of someone's "want" would be an abomination.

3 What I say in this paragraph applies not only to cases in which "to *X*" refers to a possible action or inaction. It also applies to cases in which "to *X*" refers to a first-order desire and in which the statement that "*A* wants to *X*" is therefore a shortened version of a statement – "*A* wants to want to *X*" – that identifies a desire of the second order.

tries to do. For it may correctly be said that A wants to X even when his desire to X is only one among his desires and when it is far from being paramount among them. Thus, it may be true that A wants to X when he strongly prefers to do something else instead; and it may be true that he wants to X despite the fact that, when he acts, it is not the desire to X that motivates him to do what he does. On the other hand, someone who states that A wants to X may mean to convey that it is this desire that is motivating or moving A to do what he is actually doing or that A will in fact be moved by this desire (unless he changes his mind) when he acts.

It is only when it is used in the second of these ways that, given the special usage of "will" that I propose to adopt, the statement identifies A's will. To identify an agent's will is either to identify the desire (or desires) by which he is motivated in some action he performs or to identify the desire (or desires) by which he will or would be motivated when or if he acts. An agent's will, then, is identical with one or more of his first-order desires. But the notion of the will, as I am employing it, is not coextensive with the notion of first-order desires. It is not the notion of something that merely inclines an agent in some degree to act in a certain way. Rather, it is the notion of an *effective* desire – one that moves (or will or would move) a person all the way to action. Thus the notion of the will is not coextensive with the notion of what an agent intends to do. For even though someone may have a settled intention to do X, he may nonetheless do something else instead of doing X because, despite his intention, his desire to do X proves to be weaker or less effective than some conflicting desire.

Now consider those statements of the form "A wants to X" which identify second-order desires – that is, statements in which the term "to X" refers to a desire of the first order. There are also two kinds of situation in which it may be true that A wants to want to X. In the first place, it might be true of A that he wants to have a desire to X despite the fact that he has a univocal desire, altogether free of conflict and ambivalence, to refrain from X-ing. Someone might want to have a certain desire, in other words, but univocally want that desire to be unsatisfied.

Suppose that a physician engaged in psychotherapy with narcotics addicts believes that his ability to help his patients would be enhanced if he understood better what it is like for them to desire the drug to which they are addicted. Suppose that he is led in this way to want to have a desire for the drug. If it is a genuine desire that he wants, then what he wants is not merely to feel the sensations that addicts characteristically feel when they are gripped by their desires for the drug. What the physician wants, insofar as he wants to have a desire, is to be inclined or moved to some extent to take the drug.

14

It is entirely possible, however, that, although he wants to be moved by a desire to take the drug, he does not want this desire to be effective. He may not want it to move him all the way to action. He need not be interested in finding out what it is like to take the drug. And insofar as he now wants only to *want* to take it, and not to *take* it, there is nothing in what he now wants that would be satisfied by the drug itself. He may now have, in fact, an altogether univocal desire *not* to take the drug; and he may prudently arrange to make it impossible for him to satisfy the desire he would have if his desire to want the drug should in time be satisfied.

It would thus be incorrect to infer, from the fact that the physician now wants to desire to take the drug, that he already does desire to take it. His second-order desire to be moved to take the drug does not entail that he has a first-order desire to take it. If the drug were now to be administered to him, this might satisfy no desire that is implicit in his desire to want to take it. While he wants to want to take the drug, he may have *no* desire to take it; it may be that *all* he wants is to taste the desire for it. That is, his desire to have a certain desire that he does not have may not be a desire that his will should be at all different than it is.

Someone who wants only in this truncated way to want to X stands at the margin of preciosity, and the fact that he wants to want to X is not pertinent to the identification of his will. There is, however, a second kind of situation that may be described by "A wants to want to X"; and when the statement is used to describe a situation of this second kind, then it does pertain to what A wants his will to be. In such cases the statement means that A wants the desire to X to be the desire that moves him effectively to act. It is not merely that he wants the desire to X to be among the desires by which, to one degree or another, he is moved or inclined to act. He wants this desire to be effective – that is, to provide the motive in what he actually does. Now when the statement that A wants to want to X is used in this way, it does entail that A already has a desire to X. It could not be true both that A wants the desire to X to move him into action and that he does not want to X. It is only if he does want to X that he can coherently want the desire to X not merely to be one of his desires but, more decisively, to be his will.[4]

4   It is not so clear that the entailment relation described here holds in certain kinds of
    cases, which I think may fairly be regarded as nonstandard, where the essential dif-
    ference between the standard and the nonstandard cases lies in the kind of description
    by which the first-order desire in question is identified. Thus, suppose that A admires B
    so fulsomely that, even though he does not know what B wants to do, he wants to be
    effectively moved by whatever desire effectively moves B; without knowing what B's
    will is, in other words, A wants his own will to be the same. It certainly does not follow
    that A already has, among his desires, a desire like the one that constitutes B's will. I

Suppose a man wants to be motivated in what he does by the desire to concentrate on his work. It is necessarily true, if this supposition is correct, that he already wants to concentrate on his work. This desire is now among his desires. But the question of whether or not his second-order desire is fulfilled does not turn merely on whether the desire he wants is one of his desires. It turns on whether this desire is, as he wants it to be, his effective desire or will. If, when the chips are down, it is his desire to concentrate on his work that moves him to do what he does, then what he wants at that time is indeed (in the relevant sense) what he wants to want. If it is some other desire that actually moves him when he acts, on the other hand, then what he wants at that time is not (in the relevant sense) what he wants to want. This will be so despite the fact that the desire to concentrate on his work continues to be among his desires.

II

Someone has a desire of the second order either when he wants simply to have a certain desire or when he wants a certain desire to be his will. In situations of the latter kind, I shall call his second-order desires "second-order volitions" or "volitions of the second order." Now it is having second-order volitions, and not having second-order desires generally, that I regard as essential to being a person. It is logically possible, however unlikely, that there should be an agent with second-order desires but with no volitions of the second order. Such a creature, in my view, would not be a person. I shall use the term "wanton" to refer to agents who have first-order desires but who are not persons because, whether or not they have desires of the second order, they have no second-order volitions.[5]

The essential characteristic of a wanton is that he does not care about his will. His desires move him to do certain things, without its being true of him either that he wants to be moved by those desires or that he prefers to be moved by other desires. The class of wantons includes all nonhuman animals that have desires and all very young children. Perhaps

shall not pursue here the questions of whether there are genuine counterexamples to the claim made in the text or of how, if there are, that claim should be altered.

5   Creatures with second-order desires but no second-order volitions differ significantly from brute animals, and, for some purposes, it would be desirable to regard them as persons. My usage, which withholds the designation "person" from them, is thus somewhat arbitrary. I adopt it largely because it facilitates the formulation of some of the points I wish to make. Hereafter, whenever I consider statements of the form "A wants to want to X," I shall have in mind statements identifying second-order volitions and not statements identifying second-order desires that are not second-order volitions.

it also includes some adult human beings as well. In any case, adult humans may be more or less wanton; they may act wantonly, in response to first-order desires concerning which they have no volitions of the second order, more or less frequently.

The fact that a wanton has no second-order volitions does not mean that each of his first-order desires is translated heedlessly and at once into action. He may have no opportunity to act in accordance with some of his desires. Moreover, the translation of his desires into action may be delayed or precluded either by conflicting desires of the first order or by the intervention of deliberation. For a wanton may possess and employ rational faculties of a high order. Nothing in the concept of a wanton implies that he cannot reason or that he cannot deliberate concerning how to do what he wants to do. What distinguishes the rational wanton from other rational agents is that he is not concerned with the desirability of his desires themselves. He ignores the question of what his will is to be. Not only does he pursue whatever course of action he is most strongly inclined to pursue, but he does not care which of his inclinations is the strongest.

Thus a rational creature, who reflects upon the suitability to his desires of one course of action or another, may nonetheless be a wanton. In maintaining that the essence of being a person lies not in reason but in will, I am far from suggesting that a creature without reason may be a person. For it is only in virtue of his rational capacities that a person is capable of becoming critically aware of his own will and of forming volitions of the second order. The structure of a person's will presupposes, accordingly, that he is a rational being.

The distinction between a person and a wanton may be illustrated by the difference between two narcotics addicts. Let us suppose that the physiological condition accounting for the addiction is the same in both men, and that both succumb inevitably to their periodic desires for the drug to which they are addicted. One of the addicts hates his addiction and always struggles desperately, although to no avail, against its thrust. He tries everything that he thinks might enable him to overcome his desires for the drug. But these desires are too powerful for him to withstand, and invariably, in the end, they conquer him. He is an unwilling addict, helplessly violated by his own desires.

The unwilling addict has conflicting first-order desires: he wants to take the drug, and he also wants to refrain from taking it. In addition to these first-order desires, however, he has a volition of the second order. He is not a neutral with regard to the conflict between his desire to take the drug and his desire to refrain from taking it. It is the latter desire, and not the former, that he wants to constitute his will; it is the latter desire, rather than the former, that he wants to be effective and to provide the purpose that he will seek to realize in what he actually does.

The other addict is a wanton. His actions reflect the economy of his first-order desires, without his being concerned whether the desires that move him to act are desires by which he wants to be moved to act. If he encounters problems in obtaining the drug or in administering it to himself, his responses to his urges to take it may involve deliberation. But it never occurs to him to consider whether he wants the relations among his desires to result in his having the will he has. The wanton addict may be an animal, and thus incapable of being concerned about his will. In any event he is, in respect of his wanton lack of concern, no different from an animal.

The second of these addicts may suffer a first-order conflict similar to the first-order conflict suffered by the first. Whether he is human or not, the wanton may (perhaps due to conditioning) both want to take the drug and want to refrain from taking it. Unlike the unwilling addict, however, he does not prefer that one of his conflicting desires should be paramount over the other; he does not prefer that one first-order desire rather than the other should constitute his will. It would be misleading to say that he is neutral as to the conflict between his desires, since this would suggest that he regards them as equally acceptable. Since he has no identity apart from his first-order desires, it is true neither that he prefers one to the other nor that he prefers not to take sides.

It makes a difference to the unwilling addict, who is a person, which of his conflicting first-order desires wins out. Both desires are his, to be sure; and whether he finally takes the drug or finally succeeds in refraining from taking it, he acts to satisfy what is in a literal sense his own desire. In either case he does something he himself wants to do, and he does it not because of some external influence whose aim happens to coincide with his own but because of his desire to do it. The unwilling addict identifies himself, however, through the formation of a second-order volition, with one rather than with the other of his conflicting first-order desires. He makes one of them more truly his own and, in so doing, he withdraws himself from the other. It is in virtue of this identification and withdrawal, accomplished through the formation of a second-order volition, that the unwilling addict may meaningfully make the analytically puzzling statements that the force moving him to take the drug is a force other than his own, and that it is not of his own free will but rather against his will that this force moves him to take it.

The wanton addict cannot or does not care which of his conflicting first-order desires wins out. His lack of concern is not due to his inability to find a convincing basis for preference. It is due either to his lack of the capacity for reflection or to his mindless indifference to the enterprise of evaluating his own desires and motives.[6] There is only one issue in the struggle to which his first-order conflict may lead: whether the one or the other of his conflicting desires is the stronger. Since he is moved by both desires, he will not be altogether satisfied by what he does no matter which of them is effective. But it makes no difference *to him* whether his craving or his aversion gets the upper hand. He has no stake in the conflict between them and so, unlike the unwilling addict, he can neither win nor lose the struggle in which he is engaged. When a *person* acts, the desire by which he is moved is either the will he wants or a will he wants to be without. When a *wanton* acts, it is neither.

III

There is a very close relationship between the capacity for forming second-order volitions and another capacity that is essential to persons – one that has often been considered a distinguishing mark of the human condition. It is only because a person has volitions of the second order that he is capable both of enjoying and of lacking freedom of the will. The concept of a person is not only, then, the concept of a type of entity that has both first-order desires and volitions of the second order. It can also be construed as the concept of a type of entity for whom the freedom of its will may be a problem. This concept excludes all wantons, both infrahuman and human, since they fail to satisfy an essential condition for the enjoyment of freedom of the will. And it excludes those suprahuman beings, if any, whose wills are necessarily free.

Just what kind of freedom is the freedom of the will? This question calls for an identification of the special area of human experience to which the concept of freedom of the will, as distinct from the concepts of other sorts of freedom, is particularly germane. In dealing with it, my aim will be primarily to locate the problem with which a person is most immediately concerned when he is concerned with the freedom of his will.

According to one familiar philosophical tradition, being free is fundamentally a matter of doing what one wants to do. Now the notion of an

6 In speaking of the evaluation of his own desires and motives as being characteristic of a person, I do not mean to suggest that a person's second-order volitions necessarily manifest a *moral* stance on his part toward his first-order desires. It may not be from the point of view of morality that the person evaluates his first-order desires. Moreover, a person may be capricious and irresponsible in forming his second-order volitions and give no serious consideration to what is at stake. Second-order volitions express evaluations only in the sense that they are preferences. There is no essential restriction on the kind of basis, if any, upon which they are formed.

agent who does what he wants to do is by no means an altogether clear one: both the doing and the wanting, and the appropriate relation between them as well, require elucidation. But although its focus needs to be sharpened and its formulation refined, I believe that this notion does capture at least part of what is implicit in the idea of an agent who *acts* freely. It misses entirely, however, the peculiar content of the quite different idea of an agent whose *will* is free.

We do not suppose that animals enjoy freedom of the will, although we recognize that an animal may be free to run in whatever direction it wants. Thus, having the freedom to do what one wants to do is not a sufficient condition of having a free will. It is not a necessary condition either. For to deprive someone of his freedom of action is not necessarily to undermine the freedom of his will. When an agent is aware that there are certain things he is not free to do, this doubtless affects his desires and limits the range of choices he can make. But suppose that someone, without being aware of it, has in fact lost or been deprived of his freedom of action. Even though he is no longer free to do what he wants to do, his will may remain as free as it was before. Despite the fact that he is not free to translate his desires into actions or to act according to the determinations of his will, he may still form those desires and make those determinations as freely as if his freedom of action had not been impaired.

When we ask whether a person's will is free we are not asking whether he is in a position to translate his first-order desires into actions. That is the question of whether he is free to do as he pleases. The question of the freedom of his will does not concern the relation between what he does and what he wants to do. Rather, it concerns his desires themselves. But what question about them is it?

It seems to me both natural and useful to construe the question of whether a person's will is free in close analogy to the question of whether an agent enjoys freedom of action. Now freedom of action is (roughly, at least) the freedom to do what one wants to do. Analogously, then, the statement that a person enjoys freedom of the will means (also roughly) that he is free to want what he wants to want. More precisely, it means that he is free to will what he wants to will, or to have the will he wants. Just as the question about the freedom of an agent's action has to do with whether it is the action he wants to perform, so the question about the freedom of his will has to do with whether it is the will he wants to have.

It is in securing the conformity of his will to his second-order volitions, then, that a person exercises freedom of the will. And it is in the discrepancy between his will and his second-order volitions, or in his awareness that their coincidence is not his own doing but only a happy chance, that a person who does not have this freedom feels its lack. The unwilling addict's will is not free. This is shown by the fact that it is not the will he wants. It is also true, though in a different way, that the will of the wanton addict is not free. The wanton addict neither has the will he wants nor has a will that differs from the will he wants. Since he has no volitions of the second order, the freedom of his will cannot be a problem for him. He lacks it, so to speak, by default.

People are generally far more complicated than my sketchy account of the structure of a person's will may suggest. There is as much opportunity for ambivalence, conflict, and self-deception with regard to desires of the second order, for example, as there is with regard to first-order desires. If there is an unresolved conflict among someone's second-order desires, then he is in danger of having no second-order volition; for unless this conflict is resolved, he has no preference concerning which of his first-order desires is to be his will. This condition, if it is so severe that it prevents him from identifying himself in a sufficiently decisive way with *any* of his conflicting first-order desires, destroys him as a person. For it either tends to paralyze his will and to keep him from acting at all, or it tends to remove him from his will so that his will operates without his participation. In both cases he becomes, like the unwilling addict though in a different way, a helpless bystander to the forces that move him.

Another complexity is that a person may have, especially if his second-order desires are in conflict, desires and volitions of a higher order than the second. There is no theoretical limit to the length of the series of desires of higher and higher orders; nothing except common sense and, perhaps, a saving fatigue prevents an individual from obsessively refusing to identify himself with any of his desires until he forms a desire of the next higher order. The tendency to generate such a series of acts of forming desires, which would be a case of humanization run wild, also leads toward the destruction of a person.

It is possible, however, to terminate such a series of acts without cutting it off arbitrarily. When a person identifies himself *decisively* with one of his first-order desires, this commitment "resounds" throughout the potentially endless array of higher orders. Consider a person who, without reservation or conflict, wants to be motivated by the desire to concentrate on his work. The fact that his second-order volition to be moved by this desire is a decisive one means that there is no room for questions concerning the pertinence of desires or volitions of higher orders. Suppose the person is asked whether he wants to want to want to concentrate on his work. He can properly insist that this question concerning a third-order desire does not arise. It would be a mistake to claim that, because he has not considered whether he wants the second-order volition he has formed, he is indifferent to the question of whether it is with this volition or with some other that he wants his will to accord. The decisiveness of the commitment he has made means that he has decided that no further question about his second-order volition, at any higher order, remains to be asked. It is relatively unimportant whether we explain this by saying that this commitment implicitly generates an endless series of confirming desires of higher orders, or by saying that the commitment is tantamount to a dissolution of the pointedness of all questions concerning higher orders of desire.

Examples such as the one concerning the unwilling addict may suggest that volitions of the second order, or of higher orders, must be formed deliberately and that a person characteristically struggles to ensure that they are satisfied. But the conformity of a person's will to his higher-order volitions may be far more thoughtless and spontaneous than this. Some people are naturally moved by kindness when they want to be kind, and by nastiness when they want to be nasty, without any explicit forethought and without any need for energetic self-control. Others are moved by nastiness when they want to be kind and by kindness when they intend to be nasty, equally without forethought and without active resistance to these violations of their higher-order desires. The enjoyment of freedom comes easily to some. Others must struggle to achieve it.

IV

My theory concerning the freedom of the will accounts easily for our disinclination to allow that this freedom is enjoyed by the members of any species inferior to our own. It also satisfies another condition that must be met by any such theory, by making it apparent why the freedom of the will should be regarded as desirable. The enjoyment of a free will means the satisfaction of certain desires — desires of the second or of higher orders — whereas its absence means their frustration. The satisfactions at stake are those which accrue to a person of whom it may be said that his will is his own. The corresponding frustrations are those suffered by a person of whom it may be said that he is estranged from himself, or that he finds himself a helpless or a passive bystander to the forces that move him.

A person who is free to do what he wants to do may yet not be in a position to have the will he wants. Suppose, however, that he enjoys both freedom of action and freedom of the will. Then he is not only free to do what he wants to do; he is also free to want what he wants to want. It seems to me that he has, in that case, all the freedom it is possible to desire or to conceive. There are other good things in life, and he may not possess some of them. But there is nothing in the way of freedom that he lacks.

It is far from clear that certain other theories of the freedom of the will meet these elementary but essential conditions: that it be understandable why we desire this freedom and why we refuse to ascribe it to animals. Consider, for example, Roderick Chisholm's quaint version of the doctrine that human freedom entails an absence of causal determination.[7] Whenever a person performs a free action, according to Chisholm, it's a miracle. The motion of a person's hand, when the person moves it, is the outcome of a series of physical causes; but some event in this series, "and presumably one of those that took place within the brain, was caused by the agent and not by any other events" (18). A free agent has, therefore, "a prerogative which some would attribute only to God: each of us, when we act, is a prime mover unmoved" (23).

This account fails to provide any basis for doubting that animals of subhuman species enjoy the freedom it defines. Chisholm says nothing that makes it seem less likely that a rabbit performs a miracle when it moves its leg than that a man does so when he moves his hand. But why, in any case, should anyone *care* whether he can interrupt the natural order of causes in the way Chisholm describes? Chisholm offers no reason for believing that there is a discernible difference between the experience of a man who miraculously initiates a series of causes when he moves his hand and a man who moves his hand without any such breach of the normal causal sequence. There appears to be no concrete basis for preferring to be involved in the one state of affairs rather than in the other.[8]

It is generally supposed that, in addition to satisfying the two conditions I have mentioned, a satisfactory theory of the freedom of the will necessarily provides an analysis of one of the conditions of moral responsibility. The most common recent approach to the problem of understanding the freedom of the will has been, indeed, to inquire what is entailed by the assumption that someone is morally responsible for what he has done. In my view, however, the relation between moral responsibility and the freedom of the will has been very widely misunderstood. It is not true that a person is morally responsible for what he has done only

7 "Freedom and Action," in K. Lehrer (ed.), *Freedom and Determinism* (New York: Random House, 1966), pp. 11–44.
8 I am not suggesting that the alleged difference between these two states of affairs is unverifiable. On the contrary, physiologists might well be able to show that Chisholm's conditions for a free action are not satisfied, by establishing that there is no relevant brain event for which a sufficient physical cause cannot be found.

if his will was free when he did it. He may be morally responsible for having done it even though his will was not free at all.

A person's will is free only if he is free to have the will he wants. This means that, with regard to any of his first-order desires, he is free either to make that desire his will or to make some other first-order desire his will instead. Whatever his will, then, the will of the person whose will is free could have been otherwise; he could have done otherwise than to constitute his will as he did. It is a vexed question just how "he could have done otherwise" is to be understood in contexts such as this one. But although this question is important to the theory of freedom, it has no bearing on the theory of moral responsibility. For the assumption that a person is morally responsible for what he has done does not entail that the person was in a position to have whatever will he wanted.

This assumption *does* entail that the person did what he did freely, or that he did it of his own free will. It is a mistake, however, to believe that someone acts freely only when he is free to do whatever he wants or that he acts of his own free will only if his will is free. Suppose that a person has done what he wanted to do, that he did it because he wanted to do it, and that the will by which he was moved when he did it was his will because it was the will he wanted. Then he did it freely and of his own free will. Even supposing that he could have done otherwise, he would not have done otherwise; and even supposing that he could have had a different will, he would not have wanted his will to differ from what it was. Moreover, since the will that moved him when he acted was his will because he wanted it to be, he cannot claim that his will was forced upon him or that he was a passive bystander to its constitution. Under these conditions, it is quite irrelevant to the evaluation of his moral responsibility to inquire whether the alternatives that he opted against were actually available to him.[9]

In illustration, consider a third kind of addict. Suppose that his addiction has the same physiological basis and the same irresistible thrust as the addictions of the unwilling and wanton addicts, but that he is altogether delighted with his condition. He is a willing addict, who would not have things any other way. If the grip of his addiction should somehow weaken, he would do whatever he could to reinstate it; if his desire for the drug should begin to fade, he would take steps to renew its intensity.

The willing addict's will is not free, for his desire to take the drug will

9 For another discussion of the considerations that cast doubt on the principle that a person is morally responsible for what he has done only if he could have done otherwise, see my "Alternate Possibilities and Moral Responsibility," Chapter 1 in this volume.

be effective regardless of whether or not he wants this desire to constitute his will. But when he takes the drug, he takes it freely and of his own free will. I am inclined to understand his situation as involving the overdetermination of his first-order desire to take the drug. This desire is his effective desire because he is physiologically addicted. But it is his effective desire also because he wants it to be. His will is outside his control, but, by his second-order desire that his desire for the drug should be effective, he has made this will his own. Given that it is therefore not only because of his addiction that his desire for the drug is effective, he may be morally responsible for taking the drug.

My conception of the freedom of the will appears to be neutral with regard to the problem of determinism. It seems conceivable that it should be causally determined that a person is free to want what he wants to want. If this is conceivable, then it might be causally determined that a person enjoys a free will. There is no more than an innocuous appearance of paradox in the proposition that it is determined, ineluctably and by forces beyond their control, that certain people have free wills and that others do not. There is no incoherence in the proposition that some agency other than a person's own is responsible (even *morally* responsible) for the fact that he enjoys or fails to enjoy freedom of the will. It is possible that a person should be morally responsible for what he does of his own free will and that some other person should also be morally responsible for his having done it.[10]

On the other hand, it seems conceivable that it should come about by chance that a person is free to have the will he wants. If this is conceivable, then it might be a matter of chance that certain people enjoy freedom of the will and that certain others do not. Perhaps it is also conceivable, as a number of philosophers believe, for states of affairs to come about in a way other than by chance or as the outcome of a sequence of natural causes. If it is indeed conceivable for the relevant states of affairs to come about in some third way, then it is also possible that a person should in that third way come to enjoy the freedom of the will.

10 There is a difference between being *fully* responsible and being *solely* responsible. Suppose that the willing addict has been made an addict by the deliberate and calculated work of another. Then it may be that both the addict and this other person are fully responsible for the addict's taking the drug, while neither of them is solely responsible for it. That there is a distinction between full moral responsibility and sole moral responsibility is apparent in the following example. A certain light can be turned on or off by flicking either of two switches, and each of these switches is simultaneously flicked to the "on" position by a different person, neither of whom is aware of the other. Neither person is solely responsible for the light's going on, nor do they share the responsibility in the sense that each is partially responsible; rather, each of them is fully responsible.

3

Coercion and moral responsibility

On some actions praise indeed is not bestowed, but pardon is, when one does what he ought not under pressure which overstrains human nature.

Aristotle, *Nicomachean Ethics* III, 1, 1110a

I

The courts may refuse to admit in evidence, on the grounds that it was coerced, a confession which the police have obtained from a prisoner by threatening to beat him. But the prisoner's accomplices, who are compromised by his confession, are less likely to agree that he was genuinely coerced into confessing. They may feel, perhaps justifiably, that he made a reprehensible choice and that he acted badly: he ought to have accepted the beating rather than to have betrayed them. Thus sometimes, though not always, the use of the term "coercion" conveys an exclusion of moral responsibility. A person who acts under coercion is for that reason regarded as not having acted freely, or of his own free will. It may be established that a person is not to be credited or blamed for what he has done, then, by showing that he was "coerced" into doing it.

A person is sometimes said to have been coerced even when he has performed no action at all. Suppose that one man applies intense pressure to another man's wrist, forcing him to drop the knife in his hand. In this case, which involves what may be called "physical coercion," the victim is not made to act; what happens is that his fingers are made to open by the pressure applied to his wrist. It may in certain situations be difficult, or even impossible, to know whether or not an action has been performed. Perhaps it will be unclear whether the man dropped the knife because his fingers were forced open or because he wished to avoid a continuation of the pressure on his wrist. Or suppose that a man is being severely tortured in order to compel him to reveal a password, and that at a certain point he utters the word. There may be no way of discovering whether he spoke the word in submission to the threat of further pain, or whether – his will having been overcome by the agony which he had already suffered – the word passed involuntarily through his lips.

I propose to consider those cases of coercion in which the victim is made to perform an action, by being provided with a certain kind of motive for doing so, but which resemble cases of physical coercion in that the victim is not to be regarded as morally responsible for what he has been coerced into doing. We might say that in instances of physical coercion the victim's body is used as an instrument, whose movements are made subject to another person's will. In those instances of coercion that concern me, on the other hand, it is the victim's will which is subjected to the will of another. How, in those cases, does coercion affect its victim's freedom? What basis does it provide for the judgment that he is not morally responsible for doing what he is made to do?

There are various ways in which one person may attempt to motivate another to perform a certain action. I shall confine my attention to only two of them: issuing a conditional threat and making a conditional offer. In each of these, the one person (P) proposes to bring about a certain state of affairs (C) if the other person (Q) performs a certain action (A). Whether a person who makes a proposal of this sort is actually making either a threat or an offer depends in part on his motives, intentions, and beliefs. Considerations of the same kinds are also relevant in interpreting the subsequent response of the person to whom the threat or offer is made. But, to simplify my discussion, I shall generally ignore these factors. When I speak of someone as making a threat or an offer, it is to be assumed that he satisfies all the necessary conditions for doing so that pertain to his motives, intentions, and beliefs; and similarly when I speak of someone as submitting to or defying a threat or as accepting or declining an offer. It is also to be assumed that all threats and offers are credibly firm: everyone involved has sufficient reason to believe that the proposals in question will be carried out if their conditions are fulfilled.

The proposals in which conditional threats and offers are formulated are, in fact, often implicitly or explicitly *bi*conditional. When P proposes to bring about C if Q does A, he often also states or implies that he will not bring C about if Q does not do A. This need not be so. P may leave it open that he will do what he threatens or offers to do even if Q performs some action other than the one with which P's proposal is concerned. But when a highwayman tells a traveller that it's his money or his life, biconditionality is presumably intended: the highwayman will kill the traveller if the traveller refuses to hand over his money, while he will spare his life otherwise. And when an employer offers to pay someone a certain salary for doing a certain job, it will often be clear to the prospective employee that the salary will not be paid to him if he declines the offer.[1]

It may seem reasonable to construe every biconditional proposal that makes either a threat or an offer as necessarily making both. When the highwayman threatens to kill the traveller, he may seem by the same token to be offering the traveller his life in exchange for his money; and the employer, when he offers someone a position, may seem thereby to be implicitly threatening to withhold money from that person unless he takes the job in question. I agree with Nozick, however, in rejecting the view that any biconditional proposal making a threat or an offer is also making a corresponding offer or threat.[2] Surely a merchant is not ordinarily to be regarded as threatening his customers, even by implication, when he offers his goods for sale, although his offer to sell is naturally combined with a proposal to withhold the goods if the customer declines to pay his price.

Threats and offers differ in a number of ways. A person who fulfills the condition of an offer often has the option of declining to accept what he has been offered in return, while this option is characteristically not available to someone who fulfills the condition of a threat. It may be sensible for a person who has received an offer to shop around for a better one, but someone to whom a threat has been made has no such correspondingly sensible alternative. Threatening a person is generally thought to require justification, while there is no similar presumption against the legitimacy of making someone an offer.

The most fundamental difference between threats and offers, however, is this: a threat holds out to its recipient the danger of incurring a penalty, while an offer holds out to him the possibility of gaining a benefit. Given that one half of a biconditional proposal is a threat, then, the other half is an offer if and only if withholding the threatened penalty would be tantamount to conferring a benefit; and given that one half of a biconditional is an offer, the proposal joined with it is a threat if and only if withholding the offered benefit would be tantamount to imposing a penalty. But what are the characteristics of penalties and benefits, and under what conditions is withholding the one equivalent to imposing or

1 I shall not discuss complex proposals, in which P proposes to bring about a certain consequence if Q does A and to do something other than merely refrain from bringing about that consequence if Q does not do A.

2 Robert Nozick, "Coercion," in S. Morgenbesser, P. Suppes, and M. White (eds.), *Philosophy, Science, and Method: Essays in Honor of Ernest Nagel* (New York: St. Martin's Press, 1969), p. 447. I am very greatly indebted to this splendid essay, which has provided an indispensable basis for my own examination of some of the topics with which it deals. Although I am critical of several of Nozick's views, my essay follows his in a number of ways which will readily be apparent to anyone who is familiar with both.

conferring the other? What determines whether P's proposal to bring about C if and only if Q does A includes only an offer, or only a threat, or both at once?

Nozick suggests the following criterion for distinguishing threats and offers. If C "makes the consequences of Q's action worse than they would have been in the normal and expected course of events," then P's proposal is a threat; if C makes the consequences better, the proposal is an offer. He adds in explication that "the term 'expected' is meant to shift or straddle *predicted* and *morally required.*"[3] Now this criterion requires the course of events when Q does A and P brings about C to be compared with another course of events in which Q does A. But it is not entirely clear how to identify this second course of events, which provides the baseline for evaluating the import of P's proposal. What are the "normal and expected" consequences when Q does A, with which the consequences when P brings about C are to be compared?

Nozick's criterion permits a variety of interpretations. Let us consider the interpretation he himself gives it when he applies it in his examination of the following two situations:

(1) P is Q's usual supplier of drugs, and today when he comes to Q he says that he will not sell them to Q, as he normally does, for twenty dollars, but rather will give them to Q if and only if Q beats up a certain person.

(2) P is a stranger who has been observing Q, and knows that Q is a drug addict. Both know that Q's usual supplier of drugs was arrested this morning and that P had nothing to do with his arrest. P approaches Q and says that he will give Q drugs if and only if Q beats up a certain person.[4]

Nozick believes that the second of these situations involves no threat but only an offer. "In the normal course of events," he explains, P2 "does not supply Q with drugs at all, nor is he expected to do so." If P2 does not give Q drugs "he is not *withholding* drugs from Q nor is he *depriving* Q of drugs." He is merely "offering Q drugs," therefore, "as an inducement to beat up the person." On the other hand, Nozick maintains that the first situation involves both an offer and a threat. Since "the normal course of events is one in which [P1] supplies Q with drugs for money," the terms of his proposal mean that he will make things worse than normal for Q in the event that Q does not beat up the person. Therefore, P1 is threatening Q. He is also, of course, making him an offer: since Q does not normally get drugs from P1 for beating up the person, the desirability to Q of performing this action is enhanced by P1's proposal.[5]

3 *Op. cit.*, p. 447. Nozick does not comment on the distinction between "normal" and "predicted."
4 Ibid.
5 Ibid., pp. 447–8.

In my opinion, what Nozick says about these two situations is mistaken. P1's proposal does indeed, as he maintains, include both a threat and an offer. But the criterion he employs for identifying threats and offers leads him to give an incorrect account of why the proposal has this dual character. Moreover, when this criterion is replaced with a more satisfactory one, it becomes apparent that Nozick is also mistaken in regarding P2's proposal as only an offer. The fact is that P2's proposal includes not only an offer but a threat as well. And it does so in virtue of the same features that make part of P1's proposal a threat.

If P1's proposal were to be construed for the reason Nozick cites as threatening Q with a penalty, then a butcher would be threatening his customers with a penalty whenever he raised his price for meat. What P1 does when he substitutes his new proposal for his old one is, after all, simply to raise his price for the drug. Instead of requiring Q to give him twenty dollars for it, as before, he now requires Q to do something in order to get the drug which (we are to suppose) Q likes doing less than he likes giving P1 twenty dollars. Now surely the butcher is not proposing to penalize his customers just because he tells them that he is changing his price to their disadvantage. The likelihood is that when he does this he is still making only an offer, though a less attractive one than before.[6] Thus the fact that P1 makes the addict's situation worse than it had been by changing the terms on which he proposes to sell him drugs cannot be, as Nozick claims, what accounts for the fact that P1's proposal is a threat. Nozick's criterion, as he himself interprets it, is not acceptable: it fails to preserve the distinction between threatening to penalize someone and worsening his options by making him a poorer offer than before.

To decide whether P1 and the butcher are making threats or offers it is not essential to consider, as Nozick recommends, how what they propose to do compares with what they *used* to do. Rather, it is necessary to consider how the courses of events their current proposals envisage compare with what would *now* happen but for their proposed interventions. And the question of what would now happen without these interventions is not to be answered by citing the terms of the butcher's and

6 It may be objected that, despite my desire to leave such considerations to one side, the butcher's motives must be taken into account. But even if we suppose that part of the butcher's reason for raising his price is that he wants to make things worse for his customers (cf. Nozick's condition 3', op. cit., p. 442), it does not follow that his proposal is a threat. The proposal may still be just an offer, despite the fact that it is (intended to be) so unattractive as to dissuade the butcher's customers from doing business with him. Of course, the butcher's proposal *may* be a threat. But if it is, it is not because it is (intended to be) less favorable to the customers than an earlier proposal. It is because of other circumstances, which I will discuss below.

P_I's earlier proposals. For those terms are entirely cancelled by the terms which have replaced them. When they make their new proposals, P_I and the butcher actually do two things: they wipe out their earlier proposals, and they set new terms. Since the terms of the old proposals are withdrawn and a fresh start made, there is no basis for the supposition, which alone would justify Nozick's procedure, that the earlier proposals serve to define what would now happen if the terms of the current proposals should not be carried out.

I am not suggesting that the terms on which people have had dealings in the past can have no bearing whatever on the evaluation of the terms governing their current dealings. Those earlier terms may, as I will explain later, have a certain current relevance. Moreover, I am not suggesting that the terms of a prior proposal never define the appropriate baseline against which the course of events envisaged by a current proposal is to be measured. Imagine that a prosecutor says he will ask for the death penalty if the defendant pleads innocent, and that he later proposes to ask for a lesser penalty if the defendant pleads innocent *if* the defendant gives him useful evidence against another person. Here the prosecutor's earlier proposal does define the baseline for evaluating his later one; it remains decisively relevant to the question of what will happen if the defendant should reject the later proposal. But this is because, unlike what occurs in the situations involving the addict and the butcher's customer, the prosecutor's second proposal does not entirely cancel the terms of his first.

In order to evaluate a proposal by P to intervene in the course of events that is initiated when Q does A, we need to know whether this intervention by P will leave Q better off or worse off than he would be without it. Measuring the impact of the proposal just requires, therefore, that we compare the course of events when P intervenes according to the terms of his proposal with what will happen if this intervention is subtracted from that course of events. This comparison leaves out of account the terms of any proposal which is canceled by P's current proposal, and it takes into account the terms of any proposal which is left still intact.[7]

Proceeding in this way avoids Nozick's error, and it is correct so far as

---

7   Suppose that P offers to pay Q a certain amount of money for coming to work for him. Nozick's criterion would have us compare this with the "normal and expected" consequences of Q's coming to work for P. But what is "normal" or "to be expected" when Q comes to work for P? Perhaps the best answer is that P pays Q a fair wage for his work. Clearly, however, the appropriate comparison is not between what P says he will pay Q and what it would be fair for him to pay Q (or what people normally get for such work, or what Q normally gets, or what Q normally gets from P, or what P normally pays, or what P normally pays Q). It is between P's giving Q what he says he will give him, and P's giving Q nothing for his work.

it goes. But it does not take us to the end of the matter, for it does not enable us to deal satisfactorily with situations in which what P proposes is that he will *not* intervene in a certain way in the course of events initiated by Q's action. Beating up someone and getting drugs from P1 is more desirable, from the addict's point of view, than doing the same thing without getting drugs from P1. So P1's proposal to give the addict drugs if and only if he beats up the person includes an offer, albeit not so good an offer as the one in terms of which P1 and the addict used to do business. The butcher's proposal to his customer similarly includes an offer: it is better for the customer to get meat for his money, even though it is less meat than he formerly got for the same money, than to give the butcher money and get no meat. But suppose that the addict declines to beat up anyone, and that the customer declines to pay the butcher.

The course of events then envisaged by the two proposals are: P1 gives the addict no drugs, and the butcher gives the customer no meat. In the eventualities in question, P1 and the butcher propose not to intervene at all. They will neither add to nor subtract from the courses of events that would occur if they were entirely unaware of what the addict and the customer were doing or not doing, and if they made no response whatever to their actions. It would nonetheless be a mistake to conclude that their proposals − to give the addict no drugs and to give the customer no meat − are of the same nature. On the contrary, P1 threatens the addict when he proposes not to give him drugs if the addict declines to beat up the person, while the butcher makes no corresponding threat. How are we to account for the fact that a proposal to refrain from conferring a certain benefit is in the one case a threat and in the other case not?

It will be helpful to approach this problem by focusing attention on certain things which we are inclined to take quietly for granted when we think about the situations in which P1 and the butcher are involved. Thus consider how differently P1's biconditional proposal to the addict will strike us if we suppose that there is an enormous oversupply of drugs in the market and that the addict has convenient access to numerous sellers whose prices are quite a bit lower than P1's. Consider also how differently the butcher's proposal will strike us if we suppose both that his customer will starve if the butcher does not give him meat and that the butcher's price is outrageously high. Changing our assumptions concerning the two situations in these ways would, it seems to me, lead us to alter our evaluations. We would no longer regard P1 as threatening the addict but only as making him a rather unattractive offer. And we would construe the butcher's proposal to his customer as including not only an offer but a substantial threat as well.

We find no element of threat in the butcher's proposal to raise his price as long as we suppose that he is not, in making this proposal, taking improper advantage of a situation in which he has the customer in his power. His proposal acquires the character of a threat, on the other hand, when three conditions are satisfied. First, the customer is *dependent* on the butcher for meat: he cannot readily obtain it from another source. Second, the customer *needs* meat: it is essential either for preventing what he would regard as a significant deterioration of his welfare or for preventing his continuation in what he would regard as an undesirable condition. Third, the butcher *exploits* the customer's dependency and need; he demands for his meat an unfair or improper price. When the first two of these conditions are satisfied, the butcher has the customer in his power. If he then offers meat at an exploitative price, his proposal to refrain from giving the customer meat if the customer does not pay what he asks is a threat.

It is hardly plausible to regard P's proposal to refuse Q a certain benefit as tantamount to a threat – even a weak or ineffective threat – to penalize him, unless Q cannot easily obtain an equivalent benefit elsewhere. For only in that case does Q have any reason to be interested in whether he gets the benefit from P or not, and a penalty to which it is reasonable to be entirely indifferent is not a penalty at all.[8] As for the second of the three conditions I have specified, suppose that P proposes to give Q a million dollars if and only if Q performs a certain action, that Q has no other chance of acquiring so much money, and that P's offer is in some way unfair or improper. The proposal still does not include a threat because (let us presume) the maintenance of Q's welfare above a level he regards as undesirable is not contingent upon his having a million dollars. While he may come to want the money badly once P's proposal makes it seem within his grasp, he does not need it. The point of the third condition is that without it someone with monopolistic control over a necessity would be issuing a threat if he asked any price whatever for the benefit he controls. But it would be unreasonable to construe the suppliers of electricity as threatening the public, despite their monopolistic control over a necessity, even when they proposed to

---

8 Suppose that the customer could in fact get comparable meat from other nearby butchers, but only at the same unreasonably high price or at even higher prices. In that case too the butcher would be making a threat when he raised his price, whether or not he did so in collusion with the others, because the customer would actually have no useful option apart from the ones which the butcher's proposal defines. His dependency on the butcher is therefore not significantly relieved by the fact that he has other alternatives. But perhaps it ought to be said that, in virtue of those other alternatives, the butcher does not have him so closely in *his* power.

sell electricity at a philanthropic price – a price far below their own cost, let us say, and well within everyone's ability to pay.

When considering whether the price asked for a benefit is exploitative, it may be appropriate to take into account the price at which similar benefits have been conferred in the past. Further, the history of the relationship between two people may shed light on the question of whether one of them is dependent for some necessity on the other. Moreover, the fact that one person has customarily been willing to transact with another at a given price may, under certain conditions, create an obligation for him to continue to maintain that price even when it would be fair and proper for someone else to set a higher price. Perhaps there are also other ways in which the past may have a significant bearing on the question of whether the obverse of a current offer is a threat. But none of these considerations justifies Nozick's claim that while $P1$'s proposal to the addict is both a threat and an offer, the proposal $P2$ makes to the addict is an offer only.

$P1$'s proposal does not include a threat unless we suppose that the addict is dependent on him for drugs, that the addict needs drugs, and that the price $P1$ asks is exploitative. It seems as reasonable to make these suppositions concerning the second of Nozick's two situations as to make them concerning the first. $P2$'s proposal is plainly an offer, since it envisages a beneficial intervention by $P2$ in a course of events which would be less attractive to the addict if it were not to include this intervention. But the proposal also includes a threat, for the very same reason that there is a threat in $P1$'s proposal.

With his regular supplier in the hands of the police, the addict will recognize that he is dependent on $P2$ for drugs as soon as $P2$ reveals his readiness to supply them. The fact that $P2$ has not in the past given the addict drugs is not pertinent to the question of whether $P2$ is making a threat or an offer.[9] What counts is that $P2$ gets the addict in his power by making him understand that he must choose between doing what $P2$ asks and going without the drugs he needs. Moreover, there is no reason to think the price in question fairer or more proper when $P2$ sets it on the drugs than when $P1$ does so. What makes this price unfair or improper when $P1$ demands it is not that it is higher than his usual price for drugs – price increases are not inherently exploitative – but that it requires the addict to perform a wrongful and risky action. The action has these same characteristics, of course, when it is required by $P2$. Assuming that $P1$ exploits the addict when he raises his price, then, $P2$ also exploits him when he sets that higher price for their initial transaction.

---

9 This fact may none the less mean that $P2$ acts less reprehensibly than $P1$.

Withholding a benefit is, under the conditions I have sketched, tantamount to imposing a penalty. Under what conditions does withholding a penalty confer a benefit? Suppose that someone has stolen five thousand dollars, that he has already spent all but one hundred of it, that he has been convicted of his crime, and that the judge proposes to send him to prison for ten years if and only if he refuses to pay a fine of fifty dollars. Here the judge is threatening to penalize the criminal by imprisoning him if he does not pay the fine, but he is also offering the criminal a benefit – his freedom – if he does pay it. The judge's proposal offers a benefit because the price it sets for withholding the penalty it threatens is a very good one. The proposal gives the criminal an opportunity to get a bargain – this being the contrary of exploitation (there is evidently no antonym of "exploited") – since the price it asks for his freedom is below the price that might fairly and properly have been asked for it. Generally: P's proposal to withhold a threatened penalty amounts to the offer of a benefit if P has Q in his power so far as the penalty is concerned – i.e., Q has no ready means of avoiding the penalty except on P's terms, and the penalty would deprive him of something he needs – and if P's price for withholding the penalty is lower than the price it would be fair and proper for P to demand. Just as P exploits Q when he takes unfair advantage of the fact that he has Q in his power, so P benefits Q when he takes less advantage of his power over him than it would be fair or proper for him to take.

There are three ways in which P may penalize Q for doing A. First, P may intervene in the course of events initiated when Q does A by adding to it something which it would not have included but for his intervention, and which makes the resulting course of events less desirable to Q than it would have been without this intervention by P.

Second, he may intervene in the course of events initiated when Q does A by subtracting from it something which it would have included but for his intervention, and whose absence makes the resulting course of events less desirable to Q than it would have been without this intervention by P. This rather unwelcomely implies that P is threatening to penalize Q for speaking when he proposes to turn off his hearing aid if Q says another word. The example is Nozick's, and we might attempt to cope with it by adapting a suggestion of his: P's intervention imposes a penalty on Q only if it leaves Q worse off, having done A, than Q would have been if he had not done A and P had not intervened.[10] But invoking this criterion would mean that whenever P threatens to penalize Q for doing A, it is necessarily better for Q to refrain from doing A than to

---

10 Op. cit., p. 443.

do it and incur the penalty. It seems undesirable to build this into the notion of a penalty; clearly, some penalties are ineffective. I am willing to accept the implication that in the hearing aid example, P penalizes Q by turning off his hearing aid. After all, "I stopped talking because he threatened to turn off his hearing aid" seems at least marginally acceptable.

Third, P may, without adding or subtracting from the course of events initiated by Q's doing A, unfairly or improperly make it a consequence of Q's action that Q does not get something he needs. We cannot, without intolerable artificiality, say that the addict gets drugs from P2 when he declines to beat up the person unless P2 intervenes to subtract his getting them from the course of events which follows. It is not by an "intervention" of this sort that P2 penalizes the addict for not beating up the person. Rather, it is by making it a consequence of the addict's refusal to beat up the person that the addict gets no drugs. This is equivalent to setting on drugs the exploitative price that the addict beats up the person. Having to do without drugs would not be a *consequence* of the addict's refusal to beat up the person (though it might be a *sequel* to it) if P2 did not make it such. It is possible, accordingly, to construe P's withholding a benefit or penalty from Q as a particular sort of intervention by him – one which has, as it were, low visibility – in the course of events initiated when Q does A.

There are also three ways, corresponding to these in a manner which should be clear, in which P may confer a benefit on Q for doing A.

Offering someone a benefit for performing a certain action enhances the desirability to him of performing it, while threatening to penalize him for performing it reduces its desirability to him. An offer (threat) will be *superfluous* if it enhances (reduces) the desirability of an action which is already more (less) desirable than its alternative. It will be *ineffective* if it enhances (reduces) the desirability of an action without succeeding in making it more (less) desirable than its alternative. Superfluous and ineffective offers and threats are, of course, threats or offers nonetheless.

II

But what is coercion? Coercing someone into performing a certain action cannot be, if it is to imply his freedom from moral responsibility, merely a matter of getting him to perform the action by means of a threat. A person who is coerced is *compelled* to do what he does. He has *no choice* but to do it. This is at least part of what is essential if coercion is to relieve its victim of moral responsibility – if it is to make it inappropriate either to praise him or to blame him for having done what he was coerced into doing. Now it is not necessarily true of a person who decides to avoid a penalty with which he has been threatened that he is compelled to do so or that he has no other choice. Nor is it true that a person bears no moral responsibility for what he has done just because he does it in submission to a threat. Such a person may be described as acting "under duress"; but not all duress is coercion.

It might be suggested that someone is coerced if, in addition to his acting in order to avoid a threatened penalty, two further conditions are satisfied: (1) the penalty with which he is threatened renders the action against which the threat is issued *substantially* less attractive to him than it would have been otherwise; and (2) he believes that he would be left worse off by defying the threat than by submitting to it.[11] Adding these conditions does not, however, serve adequately to identify instances of coercion.

Suppose that P threatens to step on Q's toe unless Q sets fire to a crowded hospital, and that Q sets the fire in order to keep P off his toe. This does not satisfy the first condition, which excludes trivial threats: the penalty Q seeks to avoid by submitting to P's demand is not a substantial one. Suppose instead, then, that P threatens to break Q's thumb unless Q sets fire to the hospital, and that Q submits to this threat. Here the penalty with which P threatens Q is substantial: any course of action is rendered substantially less attractive to a person if it leads him to a broken thumb than it would if it did not involve this consequence. Thus the first condition is now satisfied. It may be, moreover, that the second condition is satisfied too. Suppose that Q thinks he will not be apprehended or punished for setting fire to the hospital, and that he does not expect to be troubled very greatly by his conscience for doing so. Then he may well believe that he would be left worse off by defying P's threat and having his thumb broken than by doing what P demands of him. Even if both conditions are satisfied in this way, however, it does not seem appropriate to describe Q as being coerced into setting the fire.

Why are we disinclined to regard Q as being coerced even when we suppose that he believes he will suffer substantially more by defying P's threat than by submitting to it? One suggestion would be that it is because we think that since Q must realize that it is better to suffer even a

11 These two conditions are based on Nozick's conditions 2' and 7 (op. cit., pp. 442, 443), which are the only items in his list of the necessary and sufficient conditions for coercion which bear on the distinction between coercive threats and threats which are effective but not coercive. It must be noted, however, that Nozick does not purport to define conditions for the exclusion of moral responsibility. His use of the term "coercion" differs, therefore, from mine.

broken thumb than to set fire to a hospital, he cannot believe that his submission to P's threat is justifiable or reasonable. We might, accordingly, consider revising the second condition to make it require that Q believes it would be unreasonable for him to defy P's threat, or believes that he is justified in submitting to it.

Now the satisfaction of this revised condition would ensure that a person who has been coerced into performing a certain action *believes* that he cannot properly be *blamed* for having performed it. But the criterion of coercion for which we are looking must do more than this. It must ensure that a coerced person cannot properly be held *morally responsible at all* for what he has been coerced into doing. And this would not be accomplished even by strengthening (2) still further so that it required Q to believe *correctly* that he is justified in submitting to P's threat, or that it would be unreasonable for him to defy it. In fact the satisfaction of the second condition in any plausible version is neither necessary for coercion nor, even in conjunction with the satisfaction of the first condition, sufficient for it.

Suppose P threatens to take from Q something worth one hundred dollars to Q unless Q gives him something which Q values at fifty dollars. The penalty of losing something worth one hundred dollars is a substantial one. Moreover, we may plausibly suppose, Q both believes that he will be left worse off by defying P's threat than by submitting to it, and is correct in thinking that it would be quite justifiable for him to submit. But while Q may well choose to submit to this threat, nothing *compels* him to do so. The choice between the alternatives with which P's threat confronts him is entirely up to him. He must, of course, choose between them; he must decide whether to do what P demands and escape the penalty, or whether to refuse to do it and incur the penalty. He is free, however, to make either decision. And while he may decide that it is both in his best interests and entirely reasonable for him to do what P demands of him, he could have decided to do otherwise. The choice is his own, and there is no basis for claiming that he bears anything less than full moral responsibility for whichever decision he makes.

We do sometimes describe a person as having had no choice when the alternative he chose was plainly superior to his other alternatives. What we mean then is that he had no *reasonable* choice – that no other choice than the one he made would have been reasonable. But to have no choice in this sense does not imply that a person deserves neither credit nor blame for what he does. Indeed, a person may well be praiseworthy for having made a plainly reasonable choice. Now coercion requires something more special than this. It requires that the victim of a threat should have no alternative to submission, in a sense in which this implies

not merely that the person would act reasonably in submitting and therefore is not to be blamed for submitting, but rather that he is not morally
responsible for his submissive action.

This requirement can only be satisfied when the threat appeals to
desires or motives which are beyond the victim's ability to control, or
when the victim is convinced that this is the case.[12] If the victim's desire
or motive to avoid the penalty with which he is threatened is – or is
taken by him to be – so powerful that he cannot prevent it from leading
him to submit to the threat, then he really has no alternative other than
to submit. He cannot effectively choose to do otherwise. It is only then
that it *may* be proper to regard him as bearing no moral responsibility for
his submission. Whether or not it *is* in fact proper to regard him so – i.e.,
as being genuinely coerced – depends upon whether a still further condition, which I shall discuss later, is also satisfied.

A person may be quite incapable of defying a threat which he knows it
would be more reasonable for him to defy. Suppose that someone is
pathologically terrified of being stung by a bee. He may be coerced into
performing some action by the threat that he will otherwise be stung,
even though he himself recognizes that it would be more reasonable for
him to suffer the sting than to perform the action. I am not maintaining
that coercion occurs only when the victim of a threat is driven headlong
into submission by a wave of panic. He may be coerced into doing what
is demanded of him when he judges quite calmly that the penalty he
faces is one which he could not bring himself to accept.

Nor am I suggesting that a person is susceptible to coercion only
because he has, as it were, a repertoire of fears so imperious that he can
be made to do anything you like by a threat which arouses one of them.
The extent to which a person is in command of himself varies considerably from one situation to another. A man who is easily coerced by a
threat of death into giving his money to a thief, for example, may un-
hesitatingly defy the same threat of death when it is not his money but
the life of his child that is at stake. It does not follow from the fact that
this man was capable of resistance in the latter situation that he was not
coerced in the former.

It should not be assumed that the difference between these two situations is simply that the man judged it reasonable to avoid the penalty of
death in the one, and that he judged it reasonable to accept that penalty

12 I shall not consider whether, or in what ways, the victim's conviction here must be
justifiable. In what follows I shall in any case, for the sake of convenience, refer simply
to the victim's ability to control his desires or motives rather than to the full dis-
junctive condition formulated above, assuming that the bearing of the missing disjunct
will be apparent.

in the other. He may well have made these judgments. But what is essential so far as the question of coercion is concerned is the difference in the extents to which he was able in the two situations to mobilize his potential strength. Realizing that the cost of pursuing a certain course of action exceeds the gain will lead a person to think that pursuing the course of action would be unreasonable. But it may also tend to block his access to all his energies, and to make it actually impossible for him to pursue it. Knowing that what would be lost is too precious to lose, on the other hand, may enable him to find resources within himself upon which he is incapable of drawing in less portentous contexts. A person's evaluations may not only affect his judgments concerning what it is reasonable for him to do. They may also have an effect upon what he is capable of doing.

Faced with a coercive threat, the victim has no choice but to submit: he cannot prevent his desire to avoid the penalty in question from determining his response. When he decides that it is reasonable for him to submit to a threat which is not coercive, his submission is not in this way made inescapable by forces within himself which he is unable to overcome. Sometimes we speak of threats as coercive even when we have no particular evidence that their victims are incapable of defying them. This is because there are certain penalties which we do not expect anyone to be able to choose to incur. A person who surpasses this expectation thereby performs not merely rightly or wrongly but with a certain heroic quality.

We do on some occasions find it appropriate to make an adverse judgment concerning a person's submission to a threat, even though we recognize that he has genuinely been coerced and that he is therefore not properly to be held morally responsible for his submission. This is because we think that the person, although he was in fact quite unable to control a certain desire, ought to have been able to control it. There are two considerations which may underlie and account for an opinion of this kind. We may believe that the person is morally responsible for his own inability to defy the threat; it may seem to us that it is because of something he himself has done, and which he is morally responsible for having done, that he is now unable to defy the threat. The other consideration is only in a rather special sense a matter of moral judgment. It is fundamentally a matter of our lack of respect for the person who has been coerced. It may be that we have a low opinion of someone who is incapable of defying a threat of the kind in question; and our judgment that he ought to have been able to defy it may express this feeling that he is not much of a man. This has nothing to do with judging him as deserving blame — if he should feel anything, it is not guilt but shame — and it is entirely compatible with the belief that he had actually no choice but to do what he did. Indeed it depends upon this belief. It is just because we recognize that we cannot expect better from him that we hold him in a certain contempt.

A coercive threat arouses in its victim a desire – i.e., to avoid the penalty – so powerful that it will move him to perform the required action regardless of whether he wants to perform it or considers that it would be reasonable for him to do so. Now an offer may also arouse in the person who receives it a desire – i.e., to acquire the benefit – which is similarly irresistible. This suggests that a person may be coerced by an offer as well as by a threat. It would be too hasty, however, to conclude that an offer is coercive whenever its recipient is incapable of declining the benefit it enables him to acquire. For it is only a *necessary* condition of coercion that a person should have or be convinced that he has no choice but to submit. Even if someone is unable to withstand the motivating force of his desire for a benefit which he is offered, accordingly, the offer may not be coercive.

Suppose that a person receives an offer inviting him to perform an action which he already wanted and intended to perform; suppose further that the benefit the offer holds out to him is something which he has long hoped for but never been able to obtain, and which he thinks it would be entirely reasonable for him to have; and suppose, still further, that what actually moves him to perform the action in question is his desire for that benefit. This desire may well be too strong for him to withstand. But our supposition is not only that the action is one which he himself wants to perform. We are also supposing that the desire which finally motivates him when he performs the action is one by which he in no way resents being motivated. He has no desire or inclination to resist the desire which moves him into compliance with the terms of the offer, nor does he in any way regret being motivated by it.

Surely this person is not coerced. For coercion must involve a violation of its victim's autonomy. The victim of coercion is necessarily either moved in some way against his will or his will is in some way circumvented, and this condition is not satisfied in the situation at hand. Neither in what he does nor in the motive with which he does it is the autonomy of the person in this situation impaired because of the offer to which he responds. The fact that the desire which moves him is irresistible is also consistent with his autonomy, since he identifies himself wholeheartedly with this desire. Its thrust – though in fact beyond his capacity to control – in no way diverts him from the pursuit of his own aims.

An offer is coercive, on the other hand, when the person who receives it is moved into compliance by a desire which is not only irresistible but which he would overcome if he could.[13] In that case the desire which drives the person is a desire by which he does not want to be driven. When he loses the conflict within himself, the result is that he is motivated against his own will to do what he does. Thus a man who prefers fame to obscurity but who does not want to be motivated by this preference may nonetheless find that he cannot bring himself to decline an offer to make him famous, despite his best efforts to overcome his desire to seek fame. This man is coerced into doing whatever he does to comply with the terms of the offer, regardless of whether or not it is something which he already wanted and intended to do. For his will when he acts is a will he does not want to be his own. He acts under a compulsion which violates his own desires.[14]

The irresistibility of the desire that a *threat* arouses is similarly, of course, insufficient in itself to make the threat coercive. A coercive threat, like a coercive offer, is only coercive because it also violates its victim's autonomy. Now a person's autonomy may be violated by a threat in the same way in which this violation is accomplished by a coercive offer. Thus the man who is uncontrollably terrified of being stung by a bee may be threatened with this penalty and succumb to his fear despite his best efforts to overcome it. In that case he is moved against his own will to submit to the threat, and this entails that he is coerced regardless of his attitude towards the action he performs in submission to it.

Irresistible threats are coercive, however, even when they do not lead their victims to this kind of inner defeat. Indeed, the condition that coercion must involve a violation of its victim's autonomy is satisfied by *every* effective threat. Although a person is coerced into acting as he does only when he is motivated to act by an irresistible desire, he acts in some

---

13 Nozick denies that offers may be coercive – indeed, he defines coercion in terms of threats – but he does not take into account the kinds of considerations which lead me to construe some offers as coercive. He limits his discussion at crucial points to what he calls "the Rational Man": someone who is "able to resist those temptations which he thinks he should resist" (op. cit., p. 460). This keeps him, of course, from even considering the kinds of threats and the kinds of offers which I regard as peculiarly coercive. His use of the term "temptation," incidentally, strikes me as somewhat imprecise. Presumably his Rational Man is capable not only of resisting temptation but also of subduing those desires and impulses which, while he is not at all *tempted* to give in to them, threaten to overwhelm his efforts to direct his behavior entirely in accordance with the dictates of his reason.

14 For further adumbration of some of the concepts employed here and below, see my "Freedom of the Will and the Concept of a Person," in this volume. That essay develops a conception of the freedom of the will in terms of which coercion, as here understood, may be said to deprive its victim of free will.

way against his own will when he submits to *any* threat. In submitting to a threat, a person invariably does something which he does not really want to do. Hence irresistible threats, unlike irresistible offers, are necessarily coercive.

How are we to account for this? What is it about an effective threat which entails a violation of its victim's autonomy? The answer may seem obvious when the victim is made by the threat to perform an action which he would otherwise have preferred not to perform. But sometimes a threat will coincide with its victim's own desires and move him in just the same direction in which they would otherwise have moved him. Consider a man who, in an expansively benevolent frame of mind, decides to go for a walk and to give the money in his pocket to the first person he meets on the road. The first person he meets points a pistol at his head and threatens to kill him unless he hands over his money. The man is terrified, he loses touch with his original intention in the midst of his fear, and he hands over his money in order to escape death.

Here the action performed is one which the agent wanted and intended to perform; if he had not been coerced, he would have performed the action on his own. Moreover, he would not have defied the threat even if he had been capable of doing so; on the contrary, since he really does prefer to give up his money than to die, he would doubtless have fought against any impulse toward defiance which might have arisen in him. In what, then, does the coercion consist? Wherein is the man's autonomy impaired?

It is true that the man genuinely prefers being moved by the desire to save his life than by the desire to keep his money; he prefers to submit to the threat rather than to defy it. These are not, however, his only alternatives: submission and defiance are not the only possible responses to a threat. It is also possible that a person who receives a threat should be unmoved by it, and that he should abstain from taking it into account. In the present case, the man might thus have handed over his money with his original benevolent intention rather than with the intention of saving his life. He would then have *complied* with the threat, but he would not have been coerced into doing so. His motive in acting would have been just the motive from which he wanted to act, and there would have been no violation of his autonomy at all.

It seems that a threat is only coercive, then, when the motive from which it causes its victim to act is a motive from which he would prefer not to act. But actually, this formulation of the condition is not quite correct. Suppose that P threatens to penalize Q for doing A, that Q all along wanted and intended to refrain from doing A, but that the threat so infuriates Q that he is moved irresistibly – despite his best efforts to overcome his spiteful rage – to *defy* the threat and hence to do A. In this case the threat seems to cause Q to act from a motive by which he would prefer not to be moved. But, while his autonomy is indeed violated by the fury which overwhelms him, he is surely not coerced by P into doing A. Evidently a threat is only coercive when it causes its victim to perform, from a motive by which he would prefer not to be moved, an action which *complies* with the threat.

Now why is it invariably true that a person's motive when he submits to a threat is one by which he would prefer not to be moved?[15] It is not an adequate answer, or at least not an adequately precise one, that he is always in such cases moved by fear. For a person's motive in acting to acquire a benefit may be altogether his own, and it is difficult to specify whatever differences there may be between a desire to acquire a benefit and a fear of missing it. A somewhat better answer is that a person who submits to (and who does not merely comply with) a threat necessarily does so in order to avoid a penalty. That is, his motive is not to improve his condition but to keep it from becoming worse. This seems sufficient to account for the fact that he would prefer to have a different motive for acting.[16] It also suggests why there is a *prima facie* case against threatening people and why threats, unlike offers, are generally thought to require justification. Someone to whom a threat is made has nothing to gain from it and everything to lose. A threat, unlike an offer, exposes a person to the risk of an additional penalty without providing him with any opportunity to acquire a benefit which would otherwise not have been available to him.

When P coerces Q into doing A, then Q does not do A freely or of his

---

15   Nozick points out (op. cit., pp. 46ff.) that it is in the nature of threats that a person will not think it in his interest to be threatened (he explains plausibly how apparent counterexamples to this may be handled). The use to which he thinks this point can be put, however, is not altogether clear to me. The mere fact that a person is in a situation in which he would prefer not to be certainly does not, in itself, entail that he is less than fully autonomous in whatever choice he makes among the alternatives with which the situation provides him. For a person may defy a threat or, in the manner described above, comply with it without submitting to it; and in those events his autonomy is not impaired at all, despite the fact that he would not have chosen to be threatened. The focus of Nozick's discussion is somewhat blurred, I think, by the example he discusses. It is not an example of a threat at all, but concerns someone whose leg has been broken and who is choosing between having a decorated cast or an undecorated one put on the broken leg. This choice is unlike the choices often available to people who have been threatened, for it may be open to them to act as though the threat had not been made.

16   For a suggestive discussion of this and related points, see Gerald Dworkin, "Acting Freely," *Nous*, IV (1970), pp. 367–83.

own free will. It is also true in a sense that P subjects Q to his will, or that he replaces Q's will with his own: Q's motive is not one which Q wants, but one which P causes him to have. Now we do not speak of coercion except when one person imposes his will in this way upon another. We have good reasons for especially noticing the roles played in our lives by the actions of other men and for distinguishing them from the roles played by circumstances of other kinds. Our ways of coping with and of regulating these two sorts of conditions are very different. But the effect of coercion on its victim, in virtue of which the victim's autonomy or freedom is undermined, is not essentially due to the fact that he is subjected to the will of another.

Consider the following two situations. Suppose first that a man comes to a fork in the road, that someone on a hillside adjoining the left-hand fork threatens to start an avalanche which will crush him if he goes that way, and that the man takes the fork to the right in order to satisfy a commanding desire to preserve his own life. Next, suppose that when the man comes to the fork he finds no one issuing threats but instead notices that on account of the natural condition of things he will be crushed by an avalanche if he takes the left-hand fork, and that he is moved irresistibly by his desire to live to proceed by the fork to the right. There are interesting differences between these situations, to be sure, but there is no basis for regarding the man as acting more or less freely or of his own free will in the one case than in the other. Whether he is morally responsible for his decision or action in each case depends not on the source of the injury he is motivated to avoid but on the way in which his desire to avoid it operates within him.[17]

We do tend, of course, to be more resentful when another person places obstacles in our way than when the environment does so. What accounts for this greater resentment is not, however, the love of liberty. It is pride; or, what is closely related to pride, a sense of injustice. Only another person can *coerce* us, or interfere with our *social* or *political* freedom, but this is no more than a matter of useful terminology. When a person chooses to act in order to acquire a benefit or in order to escape

---

17 The argument might be made that it is always to some extent desirable that a threat should be defied, regardless of its terms, and that there is no corresponding *prima facie* desirability to defying the natural environment. If an argument of this kind should be sound, it would be more difficult to justify an action performed in order to avoid a threatened penalty than to justify one performed in order to escape being comparably injured by the natural environment. But it would not mean that a person's moral responsibility for what he does is affected differently depending on whether his motives are motives another person has caused him to have or whether they arise from his encounter with natural conditions in which no other person has intervened.

an injury, the degree to which his choice is autonomous and the degree to which he acts freely do not depend on the origin of the conditions which lead him to choose and to act as he does. A man's will may not be his own even when he is not moved by the will of another.[18]

18 This essay would be less defective than it is if I had known better how to accommodate the valuable comments concerning an earlier version of it which were made to me by Peter Hacker, Anthony Kenny, Sidney Morgenbesser, and Joseph Raz.

4

Three concepts of free action

There are many situations in which a person performs an action because he prefers it to any other among those he thinks are available to him, or because he is drawn more strongly to it than to any other, and yet is reluctant nonetheless to describe himself without qualification as having acted willingly. He may acknowledge that he did what in *some* sense he wanted to do, and that he understood well enough what he wanted and what he did. But at the same time he may think it pertinent and justifiable to dissociate himself in a way from his action – perhaps by saying that what he did was not something he *really* wanted to do, or that it was not something he really *wanted* to do. Situations of this sort fall into several distinct types.

In situations of Type A, the person's feeling that he acted unwillingly derives from the fact that the external circumstances under which he acted were, as he perceived them, discordant with his desires. It is nearly always possible, of course, for a person to imagine being in a situation that he would like better than the one he is actually in. There is, however, a substantial difference – often easy enough to discern, though difficult to explicate precisely – between recognizing that a state of affairs is less than ideal and being actively discontented by it or resistant to it. The discordance between reality and desire that characterizes situations of Type A gives rise to the latter, and not merely to the former: it is not just that there is another imaginable situation in which the agent would prefer to be, but that he regrets or resents the state of affairs with which he must in fact contend.

Suppose someone's reason for having performed a certain action was that he regarded it as the least of various evils among which he had to choose. Given the alternatives he confronted, he preferred without reservation the one he pursued. That provides the warrant for describing him as having done what he wanted to do. But the alternatives he confronted comprised a set from which he did not want to have to choose; he was discontented with the necessity of having to make that choice. It is this discrepancy, between the world as it was and as he wanted it to be, that supports his claim that he did not act altogether willingly.

In situations of Type B, it is the inner circumstances of his action that are discordant with the agent's desires. What motivates his action is a desire by which, given the alternatives he confronts, he does not want to be moved to act. There is a conflict within him, between a first-order desire to do what he actually does and a second-order volition that this first-order desire not be effective in determining his action. In other words, he wants to be motivated effectively, with respect to the alternatives he faces, by some desire other than the one that actually moves him to act as he does.

This person's denial that he has acted altogether willingly reflects his sense that in the conflict from which his action emerged he was defeated by a force with which, although it issued from inside of him, he did not identify himself. For instance, he may have struggled unsuccessfully against a craving (effective first-order desire) to which he did not want to succumb (defeated second-order volition). Then his effort to dissociate himself from what he has done expresses his view of himself as having been helpless in the face of a desire that drove him unwillingly, regardless of his preference for another action, to do what he did.

Worldly misfortune and inner conflict, of the kinds in question here, bear differently upon the moral responsibilities of agents who are beset by them. In virtue of the discrepancy between the desire that motivates his action and the desire by which he wants to be motivated, the agent in a situation of Type B may not be morally responsible for what he does. The desire that moves him is in one way, to be sure, indisputably his. But it moves him to act against his own will, or against the will he wants. In this respect it is alien to him, which may justify regarding him as having been moved passively to do what he did by a force for which he cannot be held morally responsible.

On the other hand, the fact that someone confronts alternatives from which he does not want to have to choose has in itself no effect at all upon his moral responsibility for the action he elects to perform. There is no reason why a person should not be found meritorious or blameworthy — in other words, be considered morally responsible — for how he acts in situations he would prefer to have avoided, as well as for his behavior in situations that he is pleased to be in. Thus the fact that a person acts in a situation of Type A provides no basis whatever for denying that he is morally responsible for what he does.

Situations of Type A include many in which the agent is threatened with a penalty, which will be imposed either by another person or by impersonal forces, unless he performs a certain action. Now if we assume that being *coerced* into doing something precludes being morally responsible for doing it, then a threat is not coercive when the threatened person believes correctly that he can defy it if he chooses to do so. For in that case the action he performs if he submits to the threat will be one to which he thinks he has an alternative; he performs it, therefore, because he himself decides to do so. And his action is consequently meritorious or blameworthy – that is, he *is* morally responsible for performing it – according to whether or not performing it is, given the circumstances in which he chooses to perform it, morally preferable to defiance.

Coercive threats, on the other hand, involve penalties that the recipient of the threat cannot effectively choose to incur. His inclination to avoid the undesirable consequence he faces is irresistible; it is impossible for him to bring himself to accept that consequence. When it is the irresistibility of this inclination or desire that accounts for the action he performs, then the recipient of a threat is not morally responsible for what he does – no more than someone is morally responsible for the performance of an action that is accounted for by an irresistible compulsion that originates within himself.

The situation of a person who succumbs to a threat because he is unable to defy it is not, accordingly, of Type A. Nor is it necessarily of Type B either, since there is no reason to assume that a person who acts because of the irresistibility of a desire would prefer, given his alternatives, to be motivated by some different desire. The situation is thus of a distinguishable type, C, whose special characteristic is that the agent acts because of the irresistibility of a desire without attempting to prevent that desire from determining his action. (The agent in a situation of Type C is in certain respects analogous to what I have elsewhere called a "wanton," which may in part account for the repugnance of coercion.) He is not defeated by the desire, as in situations of Type B, since he does not oppose a second-order volition to it. Nor is he autonomous within the limits of an unsatisfactory set of alternatives, as in situations of Type A, since his action does not result from an effective choice on his part concerning what to do.

In the light of some of Locke's remarks,[1] two points need to be made particularly clear in connection with situations of Type C. First, a person may act to satisfy a desire that he cannot in fact resist, and yet it may not be the desire's irresistibility that accounts for his action. He may be unaware that the desire is irresistible, for instance, and perform for reasons unconnected with his inability to resist it the very action to which he would otherwise be driven. In that case, his situation is not of Type C. Second, the fact that someone acts because of the irresistibility of a

---

1   Don Locke, "Three Concepts of Free Action: I," *Proceedings of the Aristotelian Society*, supp. vol. XLIX (1975), pp. 95–112. This essay was written as a response to Locke's.

desire does not mean that he acts in a panic or with a great rush of feeling. A person may believe of himself that he cannot resist a certain desire, and therefore proceed in calm resignation to satisfy it, without experiencing the uncontrollable compulsive thrust that he might indeed encounter if he should attempt to refuse it satisfaction.

Both in situations of Type B and of Type C, the agent is moved to act without the concurrence of a second-order volition: in the former case because his second-order volition is defeated, and in the latter because no second-order volition plays a role in the economy of his desires. On the other hand, the agent in a situation of Type A endorses the desire that moves him to act. Despite his dissatisfaction with a state of affairs in which he finds the desire to merit his endorsement, he is satisfied, given that state of affairs, to be moved by the desire. Thus his action is in accordance with a second-order volition, and the unwillingness with which he acts is of a different character than the unwillingness with which agents act in situations of Types B and C. This difference is reflected in the fact that he may be morally responsible for what he does, whereas they are not.

Let us consider whether it is possible to identify the class of free actions with the class – call it "W" – of actions that are *not* performed in situations of Type B or Type C, assuming that all actions in this class are performed with appropriate understanding and intent. Notice that W resembles the class of willing actions defined by Locke's notion of willingness. However, W is broader than that class: it includes not only all members of the latter but also actions performed in situations of Type A.

II

Because of this difference between the two classes, Locke's claim that willingness cannot be a *necessary* condition for free action has no force against the view that free actions must be members of W. In support of his claim Locke adduces the example of a person who acts in order to do what he takes to be his duty, but who wishes that the action he performs were not morally required of him. Locke observes that while this person acts unwillingly, "it would be implausible to suggest that he therefore acts unfreely, let alone that he lacks responsibility for doing as he does." But since the situation of the reluctant moralist is of Type A, and not of Type B or Type C, his action belongs to W. Thus Locke's observation that he acts both freely and responsibly raises no difficulties for the view that membership in W is a necessary condition for free action.

Locke also maintains that willingness cannot be a *sufficient* condition for free action. The support he provides for this claim loses none of its pertinence on account of the difference between his class of willing actions and W. He argues that if willingness is taken to be sufficient for free action – his point can be made equally if membership in W is regarded as sufficient – then a willing addict acts freely when he takes the drug to which he is addicted while an unwilling addict does not. This conclusion does indeed follow, and Locke asserts that it is "implausible given that both are addicts."

But wherein lies its implausibility? The fact that both are addicts means just that neither can refrain from taking the drug or, if one likes, that neither is free to refrain from taking it. This hardly settles the question. For it is far from apparent that a person who is not free to refrain from performing a certain action cannot be free to perform it, or that he cannot perform it freely. Why, after all, should a person's freedom with respect to the performance of one action be thought to have anything essentially to do with his freedom with respect to the performance of another? Evidently, however, Locke takes it for granted that doing something freely entails being able to refrain from or to avoid doing it. Later in his essay he adopts this assumption more openly and makes it central to his own account of free action. Yet nowhere in his essay does he provide any argument to support it.

It is to my mind very implausible to maintain, as Locke also does, that the two addicts have equal moral responsibility for taking the drug. I believe it is decisive, in this connection, that the willing addict's addiction may play no role at all in the explanation of his action. What explains his taking the drug may in fact be, especially if he is unaware of being addicted, exactly the same as what explains the taking of a drug by a non-addict who takes it simply because he unreservedly likes taking it. In that case, surely, the moral responsibility of the willing addict for his action corresponds to that of the non-addict who takes the drug, rather than to that of the unwilling addict who takes it and whose taking it is explicable only in terms of his addiction.

What the willing addict's action reveals about him is the same as what is revealed by the action of the non-addict. It is not the same as what the action of the unwilling addict reveals. The moral significance of the willing addict's action is therefore the same as that of the non-addict's action, it seems to me, and different from the moral significance of what the unwilling addict does. Notice, by the way, that the actions of the willing addict and of the non-addict both belong to W, while that of the unwilling addict does not.

In evaluating the moral responsibilities of the willing and unwilling addicts, Locke tends to ignore the distinction between performing an action one is unable to avoid performing and performing an action *be-*

cause one is unable to avoid performing it. This is apparently what makes it possible for him erroneously to regard the problem of assessing moral responsibility in the case of the two addicts as a relevant analogue to the problem of assessing it in the case of the two hijacked pilots. His comment about the pilots – that it would be odd to ascribe to the willing pilot some responsibility for flying to Cuba that is not ascribable equally to the unwilling pilot – does not, as he thinks, support his claim that the responsibilities of the two addicts are the same.

Both pilots, as Locke describes them, act for the same reason – to avoid being shot – even though one of them is glad to have this reason for flying to Cuba while the other is not. Now it is precisely because they act for the same reason, or because their actions have the same explanation, that the pilots are equally responsible for what they do. In this crucial respect, of course, their case differs from the case of the two addicts; for what accounts for the action of the one addict is not what accounts for the action of the other. If we were to suppose that the willing pilot flew to Cuba because he wanted to see his mistress in Havana, and that the desire to avoid being shot was not what actually motivated him, then the case of the two pilots *would* be more pertinently like that of the two addicts. But then we would also, I believe, judge the responsibility of the willing pilot to differ from the responsibility of the unwilling one.

Locke's discussions of the addicts and pilots do not establish any basis for rejecting the identification of W with the class of free actions, or for accepting his claim that free actions must be avoidable. It is clear that the unwilling addict acts neither freely nor responsibly, when he takes the drug, and that the willing addict is no more able than he is to avoid taking it. The two addicts differ, however, in what leads each to his action. In virtue of that difference, their moral responsibilities for those actions differ. The view that there is no difference in the freedom with which they act gains no support, therefore, from considerations having to do with moral responsibility.

III

It appears that actions belonging to W might be performed by an individual whose mental life and physical behavior were determined by some sort of manipulation of his physiological condition by Locke's Devil/neurologist. Identifying W with the class of free actions would therefore apparently mean allowing that the D/n could ensure that his subject acted freely. Is this objectionable?

Let us distinguish two fundamentally different states of affairs, ignoring the difficult problems connected with the possibilities of mixed and borderline cases. In the first state of affairs the D/n manipulates his subject on a continuous basis, like a marionette, so that each of the subject's mental and physical states is the outcome of specific intervention on the part of the D/n. In that case the subject is not a person at all. His history is utterly episodic and without inherent connectedness. Whatever identifiable themes it may reveal are not internally rooted; they cannot be understood as constituting or belonging to the subject's own nature. Rather, they are provided gratuitously by an agency external to the subject. To be sure, the subject's instantaneous states of mind may be as rich as those of a person; they may include second-order desires and volitions, or have even more complex structures. But the subject has no character or dispositions of his own, and there is no reason to expect from him — except derivatively, insofar as there is reason to expect it from the D/n — even the minimum of continuity and intelligibility essential to being a person. Instances of his behavior can reasonably be excluded from membership in W, I believe, on the ground that since he lacks all autonomy they cannot legitimately be ascribed to him as his actions.

The other possibility is that the D/n provides his subject with a stable character or program, which he does not thereafter alter too frequently or at all, and that the subsequent mental and physical responses of the subject to his external and internal environments are determined by this program rather than by further intervention on the part of the D/n. In that case there is no reason for denying that instances of the subject's behavior may be members of W. Nor, in my opinion, are there compelling reasons either against allowing that the subject may act freely or against regarding him as capable of being morally responsible for what he does.

He may become morally responsible, assuming that he is suitably programmed, in the same way others do: by identifying himself with some of his own second-order desires, so that they are not merely desires that he happens to have or to find within himself, but desires that he adopts or puts himself behind. In virtue of a person's identification of himself with one of his own second-order desires, that desire becomes a second-order volition. And the person thereby *takes* responsibility for the pertinent first- and second-order desires and for the actions to which these desires lead him.

Locke suggests that the subject of a D/n cannot be regarded as acting freely because it is not up to the subject, or within the subject's control, what he does or what desires and second-order volitions he has. Evidently he construes the notions "up to X" and "within X's control" in such a way that nothing is up to a person, or within that person's control, if someone else determines its occurrence. In my view these notions are to be construed differently, at least in the present context. What is at stake in their application is not so much a matter of the causal origins of the states of affairs in question, but X's activity or passivity with respect to those states of affairs.

Now a person is active with respect to his own desires when he identifies himself with them, and he is active with respect to what he does when what he does is the outcome of his identification of himself with the desire that moves him in doing it. Without such identification the person is a passive bystander to his desires and to what he does, regardless of whether the causes of his desires and of what he does are the work of another agent or of impersonal external forces or of processes internal to his own body. As for a person's second-order volitions themselves, it is impossible for him to be a passive bystander to them. They *constitute* his activity – i.e., his being active rather than passive – and the question of whether or not he identifies himself with them cannot arise. It makes no sense to ask whether someone identifies himself with his identification of himself, unless this is intended simply as asking whether his identification is wholehearted or complete.

This notion of identification is admittedly a bit mystifying, and I am uncertain how to go about explicating it. In my opinion, however, it grasps something quite fundamental in our inner lives, and it merits a central role in the phenomenology and philosophy of human mentality. Instead of attempting to provide the analysis the notion requires, I shall limit myself to a declaration: to the extent that a person identifies himself with the springs of his actions, he takes responsibility for those actions and acquires moral responsibility for them; moreover, the questions of how the actions and his identifications with their springs are caused are irrelevant to the questions of whether he performs the actions freely or is morally responsible for performing them.

The fact that the D/n causes his subject to have and to identify with certain second-order desires does not, then, affect the moral significance of the subject's acquisition of the second-order volitions with which he is thereby endowed. There is no paradox in the supposition that a D/n might create a morally free agent. It might be reasonable, to be sure, to hold the D/n too morally responsible for what his free subject does, at least insofar as he can fairly be held responsible for anticipating the subject's actions. This does not imply, however, that full moral responsibility for those actions may not also be ascribable to the subject. It is quite possible for more than one person to bear full moral responsibility for the same event or action.

IV

An action may belong to W even when the agent performs it under duress — that is, in submission to a threat, but where the agent's submission does not result from the irresistibility of his desire to avoid the penalty with which he is threatened. If W is identified with the class of free actions, then of course it follows that actions may be performed freely even when they are performed under duress. This has a rather jarring sound. It must be noted, however, that the consequence would evidently not be unacceptable to Locke.

He is prepared to allow that a bank clerk acts freely when, in order to avoid being shot, the clerk submits to the demands of an armed raider. And he explains that the clerk may be said to act freely because "it is his decision and his decision alone whether to hand over the funds or risk his life, and which he does will depend on him, his wishes and preferences, not on anyone else, not even on the raider." Locke apparently does not suppose that the clerk is stampeded by his desire to avoid being shot, or that his action derives from a belief that he cannot avoid succumbing to this desire. In other words, he construes the clerk's situation to be of Type A and his action to belong to W: the clerk acts under duress, but he is not coerced.

On this assumption the point of characterizing the clerk as acting freely, even though he can hardly be said to act willingly, is just that the clerk's action is not due to his being inescapably forced to act as he does. His action results from a decision to which he has, or thinks he has, an available alternative. Thus it expresses a genuine choice on his part. It is plainly irrelevant to the genuineness of this choice whether or not the clerk is correct in his belief that he could refrain from or avoid handing over the funds if he preferred that alternative. Insofar as the freedom of the clerk's action rests upon its derivation from a genuine choice on his part, as Locke suggests, freedom of action appears not to require avoidability.

Although Locke regards the clerk as acting freely, he does not think him morally responsible for his action. In Locke's opinion, indeed, it is an error to suppose that there is any necessary connection at all between the concepts of free action and moral responsibility. His reasons for holding this opinion, however, are not convincing.

To support the position that acting freely is not a necessary condition for moral responsibility Locke claims that a speeding driver may be morally responsible for hitting a child who runs out from behind a parked car, despite the fact that the driver does not freely hit the child. But this claim seems incorrect. Other things being equal, the driver is no more blameworthy than if he had missed the child; and he is far less blameworthy than someone who freely hits a child with his car. These considerations indicate that the speeder is not morally responsible for hitting the child at all. What he is responsible for is something like driving recklessly, and there is no reason to doubt that he does this freely. The example does not, then, undermine the view that acting freely is a necessary condition for moral responsibility.

And what of the bank clerk? It is true that we would probably not blame him for submitting to the demands of the armed raider. Locke evidently supposes that this is because we do not think him morally responsible for his action, and that if free action were tied to moral responsibility we would consequently have to say (wrongly, in his judgment) that the clerk does not act freely. But assuming that we do regard the clerk as acting freely, the reason we refrain from blaming him is not that we think he bears no moral responsibility for his submission to the raider. It is that we judge him to act reasonably when he gives up the bank's money instead of his own life, and so we find nothing blameworthy in what he does. Thus the example does not show, as it is presumably intended to do, that a person may act freely without being morally responsible for what he does.

V

Given the roles played by freedom and related concepts in our general conceptual scheme, and the reflections of these roles in linguistic custom, it would not be unreasonable to require that the concept of free action be understood in such a way that a person can bear no moral responsibility except for what he has done freely. On the same basis, it would be equally reasonable to require that no action be construed as having been performed freely if it was performed under duress, or under duress of a certain degree of harshness. Locke's analysis, according to which free actions are those that are avoidable, satisfies neither of these requirements. Being able to avoid performing an action is not incompatible with performing the action under duress, nor is it a necessary condition for being morally responsible for performing it.

This does not mean that avoidability has nothing whatever to do with freedom. It only means that a person may act freely when he is not free to act differently. From the fact that X did A freely, in other words, it does not follow that X was free to refrain from doing A. Thus a person may be free to do what it happens that he wants to do, and do it freely, without enjoying freedom in the sense of being in a position to do whatever he might both want and be inherently able to do. It does not strike me as objectionable to say that a prisoner may come to act more freely – that is, to perform more of his actions freely – through having learned the lessons of Epictetus. But there will naturally remain as many things as before that he is not free to do, which he would be capable of doing if he were not imprisoned. Therefore it would not be correct to describe him as having been freed, or as having escaped the limitations of his imprisonment, by his study of Stoic philosophy.

Identifying W with the class of free actions, since it allows that actions may be performed both freely and under duress, fails to satisfy one of the requirements that has been suggested. It does appear to satisfy the other: membership in W is a necessary condition for a morally responsible action. In fact it is not possible to satisfy both requirements at once, because a person may be morally responsible for what he does under duress. Phrases like "did it freely" are actually used somewhat equivocally: at times they connote that the agent did what he did willingly, and at times they connote his moral responsibility for doing it. If we must have an established and univocal philosophical usage for "free action," we must decide whether it is preferable to satisfy the one requirement or to satisfy the other. So far as I can see, there is little to choose between these alternatives.

5

Identification and externality

One of the central and most difficult problems in the theory of action is often formulated in some such way as the following. What account is to be given of the difference between the sort of thing that goes on when a person raises his arm (say, to give a signal) and the sort of thing that happens when a person's arm rises (say, because of a muscular spasm) without his raising it? The question invokes a contrast between events that are actions, in which the higher faculties of human beings come into play, and those movements of a person's body – instances of behavior other than actions, or mere bodily happenings – that he does not himself make. This contrast can evidently be generalized. It is a special case of the contrast between activity and passivity, which is considerably wider in scope.

Actions are instances of activity, though not the only ones even in human life. To drum one's fingers on the table, altogether idly and inattentively, is surely not a case of passivity: the movements in question do not occur without one's making them. Neither is it an instance of action, however, but only of being active. The occurrence in human life of events that are neither actions nor mere happenings is sometimes overlooked, but it should not be surprising.[1] The contrast between activity and passivity is readily discernible at levels of existence where we are disinclined to suppose that there are actions. Thus, a spider is passive with respect to the movements of its legs when its legs move because the spider has received an electric shock. On the other hand the spider is active with respect to the movements of its legs – though it performs no action – when it moves its legs in making its way along the ground. We should not find it unnatural that we are capable, without lapsing into mere passivity, of behaving as mindlessly as the spider.

It is far from easy to explicate the difference between being active and

---

1 One result of overlooking events of this kind is an exaggeration of the peculiarity of what humans do. Another result, related to the first, is the mistaken belief that a twofold division of human events into actions and mere happenings provides a classification that suits the interests of the theory of action.

being passive, and in fact philosophers have for some time generally neglected the task. Aristotle took a step by dividing the events in a thing's history into those whose moving principle is inside the thing and those whose moving principle is outside. This is suggestive: a thing is active with respect to events whose moving principle is inside of it, and passive with respect to events whose moving principle is outside of it. But the internal-external distinction, which appears to underlie that between activity and passivity, is unfortunately no less difficult to understand. Clearly, the terms "inside" and "outside" cannot be taken in their straightforwardly spatial meanings. If a man is carried somewhere by the wind, what moves him is outside his body. If his body or some part of his body is moved by a spasm that occurs in his own muscles, he is equally passive with respect to the event although its moving principle is inside his body. To what, then, is the moving principle in this case pertinently "external"?

I shall not attempt to explore the basis of the distinction between activity and passivity. Instead, I shall consider a further extension of the scope of the distinction with which I began. The contrast between those movements of a person's body that are mere happenings in his history, and those that are his own activities, leads not only away from human life into the lower realms of creation. It also leads, in virtue of its analogues in the psychological domain, into the center of our experience of ourselves.

In our intellectual processes, we may be either active or passive. Turning one's mind in a certain direction, or deliberating systematically about a problem, are activities in which a person himself engages. But to some of the thoughts that occur in our minds, as to some of the events in our bodies, we are mere passive bystanders. Thus there are obsessional thoughts, whose provenances may be obscure and of which we cannot rid ourselves; thoughts that strike us unexpectedly out of the blue; and thoughts that run willy-nilly through our heads.

The thoughts that beset us in these ways do not occur by our own active doing. It is tempting, indeed, to suggest that they are not thoughts that *we think* at all, but rather thoughts that we *find* occurring within us. This would express our sense that, although these thoughts are events in the histories of our own minds, we do not participate actively in their occurrence. The verb "to think" can connote an activity — as in "I am thinking carefully about what you said" — and with regard to this aspect of its meaning we cannot suppose that thoughts are necessarily accompanied by thinking. It is not incoherent, despite the air of paradox, to say that a thought that occurs in my mind may or may not be something that *I think*. This can be understood in much the same way as the less jarring

statement that an event occurring in my body may or may not be something that *I do.*

It is the passions, however, that I want particularly to consider. The
fact that the very word "passion" conveys passivity presents something of
a linguistic obstacle to the comfortable application to the passions of the
distinctions with which I have been dealing. It may well be, moreover,
that this obstacle is more substantial than a mere etymology. Nonetheless I believe that there is a useful distinction to be made, however
awkward its expression, between passions with respect to which we are
active and those with respect to which we are passive. Among our passions, as among the movements of our bodies, there are some whose
moving principles are within ourselves and others whose moving principles are external to us.

This is apparently denied by Terence Penelhum. According to him,
any person who attempts to represent his desires as external to himself is
engaged in a "form of moral trickery" involving "gross literal
falsehood."[2] He condemns every representation of this kind as evasive
and inauthentic, because "it denies that some desire . . . is part of one's
ongoing history when it is" (671). Penelhum acknowledges that when a
person has a desire that he would prefer not to have, or when he is
moved to act by a desire that he does not want to move him to act, the
person may feel that his desire is somehow alien to him. In such cases,
admittedly, the person may say that he does not identify himself with the
desire. But Penelhum maintains that the desire with which a person does
not identify himself is "just as much part of him as that with which he
does" (672). His argument for this claim is a simple one: every desire
must, after all, belong to *someone,* and a desire with which a person does
not identify himself clearly does not belong to anyone else (674).

This way with the matter strikes me as being too hasty. It is not so
unequivocally obvious, it seems to me, that a human desire must be the
desire of some person. At least, I think we may say that there is an
interesting sense, distinct from the sense in which this *is* quite obvious,
in which it is not obvious at all. Suppose that one person in a lurching and
crowded vehicle is impelled against another, and that the second person
asks merely out of curiosity who it was that pushed him; then it would be
sensible enough for the first person to say that it was he who did it, and
to let the matter go at that, even though the push involved no activity on
his part. A human bodily movement, even when it is a mere happening in

---

2 Terence Penelhum, "The Importance of Self-Identity," *Journal of Philosophy* LXVIII
(1971), 670. The numbers within parentheses in the remainder of the current paragraph refer to the pages of this essay.

the history of the person whose body moves, can for certain purposes be identified appropriately as a movement of that person and of no one else. However, we find it useful to reserve a sense in which a movement of this kind is strictly attributable not to the person at all but only to his body. We acknowledge that in this strict sense there is *no person* to whom it can be attributed – no person of whom it is "just as much part of him" as his actions and his activities are. Now why may a desire not, in a similar way, be an event in the history of a person's mind without being that person's desire? Why may not certain mental movements, like certain movements of human bodies, in this sense belong to no one?

We think it correct to attribute to a person, in the strict sense, only some of the events in the history of his body. The others – those with respect to which he is passive – have their moving principles outside him, and we do not identify him with these events. Certain events in the history of a person's mind, likewise, have their moving principles outside of him. He is passive with respect to them, and they are likewise not to be attributed to him. A person is no more to be identified with everything that goes on in his mind, in other words, than he is to be identified with everything that goes on in his body. Of course, every movement of a person's body is an event in his history; in this sense it is his movement, and no one else's. In this same sense, all the events in the history of a person's mind are his too. If this is all that is meant, then it is undeniably true that a passion can no more occur without belonging to someone than a movement of a living human body can occur without being someone's movement. But this is only a gross literal truth, which masks distinctions that are as valuable in the one case as they are in the other.

Penelhum's strictures are too severe. They ignore the fact that there are, in the relation of a person to his passions, problems analogous to the more familiar problems concerning the relation of a person to the movements of his body. To insist unequivocally that every passion must be attributable to someone is thus as gratuitous as it would be to insist that a spasmodic movement of a person's body must be a movement the person makes, unless there is some other person of whom it can be said that *he* makes the movement. There is in fact a legitimate and interesting sense in which a person may experience a passion that is external to him, and that is strictly attributable neither to him nor to anyone else.

Recognizing this need not prevent us from agreeing with Penelhum that such a passion is part of the person's ongoing history. It may be noted, moreover, that declining to attribute to a person certain of the passions he experiences does not commit us to regarding those passions as altogether irrelevant in reaching a fair judgment concerning what we can expect from him. A passion is no less genuine, and its thrust is no less forceful, for being external to the person in whose history it occurs, any more than a bodily movement is less palpable in its occurrence or in its effects for being a movement that is not made by the person in whose body it occurs.

No doubt we would be providing people with opportunities for moral evasion, as Penelhum suggests, if we were to allow that it may be legitimate for someone to disclaim certain of his passions as external. For a person may of course be acting in bad faith when he denies that a passion he finds in himself is unequivocally to be attributed to him. But we routinely make room for similar evasiveness and inauthenticity already, without thinking that it is a mistake for us to do so, in our acceptance of the practice of disclaiming certain bodily movements as external. A person may dishonestly and successfully seek to escape an unfavorable judgment to which he would otherwise be subject, after all, by denying that a certain movement of his body was one that he made, and by professing that the moving principle of the physical event in question was actually quite external to him. Moreover it may be as hopelessly difficult to uncover the self-deception or the lie when someone pretends that a movement of his body is one that he did not make, as it often is to discover a person's insincerity when he maintains that a passion he experiences is not to be attributed to him. The ambition to make our tasks as moral judges less difficult is no more a good reason in the one case than it is in the other, surely, for ignoring a distinction that corresponds to a significant difference of fact.

II

We need now to consider which of the passions in a person's history *are* external to him, and to examine the conditions of their externality. A passion is especially likely to be external when it is artificially induced by such means as hypnosis or the use of drugs. In cases of this sort, the passion generally does not arise as a response to a perceived experience. It may well present itself to the person in whose history it is contrived to occur, accordingly, as discontinuous with his understanding of his situation and with his conception of himself. Even so, the person often appears by a kind of instinct to circumvent these discontinuities with rationalization: he instantaneously provides the passion with meaning, or somehow construes it as having a natural place in his experience. Then, despite its origin, the passion becomes attached to a moving principle within the person; and the person is no more a passive bystander with respect to it than if it had arisen in more integral response to his perceptions.

IDENTIFICATION AND EXTERNALITY

It is not only passions aroused by contrivance, however, that are external. Consider the following exemplary episode:

In the course of an animated but amiable enough conversation, a man's temper suddenly rushes up in him out of control. Although nothing has happened that makes his behavior readily intelligible, he begins to fling dishes, books, and crudely abusive language at his companion. Then his tantrum subsides, and he says: "I have no idea what triggered that bizarre spasm of emotion. The feelings just came over me from out of nowhere, and I couldn't help it. I wasn't myself. Please don't hold it against me."

These disclaimers may be, of course, shabbily insincere devices for obtaining unmerited indulgence. Or they may be nothing more than emphatic expressions of regret. But it is also possible that they are genuinely descriptive. What the man says may appropriately convey his sense that the rise of passion represented in some way an intrusion upon him, that it violated him, that when he was possessed by the anger he was not in possession of himself. It is in statements like the ones made by the man in this example, and in the sense of oneself. that such statements express, that we most vividly encounter the experience of externality.

Which features of episodes like this one are essential conditions or marks of externality, and which are inessential? The answer that comes most readily to mind is that passions are external to us just when we prefer not to have them, or when we prefer not to be moved by them; and that they are internal when, at the time of their occurrence, we welcome or indifferently accept them. On this account a passion is unequivocally ours when it is what we want to feel, or are willing to feel, while a passion whose occurrence in us we disapprove is not strictly ours.

Sometimes, when we disapprove of the course our passions have taken, we say that it does not represent what we "really" feel. We do not intend in this way to deny that the passions in question occur, but to indicate that we regard them as being in some manner incoherent with our preferred conception of ourselves, which we suppose captures what we are more truly than mere undistilled description. People are often inclined, at least until they reach a certain age, to construe what they really are as what they would like to be. They consider their "real" passions to be those by which they would like to be motivated, or with which they would prefer to be identified by those who know them, even though these passions may in fact be dimmer and less influential upon their behavior than others.

This equation of the real with the ideal does play a role in the way some people think about themselves. Nonetheless, the distinction between internal and external passions is not the same as the distinction between what is and what is not "real" in the sense of conforming to a person's ideal image of himself. Surely it is possible for a person to recognize that a certain passion is unequivocally attributable to him, even when he regrets this fact and wishes that the passion did not occur in him or move him at all. Perhaps after long struggle and disillusion with himself, a person may become resigned to being someone of whom he himself does not altogether approve. He no longer supposes that he is capable of bringing the course of his passions into harmony with his ideal concept of himself, and accordingly he ceases to reserve his acceptance of his passions as they are.

It is also not essential to the externality of a passion that it be of irresistible intensity. We are ordinarily led to disclaim a passion only when it happens to be one to which we would have preferred not to be subject, or when it interferes in some important way with the sovereignty of other passions that we regard as more genuinely our own. Considerations of this sort account for our interest in *calling attention to* the externality of certain passions, but they are not conditions of externality itself. There is nothing in the notion of externality that implies irresistibility or, for that matter, any particular level of relative intensity. Thus it is quite intelligible that a person should find in himself a desire with which he does not identify, and yet that he should have no difficulty whatever in preventing that desire from moving him or from usurping his will. In my example, the person regrets his inability to control his anger. This explains his eagerness to dissociate himself publicly from that passion and from the desires to which it led. Neither his inability nor his regret, however, accounts for the fact – if it was a fact – that the anger and the angry desires were not strictly his own.

III

I have maintained that the question of whether a passion is internal or external to a person is not just a matter of the person's attitude toward the passion. Still, I am reluctant to suggest that the attitudes of a person toward his passions can be dismissed as altogether irrelevant to this question. Suppose someone disclaims a passion that occurs in him on a certain occasion, but we know both that he experiences passions of this sort regularly on such occasions, and that he is quite willing and satisfied to do so. We are unlikely to treat his disclaimer very seriously, in that case, and this response seems reasonable. What is unclear is the basis on which we would rightly be skeptical.

Perhaps we think that whether or not a person is to be identified with a certain passion is, at least sometimes, up to him. Perhaps we have the idea, in other words, that there is something a person can do that makes a passion fully his own, and that there is sometimes nothing to stop him from doing this if he chooses to do it. Then we would find it difficult to understand, when a person contentedly and with predictable regularity experiences a certain passion, that he has not done whatever it takes to identify himself with it. That would explain our skepticism.

The fact that a person disapproves of a passion that occurs in him is not by itself tantamount to the passion's being an external one. For it is possible, as I have already observed, that someone should become re-signed to what he judges to be his defects. A person may acknowledge to himself that passions of which he disapproves are undeniably and un-equivocally his; and he may then cease to feel, if he ever felt, that these passions are in any way alien or that they intrude upon him. The fact that a person disapproves of a passion is not, accordingly, a sufficient condi-tion of the passion's externality to him. On the other hand, it may be that disapproval is a necessary condition of externality. It is in fact difficult to think of a convincing example in which a person to whom a passion is external nonetheless approves of the occurrence of the passion in him. And the difficulty of finding an example of this kind also tends to sup-port the conjecture that a person's approval of a passion that occurs in his history is a sufficient condition of the passion's being internal to him.

Whatever the truth about these relationships may be, it is important to notice that there is a quite basic error in thinking that the concepts of internality and externality are to be explicated *simply* in terms of a per-son's attitudes. It is fundamentally misguided to suggest that a passion's externality is entailed by the person's disapproval of it, or that its inter-nality is entailed by his approval. The trouble with this approach to the problem of understanding internality and externality is that it fails to take into account the fact that attitudes toward passions are as susceptible to externality as are passions themselves. Suppose that a person has mixed feelings about one of his passions: he is aware of having an inclination to approve of the passion and also of having an inclination to disapprove of it. Suppose he resolves this conflict by decisively adopting an attitude of disapproval toward the passion. He may find nonetheless that his inclina-tion to approve of the passion persists, though it is now external to him and not properly to be attributed to him as his own.

The fact that a person has a certain attitude toward a passion can be construed as determining either the internality or the externality of the passion, surely, only if the attitude in question is itself genuinely at-tributable to him. An attitude in virtue of which a passion is internal, or in virtue of which a passion is external, cannot be merely an attitude that a person finds within himself; it must be one with which he is to be identified. But given that the question of attribution arises not only with regard to a person's passions, but also with regard to his attitudes toward his passions, an infinite regress will be generated by any attempt to account for internality or externality in terms of attitudes. For the attitude that is invoked to account for the status of a passion will have to be an internal one; its internality will have to be accounted for by invoking a higher-order attitude – that is, an attitude toward an attitude; the internality of this higher-order attitude will have to be accounted for in terms of an attitude of a still higher order; and so on. This precludes explication of the concepts of internality and externality by appealing merely to the notion of orders of attitudes.

IV

I cannot provide a satisfactory account of what it means to characterize a passion as internal or as external. It may be possible for me to clarify these notions a bit further, however, by discussing two sorts of conflict of desire. Suppose that a person wants to go to a concert, and that he also wants to see a film. Imagine further that in the circumstances these desires conflict, so that the person must decide whether he prefers to spend his evening in the one way or in the other. Now it is likely that both the desire to see the film and the desire to go to the concert are equally internal to the person. The situation is simply one in which he wants to do two things and cannot do both of them. He would resolve the problem this conflict presents just by deciding which of the two things in question he prefers to do.

Conflicts of this kind require only that the desires at issue be ordered. Their essential feature is that the conflicting desires belong to the same ordering, though as long as the conflict is unresolved their relative positions in that ordering are unsettled. Membership in the same ordering may be explained as follows. Suppose the person decides that he actually prefers to see the film, but it turns out that he is unable to obtain a ticket. Then it would be quite natural for him to revert to his second choice and go to the concert. After all, he wants to do that too. His original decision against doing it meant only that satisfying his desire to go to the concert was lower in his ordering than satisfying his desire to see the film.

When a person suffers a conflict of the second kind, his problem is not to assign one desire that he feels to a lower position than another on a single scale. It is to reject one of the desires that he feels altogether. Conflicts between conscious and unconscious desires are typically of this kind but both of the conflicting desires may well remain conscious. Suppose that a person wants to compliment an acquaintance for some recent achievement, but that he also notices within himself a jealously spiteful desire to injure the man. It may be that, as things turn out, he finds no opportunity to make the friendly remark that he had (we may imagine) decided to make. This would not naturally lead him to see if he can salvage the satisfaction of his other desire. When a person is frustrated in his desire to see a film, he naturally turns to his second choice and goes to a concert. In the present example, however, the alternative of injuring his acquaintance is not second to the person's first choice of paying him a compliment. It is in this sense that the friendly and the jealous desires, unlike those concerning the concert and the film, do not belong to the same ordering.

There is no reason to presume that the person's desire to injure his acquaintance occurs in the first instance as an external desire, and that his desire to compliment the man occurs originally as an internal one. To be sure, it may happen that way. If it does, then the two desires will present themselves from the start as belonging to different orderings; and the person will have no conflict to resolve, though he may have to fight off the influence of the external desire. On the other hand, it may happen that, at an early stage in his confrontation of his feelings, the person finds that the one desire is no less internal to him than the other. In that case, the person himself is in conflict and not merely the desires that are occurring in his mental history. He has the problem of not knowing what he wants to do, in a familiar sense that is quite compatible with his knowing both that he wants to injure his acquaintance and that he wants to pay him a compliment, and the conflict his uncertainty manifests requires resolution.

The person cannot resolve this conflict by deciding that his first choice is to satisfy one of the conflicting desires and that satisfying the other desire is his second choice. The conflict is not one to be resolved by *ordering* the conflicting desires, in other words, but by *rejecting* one of them. In rejecting the desire to injure his acquaintance, presuming that this is what he does, the person withdraws himself from it. He places the rejected desire outside the scope of his preferences, so that it is not a candidate for satisfaction at all. Although he may continue to experience the rejected desire as occurring in his mental history, the person brings it about in this way that its occurrence is an external one. The desire is then no longer to be attributed strictly to him, even though it may well persist or recur as an element of his experience.

In a conflict of the first kind, the person's decision to go to the film does not mean that he does not want to go to the concert. It means that he does not want to go to the concert *as much* as he wants to go to the film. In the second, the person's rejection of the desire to injure his acquaintance does not mean simply that he wants to compliment him *more* than he wants to injure him. It means that he does *not* want to injure him, even though the desire to injure is something that he experiences. It would be a bit misleading to insist that since the desire to compliment prevails over the desire to injure, the situation is merely that the former is stronger than the latter. This wrongly suggests that both desires occupy positions in the same ordering, and that they differ only in strength. There is a better way, I believe, to describe the fact that the desire to compliment prevails over the desire to injure. It is to say that *the person,* who wants to pay his acquaintance a compliment, is stronger than the desire to injure him that he finds within himself.

By deciding that what he wants after all is to compliment his acquaintance, and that his desire to injure the man is finally to be excluded from the order of candidates for satisfaction, the person renders the second desire external to himself and identifies himself with the first. Here it appears to be by making a particular kind of decision that the relation of the person to his passions is established. It may be that a decision of this kind, even when it is not so visible as in the present example, lies behind every instance of the establishment of the internality or externality of passions. Or perhaps it is by referring to something more general, of which decisions are only special cases, that we must seek to understand the phenomena in question. In any event, the nature of decision is very obscure.[3]

V

The problem of attribution or of externality with regard to bodily movements is to explain what differentiates a movement that a person makes from a mere happening in the history of his body. The corresponding problem with regard to psychic phenomena concerns the nature of identification: what does it mean for a person to be identified with one rather than with another of two passions (or whatever), both of which are in the gross literal sense his? Each of these problems is, in its own realm, both fundamental and frustratingly recalcitrant. I have done little more than to suggest that they are in certain respects analogous. It remains to be seen in what important ways they may differ, and whether it is likely that they are susceptible to analogous solutions.

3 Decisions, unlike desires or attitudes, do not seem to be susceptible both to internality and to externality. Invoking them here would appear to avoid, accordingly, the difficulty considered in the preceding section.

6

The problem of action

The problem of action is to explicate the contrast between what an agent does and what merely happens to him, or between the bodily movements that he makes and those that occur without his making them. According to causal theories of the nature of action, which currently represent the most widely followed approach to the understanding of this contrast, the essential difference between events of the two types is to be found in their prior causal histories: a bodily movement is an action if and only if it results from antecedents of a certain kind. Different versions of the causal approach may provide differing accounts of the sorts of events or states which must figure causally in the production of actions. The tenet they characteristically share is that it is both necessary and sufficient, in order to determine whether an event is an action, to consider how it was brought about.

Despite its popularity, I believe that the causal approach is inherently implausible and that it cannot provide a satisfactory analysis of the nature of action. I do not mean to suggest that actions have no causes; they are as likely to have causes, I suppose, as other events are. My claim is rather that it is no part of the nature of an action to have a prior causal history of any particular kind. From the fact that an event is an action, in my view, it does not follow even that it has a cause or causes at all, much less that it has causal antecedents of any specific type.

In asserting that the essential difference between actions and mere happenings lies in their prior causal histories, causal theories imply that actions and mere happenings do not differ essentially in themselves at all. These theories hold that the causal sequences producing actions are necessarily of a different type than those producing mere happenings, but that the effects produced by sequences of the two types are inherently indistinguishable. They are therefore committed to supposing that a person who knows he is in the midst of performing an action cannot have derived this knowledge from any awareness of what is currently happening, but that he must have derived it instead from his understanding of how what is happening was caused to happen by certain earlier conditions. It is integral to the causal approach to regard actions and mere happenings as being differentiated by nothing that exists or that is going on at the time those events occur, but by something quite extrinsic to them — a difference at an earlier time among another set of events entirely.

This is what makes causal theories implausible. They direct attention exclusively away from the events whose natures are at issue, and away from the times at which they occur. The result is that it is beyond their scope to stipulate that a person must be in some particular relation to the movements of his body *during* the period of time in which he is presumed to be performing an action. The only conditions they insist upon as distinctively constitutive of action may cease to obtain, for all the causal accounts demand, at precisely the moment when the agent commences to act. They require nothing of an agent, once the specified causal antecedents of his performing an action have occurred, except that his body move as their effect.

It is no wonder that such theories characteristically run up against counterexamples of a well-known type. For example: a man at a party intends to spill what is in his glass because he wants to signal his confederates to begin a robbery and he believes, in virtue of their prearrangements, that spilling what is in his glass will accomplish that; but all this leads the man to be very anxious, his anxiety makes his hand tremble, and so his glass spills. No matter what kinds of causal antecedents are designated as necessary and sufficient for the occurrence of an action, it is easy to show that causal antecedents of that kind may have as their effect an event that is manifestly not an action but a mere bodily movement. The spilling in the example given has among its causes a desire and a belief, which rationalize the man's spilling what is in his glass, but the spilling as it occurs is not an action. That example makes trouble particularly for a causal theory in which actions are construed as essentially movements whose causes are desires and beliefs by which they are rationalized. Similar counterexamples can readily be generated to make similar trouble for other variants of the causal approach.

I shall not examine the various maneuvers by means of which causal theorists have attempted to cope with these counterexamples.[1] In my

---

[1] For discussion of the problem by adherents to the causal approach, cf. Alvin Goldman, *A Theory of Human Action* (Princeton, 1970), pp. 61–3; Donald Davidson, "Freedom to Act," in T. Honderich (ed.), *Essays on Freedom of Action* (London, 1973), pp. 153–4; Richard Foley, "Deliberate Action," *The Philosophical Review*, vol. 86 (1977), pp. 58–69. Goldman and Davidson evidently believe that the problem of avoiding the counterexamples is an empirical one, which is appropriately to be passed on to scientists. Foley's "solution" renounces the obligation to provide suitable analysis in another way: he specifies conditions for acting and, when he recognizes that they may be met by

judgment causal theories are unavoidably vulnerable to such counterexamples, because they locate the distinctively essential features of action exclusively in states of affairs which may be past by the time the action is supposed to occur. This makes it impossible for them to give any account whatever of the most salient differentiating characteristic of action: during the time a person is performing an action he is necessarily in touch with the movements of his body in a certain way, whereas he is necessarily not in touch with them in that way when movements of his body are occurring without his making them. A theory that is limited to describing causes prior to the occurrences of actions and of mere bodily movements cannot possibly include an analysis of these two ways in which a person may be related to the movements of his body. It must inevitably leave open the possibility that a person, whatever his involvement in the events from which his action arises, loses all connection with the movements of his body at the moment when his action begins.

II

In order to develop a more promising way of thinking about action, let us consider the notion that actions and mere happenings are indistinguishable in themselves. This notion is an important element in the motivation for causal theories. If it were thought that actions and mere happenings differ inherently, then it would be obvious that the way to explicate how they differ would be by identifying this inherent difference between them. It is because causal theorists think that there is no other way to differentiate between actions and mere happenings that they seek a differentiating difference among the events that precede them.

David Pears, who believes that desires play an essential causal role in the production of actions, makes this explicit:

We simply do not possess the general ability to distinguish between those bodily movements which are actions and those which are mere bodily movements without using as a criterion the presence or absence of the relevant desire. . . . It is true that there are various intrinsic characteristics of bodily movements which do give some indication of their classification. For example, a very complicated movement was probably produced by a desire. But . . . the simplicity of a movement does not even make it probable that it was not produced by a desire.

Because we cannot find any inherent characteristic of action which permits us to distinguish it reliably from mere bodily movement, we must

spasms and twitches, he simply declares that such movements are nonetheless actions if they satisfy his conditions.

therefore, in Pears's view, "classify some bodily movements as actions solely by virtue of their origins."[2]

Pears observes correctly that the movements of a person's body do not definitively reveal whether he is performing an action: the very same movements may occur when an action is being performed or when a mere happening is occurring. It does not follow from this, however, that the only way to discover whether or not a person is acting is by considering what was going on *before* his movements began – that is, by considering the causes from which they originated. In fact, the state of affairs *while* the movements are occurring is far more pertinent. What is not merely pertinent but decisive, indeed, is to consider whether or not the movements as they occur are *under the person's guidance*. It is this that determines whether he is performing an action. Moreover, the question of whether or not movements occur under a person's guidance is not a matter of their antecedents. Events are caused to occur by preceding states of affairs, but an event cannot be guided through the course of its occurrence at a temporal distance.

It is worth noticing that Pears is mistaken when he concedes that very complicated movements, though they may possibly be mere happenings, are probably to be classified as actions. The complicated movements of a pianist's hands and fingers do, to be sure, compellingly suggest that they are not mere happenings. Sometimes, however, complexity may quite as compellingly suggest the likelihood of mere bodily movement. The thrashings about of a person's body during an epileptic seizure, for example, are very complicated movements. But their complexity is of a kind which makes it appear unlikely to us that the person is performing an action.

When does complexity of movement suggest action, and when does it suggest its absence? This depends, roughly speaking, upon whether the movements in question cohere in creating a pattern which strikes us as meaningful. When they do, as in the case of the pianist, we find it difficult to imagine that the movements would have occurred, in just those complicated ways required by the meaningful pattern they have created, unless the pianist had been guiding his hands and fingers as they moved. In the epileptic's case, on the other hand, we find it unlikely that a person would have created such an incoherently complicated pattern if he had been guiding his body through its movements. A person's simple movements, as Pears notes, generally suggest neither an action nor a mere happening. This is because their patterns do not ordinarily strike us

2 David Pears, "Two Problems about Reasons for Actions," in R. Binkley, R. Bronaugh, A. Marras (eds.), *Agent, Action and Reason* (Oxford, 1971), pp. 136–7, 139.

as being in themselves either meaningful or incoherent. They do not present us on their faces with any indication of whether or not they are being guided by the person as they occur.

Complexity of body movement suggests action only when it leads us to think that the body, during the course of its movement, is under the agent's guidance. The performance of an action is accordingly a complex event, which is comprised by a bodily movement and by whatever state of affairs or activity constitutes the agent's guidance of it. Given a bodily movement which occurs under a person's guidance, the person is performing an action regardless of what features of his prior causal history account for the fact that this is occurring. He is performing an action even if its occurrence is due to chance. And he is not performing an action if the movements are not under his guidance as they proceed, even if he himself provided the antecedent causes – in the form of beliefs, desires, intentions, decisions, volitions, or whatever – from which the movement has resulted.

III

When we act, our movements are purposive. This is merely another way of saying that their course is guided. Many instances of purposive movement are not, of course, instances of action. The dilation of the pupils of a person's eyes when the light fades, for example, is a purposive movement; there are mechanisms which guide its course. But the occurrence of this movement does not mark the performance of an action by the person; his pupils dilate, but he does not dilate them. This is because the course of the movement is not under *his* guidance. The guidance in this case is attributable only to the operation of some mechanism with which he cannot be identified.

Let us employ the term "intentional" for referring to instances of purposive movement in which the guidance is provided by the agent. We may say, then, that action is intentional movement. The notion of intentional movement must not be confused with that of intentional action. The term "intentional action" may be used, or rather mis-used, simply to convey that an action is necessarily a movement whose course is under an agent's guidance. When it is used in this way, the term is pleonastic. In a more appropriate usage, it refers to actions which are undertaken more or less deliberately or self-consciously – that is, to actions which the agent intends to perform. In this sense, actions are not necessarily intentional.

When a person intends to perform an action, what he intends is that certain intentional movements of his body should occur. When these movements do occur, the person is performing an intentional action. It might be said that he is then guiding the movements of his body in a certain way (thus, he is acting), and that in doing so he is guided by and fulfilling his intention to do just that (thus, he is acting intentionally). There appears to be nothing in the notion of an intentional movement which implies that its occurrence must be intended by the agent, either by way of forethought or by way of self-conscious assent. If this is correct, then actions (i. e., intentional movements) may be performed either intentionally or not.

Since action is intentional movement, or behavior whose course is under the guidance of an agent, an explication of the nature of action must deal with two distinct problems. One is to explain the notion of guided behavior. The other is to specify when the guidance of behavior is attributable to an agent and not simply, as when a person's pupils dilate because the light fades, to some local process going on within the agent's body. The first problem concerns the conditions under which behavior is purposive, while the second concerns the conditions under which purposive behavior is intentional.

The driver of an automobile guides the movement of his vehicle by acting: he turns the steering wheel, he depresses the accelerator, he applies the brakes, and so on. Our guidance of our movements, while we are acting, does not similarly require that we perform various actions. We are not at the controls of our bodies in the way a driver is at the controls of his automobile. Otherwise action could not be conceived, upon pain of generating an infinite regress, as a matter of the occurrence of movements which are under an agent's guidance. The fact that our movements when we are acting are purposive is not the effect of something we do. It is a characteristic of the operation at that time of the systems we are.

Behavior is purposive when its course is subject to adjustments which compensate for the effects of forces which would otherwise interfere with the course of the behavior, and when the occurrence of these adjustments is not explainable by what explains the state of affairs that elicits them. The behavior is in that case under the guidance of an independent causal mechanism, whose readiness to bring about compensatory adjustments tends to ensure that the behavior is accomplished.[3] The

---

3   A useful discussion of this way of understanding purposive behavior is provided by Ernest Nagel, "Goal-directed Processes in Biology," *The Journal of Philosophy*, vol. 74 (1977), pp. 271ff. The details of the mechanisms in virtue of which some item of behavior is purposive can be discovered, of course, only by empirical investigation. But specifying the conditions which any such mechanism must meet is a philosophical problem, belonging to the analysis of the notion of purposive behavior.

activity of such a mechanism is normally not, of course, guided by us. Rather it *is*, when we are performing an action, our guidance of our behavior. Our sense of our own agency when we act is nothing more than the way it feels to us when we are somehow in touch with the operation of mechanisms of this kind, by which our movements are guided and their course guaranteed.

Explaining purposive behavior in terms of causal mechanisms is not tantamount to propounding a causal theory of action. For one thing, the pertinent activity of these mechanisms is not prior to but concurrent with the movements they guide. But in any case it is not essential to the purposiveness of a movement that it actually be causally affected by the mechanism under whose guidance the movement proceeds. A driver whose automobile is coasting downhill in virtue of gravitational forces alone may be entirely satisfied with its speed and direction, and so he may never intervene to adjust its movement in any way. This would not show that the movement of the automobile did not occur under his guidance. What counts is that he was prepared to intervene if necessary, and that he was in a position to do so more or less effectively. Similarly, the causal mechanisms which stand ready to affect the course of a bodily movement may never have occasion to do so; for no negative feedback of the sort that would trigger their compensatory activity may occur. The behavior is purposive not because it results from causes of a certain kind, but because it would be affected by certain causes if the accomplishment of its course were to be jeopardized.

IV

Since the fact that certain causes originate an action is distinct from the considerations in virtue of which it is an action, there is no reason in principle why a person may not be caused in a variety of different ways to perform the same action. This is important in the analysis of freedom. It is widely accepted that a person acts freely only if he could have acted otherwise. Apparent counterexamples to this principle – "the principle of alternate possibilities" – are provided, however, by cases that involve a certain kind of overdetermination. In these cases a person performs an action entirely for his own reasons, which inclines us to regard him as having performed it freely; but he would otherwise have been caused to perform it by forces alien to his will, so that he cannot actually avoid acting as he does.[4]

4 Cf. my "Alternate Possibilities and Moral Responsibilities," and "Freedom of the Will and the Concept of a Person," both reprinted in this volume.

Thus, suppose a man takes heroin because he enjoys its effects and considers them to be beneficial. But suppose further that he is unknowingly addicted to the drug, and hence that he will be driven to take it in any event, even if he is not led to do so by his own beliefs and attitudes. Then it seems that he takes the drug freely, that he could not have done otherwise than to take it, and that the principle of alternate possibilities is therefore false.

Donald Davidson argues to the contrary that whereas a person does intentionally what he does for his own reasons, he does not do intentionally what alien forces cause him to do. While the movements of his body may be the same in both cases, Davidson maintains that the person is not performing an action when the movements occur apart from pertinent attitudes and beliefs. Someone who has acted freely might have done the same thing even if he had not been moved on his own to do it, but only in the sense that his body might have made the same movements: "he would not have acted intentionally had the attitudinal conditions been absent." Even in the "overdetermined" cases, then, something rests with the agent: "not . . . what he does (when described in a way that leaves open whether it was intentional), but whether he does it intentionally."[5]

The issue here is not, as Davidson suggests at one point, whether a person's *action* can be intentional when alien forces rather than his own attitudes account for what he does. It is whether his *behavior* can be intentional in those circumstances. Now the behavior of the unknowing addict is plainly as intentional when he is caused to take the drug by the compulsive force of his addiction, as it is when he takes it as a matter of free choice. His movements are not mere happenings, when he takes the drug because he cannot help himself. He is then performing the very same action that he would have performed had he taken the drug freely and with the illusion that he might have done otherwise.

This example is not designed to show that Davidson is mistaken in insisting that there can be no action without intentionality, or in the absence of pertinent attitudinal conditions. Even when the addict is driven to do what he does, after all, his behavior is presumably affected both by his craving for the drug and by his belief that the procedure he follows in taking it will bring him relief. His movements, as he sticks the syringe into his arm and pushes the plunger, are certainly intentional. However, the relevant problem is not whether an action can occur apart from attitudinal conditions. It is whether it is possible that an action should be caused by alien forces alone.

5 Op. cit., pp. 149–150.

This will seem to be impossible only if it is thought that an action must have attudinal conditions among its causes. But it is not essential to an action that it have an antecedent causal history of any particular kind. Even if there can be no action in the absence of certain attitudinal conditions, therefore, it is not as prior causes that these conditions are essential. The example bears upon the point that is actually at issue, by illustrating how an action (including, of course, any requisite attitudinal constituents) may have no causes other than nonattitudinal or alien ones. Thus it confirms the falsity of the principle of alternate possibilities, by showing that a person may be caused by alien forces alone to perform an action which he might also perform on his own.

The example also suggests, by the way, that the additudinal conditions of a person's action may themselves be alien to him. There is no reason to assume that an addict who succumbs unwillingly to his craving finally adopts as his own the desire he has tried to resist. He may in the end merely submit to it with resignation, like a man who knows he is beaten and who therefore despairingly accepts the consequences defeat must bring him, rather than like someone who decides to join with or to incorporate forces which he had formerly opposed. There are also obsessional and delusional beliefs – e.g., "If I step on a crack it will break my mother's back" – which a person may know to be false but whose influence he cannot escape. So even if it were true (which it is not) that every action necessarily has attitudinal conditions among its antecedent causes, it might nonetheless be alien forces alone which bring it about that a person performs an action.

The assertion that someone has performed an action entails that his movements occurred under his guidance, but not that he was able to keep himself from guiding his movements as he did. There are occasions when we act against or independently of our wills. On other occasions, the guiding principle of our movements is one to which we are not merely resigned; rather, we have embraced it as our own. In such cases, we will ordinarily have a reason for embracing it. Perhaps, as certain philosophers would claim, our having a reason for acting may sometimes cause it to be the case that movements of our bodies are guided by us in a manner which reflects that reason. It is indisputable that a person's beliefs and attitudes often have an important bearing upon how what he is doing is to be interpreted and understood; and it may be that they also figure at times in the causal explanations of his actions. The facts that we are rational and self-conscious substantially affect the character of our behavior and the ways in which our actions are integrated into our lives.

V

The significance to *our* actions of states and events which depend upon the exercise of our higher capacities should not lead us, however, to exaggerate the peculiarity of what human beings do. We are far from being unique either in the purposiveness of our behavior or in its intentionality. There is a tendency among philosophers to discuss the nature of action as though agency presupposes characteristics which cannot plausibly be attributed to members of species other than our own. But in fact the contrast between actions and mere happenings can readily be discerned elsewhere than in the lives of people. There are numerous agents besides ourselves who may be active as well as passive with respect to the movements of their bodies.

Consider the difference between what goes on when a spider moves its legs in making its way along the ground, and what goes on when its legs move in similar patterns and with similar effect because they are manipulated by a boy who has managed to tie strings to them. In the first case the movements are not simply purposive, as the spider's digestive processes doubtless are. They are also attributable to the spider, who makes them. In the second case the same movements occur but they are not made by the spider, to whom they merely happen.

This contrast between two sorts of events in the lives of spiders, which can be observed in the histories of creatures even more benighted, parallels the more familiar contrast between the sort of event that occurs when a person raises his arm and the sort that occurs when his arm goes up without his raising it. Indeed, the two contrasts are the same. The differences they respectively distinguish are alike; and they have, as it were, the same point. Each contrasts instances in which purposive behavior is attributable to a creature as agent and instances in which this is not the case.

This generic contrast cannot be explicated in terms of any of the distinctive higher faculties which characteristically come into play when a person acts. The conditions for attributing the guidance of bodily movements to a whole creature, rather than only to some local mechanism within a creature, evidently obtain outside of human life. Hence they cannot be satisfactorily understood by relying upon concepts which are inapplicable to spiders and their ilk. This does not mean that it must be illegitimate for an analysis of human agency to invoke concepts of more limited scope. While the general conditions of agency are unclear, it may well be that the satisfaction of these conditions by human beings depends upon the occurrence of events or states which do not occur in the histories of other creatures. But we must be careful that the ways in which we construe agency and define its nature do not conceal a parochial bias, which causes us to neglect the extent to which the concept of human action is no more than a special case of another concept whose range is much wider.

7

The importance of what we care about

I

Philosophers have for some time devoted their most systematic attention primarily to two large sets of questions, each of which develops out of concern with a pervasively compelling and troublesome aspect of our lives. In the first set, which constitutes the domain of epistemology, the questions derive in one way or another from our interest in deciding *what to believe.* The general topic of those in the second set is *how to behave,* insofar as this is the subject matter of ethics. It is also possible to delineate a third branch of inquiry, concerned with a cluster of questions which pertain to another thematic and fundamental preoccupation of human existence – namely, *what to care about.*

It is not properly within the scope either of epistemology or of ethics to investigate the various distinctive conceptual questions to which this third preoccupation leads. Those disciplines need not reflect upon the nature of caring as such, nor are they obliged to consider what is implied by the fact that we are creatures to whom things matter. I shall not attempt to provide a formal and exhaustive account of the branch of inquiry that does specifically attend to such things. I propose in this essay merely to broach, in a somewhat tentative and fragmentary way, a few of its central concepts and issues.

II

There is naturally an intimate connection between what a person cares about and what he will, generally or under certain conditions, think it best for himself to do. But while the third branch of inquiry therefore resembles ethics in its concern with problems of evaluation and of action, it differs significantly from ethics in its generative concepts and in its motivating concerns. Ethics focuses on the problem of ordering our relations with *other people.* It is concerned especially with the contrast between *right* and *wrong,* and with the grounds and limits of *moral obligation.* We are led into the third branch of inquiry, on the other hand, because we are interested in deciding what to do with *ourselves* and because we therefore need to understand what is *important* or, rather, what is *important to us*.

It can hardly be disputed that, for most of us, the requirements of ethics are not the only things we care about. Even people who care a great deal about morality generally care still more about other things. They may care more, for instance, about their own personal projects, about certain individuals and groups, and perhaps about various ideals to which they accord commanding authority in their lives but which need not be particularly of an ethical nature. There is nothing distinctively moral, for instance, about such ideals as being steadfastly loyal to a family tradition, or selflessly pursuing mathematical truth, or devoting oneself to some type of connoisseurship.

The role of moral judgment in the development and pursuit of concerns like these is often quite marginal, not only in potency but in relevance as well. It goes without saying that there are many important decisions with regard to which moral considerations are simply not decisive, and which must accordingly be based, at least to some extent, upon considerations of nonmoral kinds. But even decisions that are not of this sort are also often made, of course, in the light of values or preferences other than moral ones. Moreover, it is not wholly apparent that making them in such ways is always unjustifiable.

Someone who takes morality seriously, and who believes that one of his alternatives is in fact morally preferable to the others, may nonetheless regard the importance of this fact as less than categorically preemptive. Suppose first that he does not actually know which of his alternatives is the morally best one. It might be sensible for him to decline to look into the matter at all, on the grounds that under the circumstances doing so would be too costly. That is, he might plausibly judge it more important to himself to reserve for other uses the time and the effort which a conscientious exploration and assessment of the relevant moral features of his situation would require. Whether a judgment of this kind is ever fully warranted depends upon whether or not moral considerations are necessarily so much more important than others that there is no limit to the resources which it is reasonable to spend in order to see that they get their due.

Or suppose, secondly, that the person does already know what he is morally obliged to do. He may nonetheless choose deliberately to violate this obligation — not because he thinks it is overridden by a stronger one, but because there is an alternative course of action which he considers more important to him than meeting the demands of moral rectitude. It seems to me that both in this case and in the first the subordination of moral considerations to others might be justified. In any event, it is clear in both cases that the question concerning what is most important is distinguishable from the question concerning what is morally right.

There may be some people to whom ethical considerations are not only unequivocally paramount but exclusive. If so, then nothing else has as such any importance in their lives. Their only purpose, to which they intend all their activities to contribute, is to do whatever they regard as most desirable from the point of view of morality – to maximize human welfare, perhaps, or to make society more just. This sort of over-specialization is difficult to sustain, and it is rare. But suppose that some-one will in fact accept no reason for acting except that the action in question is more likely than any other to lead to the realization of his moral ideal. It is still the case that this person's moral judgments are one thing and the fact that he cares about them so much is another. His belief that certain courses of action are dictated by ethical considerations dif-fers, in other words, from his belief that no other considerations com-pare in importance to those.

III

Providing fully articulated analyses of the concepts of caring and of importance is no easier than defining the notions – e.g., those of belief and of obligation – which are basic to the first two branches of inquiry. Indeed, the concept of importance appears to be so fundamental that a satisfactory analysis of it may not be possible at all. It is reasonable to suppose that things have importance only in virtue of the differences they make: if it would make no difference at all to anything whether a certain thing existed, or whether it had certain characteristics, then nei-ther the existence of that thing nor its characteristics would be of any importance whatever. But everything does actually make *some* difference. How is it possible, then, for anything to be genuinely unimportant? It can only be because the difference such a thing makes is itself of no importance. Thus it is evidently essential to include, in the analysis of the concept of importance, a proviso to the effect that nothing is important unless the difference it makes is an important one. Whether a useful account of the concept can be developed without running into this cir-cularity is unclear.

As for the notion of what a person cares about, it coincides in part with the notion of something with reference to which the person guides him-self in what he does with his life and in his conduct. It is not to be presumed, of course, that whenever a person's life displays over a period of time some more or less stable attitudinal or behavioral disposition, this reflects what the person cares about during that time. After all, patterns of interest or of response may be manifestations only of habits or of involuntary regularities of some other kind; and it is also possible for them to develop merely by chance. They may be discernible, therefore, even in the lives of creatures who are incapable of caring about anything.

Caring, insofar as it consists in guiding oneself along a distinctive course or in a particular manner, presupposes both agency and self-consciousness. It is a matter of being active in a certain way, and the activity is essentially a reflexive one. This is not exactly because the agent, in guiding his own behavior, necessarily does something *to* himself. Rather, it is more nearly because he purposefully does something *with* himself.

A person who cares about something is, as it were, invested in it. He *identifies* himself with what he cares about in the sense that he makes himself vulnerable to losses and susceptible to benefits depending upon whether what he cares about is diminished or enhanced. Thus he concerns himself with what concerns it, giving particular attention to such things and directing his behavior accordingly. Insofar as the person's life is in whole or in part *devoted* to anything, rather than being merely a sequence of events whose themes and structures he makes no effort to fashion, it is devoted to this.

A person might stop caring about something because he knew he could not have it. But he might nonetheless continue to like it and to want it, and to consider it both desirable and valuable. Thus caring about something is not to be confused with liking it or with wanting it; nor is it the same as thinking that what is cared about has value of some kind, or that it is desirable. It is especially to be noted that these attitudes and beliefs differ significantly from caring in their temporal characteristics. The outlook of a person who cares about something is inherently prospective; that is, he necessarily considers himself as having a future. On the other hand, it is possible for a creature to have desires and beliefs without taking any account at all of the fact that he may continue to exist.

Desires and beliefs can occur in a life which consists merely of a succession of separate moments, none of which the subject recognizes – either when it occurs or in anticipation or in memory – as an element integrated with others in his own continuing history. When this recognition is entirely absent, there *is* no continuing subject. The lives of some animals are presumably like that. The moments in the life of a person who cares about something, however, are not merely linked inherently by formal relations of sequentiality. The person necessarily binds them together, and in the nature of the case also construes them as being bound together, in richer ways. This both entails and is entailed by his own continuing concern with what he does with himself and with what goes on in his life.

Considerations of a similar kind indicate that a person can care about something only over some more or less extended period of time. It is possible to desire something, or to think it valuable, only for a moment. Desires and beliefs have no inherent persistence; nothing in the nature of wanting or of believing requires that a desire or a belief must endure. But the notion of guidance, and hence the notion of caring, implies a certain consistency or steadiness of behavior; and this presupposes some degree of persistence. A person who cared about something just for a single moment would be indistinguishable from someone who was being moved by impulse. He would not in any proper sense be guiding or directing himself at all.

Since the making of a decision requires only a moment, the fact that a person decides to care about something cannot be tantamount to his caring about it. Nor is it a guarantee that he will care about it. By making such a decision, the person forms an intention concerning what to care about. But whether that intention is truly fulfilled is quite another matter. A decision to care no more entails caring than a decision to give up smoking entails giving it up. In neither case does making the decision amount even to initiating the state of affairs decided upon unless that state of affairs actually ensues.

This would hardly be worth pointing out except that an exaggerated significance is sometimes ascribed to decisions, as well as to choices and to other similar "acts of will." If we consider that a person's will is that by which he moves himself, then what he cares about is far more germane to the character of his will than the decisions or choices he makes. The latter may pertain to what he *intends* to be his will, but not necessarily to what his will truly *is*.

The young man in Sartre's famous example is sometimes understood to have resolved his dilemma, concerning whether to remain at home and look after his mother or to abandon her and join the fight against his country's enemies, by making a radically free choice. But how significant is the fact that the young man chooses to pursue one rather than the other of his alternatives, even if we understand this choice to entail a decision on his part concerning what sort of person to be and not merely concerning what to do? It surely gives us no particular reason for thinking that he will actually become the sort of person he decides to be, nor does it even entitle us to assume that he will actually pursue the alternative he chooses.

The point is not that he might change his mind a moment after making his choice, or that he might immediately forget his decision. It is that he might be *unable* to carry out his intention. He might discover, when the chips are down, that he simply cannot bring himself to pursue the course of action upon which he has decided. Without changing his mind or forgetting anything, he might find either that he is moved irresistibly to pursue the other course of action instead or that he is similarly constrained at least to forbear from the course he has chosen. Or he might find that he is actually able to perform the actions he has chosen to perform, but only by forcing himself to do so against powerful and persistent natural inclinations. That is, he might discover that he does not have and that he does not subsequently develop the feelings, attitudes, and interests constitutive of the sort of person which his decision has committed him to being.

The resolution of the young man's dilemma does not merely require, then, that he decide what to do. It requires that he really care more about one of the alternatives confronting him than about the other; and it requires further that he understand which of those alternatives it is that he really cares about more. The difficulty he is in is due either to his not knowing which of the alternatives he cares about more, or to his caring equally about each. It is clear that in neither case is his difficulty reliably to be overcome by making a decision.

The fact that someone cares about a certain thing is constituted by a complex set of cognitive, affective, and volitional dispositions and states. It may sometimes be possible for a person, by making a certain choice or decision, effectively to bring it about that he cares about a certain thing or that he cares about one thing more than about another. But that depends upon conditions which do not always prevail. It certainly cannot be assumed that what a person cares about is generally under his immediate voluntary control.

IV

There are, of course, wide variations in how strongly and how persistently people care about things. It is also possible to discriminate different *ways* of caring, which are not reducible in any obvious manner to differences of degree. The most notable of these are perhaps the several varieties of love. Another significant distinction – which is related to but not identical with the one concerning whether or not caring can be initiated by an act of will – has to do with whether or not a person can help caring as he does. When a person cares about something, it may be entirely up to him both that he cares about it and that he cares about it as much as he does. In certain instances, however, the person is susceptible to a familiar but nonetheless somewhat obscure kind of necessity, in virtue of which his caring is not altogether under his own control.

There are occasions when a person realizes that what he cares about matters to him not merely so much, but in such a way, that it is impossible for him to forbear from a certain course of action. It was presumably on such an occasion, for example, that Luther made his famous declaration: "Here I stand; *I can do no other.*" An encounter with necessity of this sort characteristically affects a person less by impelling him into a certain course of action than by somehow making it apparent to him that every apparent alternative to that course is unthinkable. Such encounters differ from situations in which a person finds that he is unable to forbear, whether or not he wants to do so, because he is being driven to act by some desire or by some compulsion which is too powerful for him to overcome. They also differ from situations in which it is clear to the person that he must reject the possibility of forbearing because he has such a good reason for rejecting it – for instance, because to forbear strikes him as too unappealing or too undesirable a course of action to pursue.

On the other hand, encounters with necessity of the sort in question are in certain respects similar to situations like these. They resemble those of the latter type – viz., the person cannot forbear because his reasons for not doing so are too good – in that the inability to forbear is not a simple matter of deficient capacity on the part of the agent. They resemble those of the former variety – viz., the person is driven by irresistible passion or the like – in that the agent experiences himself as having no choice but to accede to the force by which he is constrained even if he thinks it might be better not to do so.

It is clear, of course, that the impossibility to which Luther referred was a matter neither of logical nor of causal necessity. After all, he knew well enough that he was in one sense quite able to do the very thing he said he could not do; that is, he had the capacity to do it. What he was unable to muster was not the *power* to forbear, but the *will*. I shall use the term "volitional necessity" to refer to constraint of the kind to which he declared he was subject. To the extent that such constraint actually does render it impossible for a person to act in any way other than as he acts, it renders it impossible by preventing him from *making use of* his own capacities. Perhaps there is a sense in which Luther, even if his declaration was true, might have been strong enough to overcome the force which obstructed his pursuit of any course of action but the one he pursued. But he could not *bring himself* to overcome that force.

A person who is subject to volitional necessity finds that he *must* act as he does. For this reason it may seem appropriate to regard situations which involve volitional necessity as providing instances of passivity. But the person in a situation of this kind generally does not construe the fact that he is subject to volitional necessity as entailing that he is passive at all. People are generally quite far from considering that volitional necessity renders them helpless bystanders to their own behavior. Indeed they may even tend to regard it as actually enhancing both their autonomy and their strength of will.

If a person who is constrained by volitional necessity is for that reason unable to pursue a certain course of action, the explanation is not that he is in any straightforward way too weak to overcome the constraint. That sort of explanation can account for the experience of an addict, who dissociates himself from the addiction constraining him but who is unsuccessful in his attempt to oppose his own energies to the impetus of his habit. A person who is constrained by volitional necessity, however, is in a situation which differs significantly from that one. Unlike the addict, he does not accede to the constraining force because he lacks sufficient strength of will to defeat it. He accedes to it because he is *unwilling* to oppose it and because, furthermore, his unwillingness is *itself* something which he is unwilling to alter.

Not only does he care about following the particular course of action which he is constrained to follow. He also cares about caring about it. Therefore he guides himself away from being critically affected by anything – in the outside world or within himself – which might divert him or dissuade him either from following that course or from caring as much as he does about following it. He cannot bring himself to overcome the constraint to which he is subject because, in other words, he does not really want to do so. The predicament of the unwilling addict is that there is something which he really wants to do, but which he cannot do because of a force other than and superior to that of his own will. In the case of the person constrained by volitional necessity, there is also something which he cannot do but only because he does not really want to do it.

The reason a person does not experience the force of volitional necessity as alien or as external to himself, then, is that it coincides with – and is, indeed, partly constituted by – desires which are not merely his own but with which he actively identifies himself. Moreover, the necessity is to a certain extent self-imposed. It is generated when someone requires himself to avoid being guided in what he does by any forces other than those by which he most deeply wants to be guided. In order to prevent himself from caring about anything as much as he cares about them, he suppresses or dissociates himself from whatever motives or desires he regards as inconsistent with the stability and effectiveness of his commitment. It is in this way that volitional necessity may have a liberating effect: when someone is tending to be distracted from caring about what he cares about most, the force of volitional necessity may constrain him to do what he really wants to do.

Whatever the pertinence and the validity of these considerations, however, they do not explain how it is possible for a person to be constrained by a necessity which is imposed upon him only by himself. To be sure, people do often force themselves to act in certain ways – for instance, when they are strongly tempted to act otherwise. But the strenuous exertion of will power in cases of those kinds is fully voluntary. The agent can discontinue it whenever he likes. On the other hand, even if volitional necessity is self-imposed there must be some respect in which it is imposed or maintained involuntarily.

The condition that it be self-imposed helps to account for the fact that it is liberating rather than coercive – i.e., the fact that it supports the person's autonomy rather than being opposed to or independent of his will. It cannot be the case, however, that the person who requires of himself that he avoid guiding himself in a certain way accomplishes the self-imposition of this requirement merely by performing a voluntary act. It must be an essential feature of volitional necessity that it is imposed upon a person involuntarily. Otherwise it will be impossible to account for the fact that the person cannot extricate himself from it merely at will – i.e., the fact that it is genuinely a kind of necessity.

It may seem difficult to understand how volitional necessity can possibly be at the same time both self-imposed and imposed involuntarily, or how it is possible to avoid the conclusion that an agent who is constrained by volitional necessity must be simultaneously both active and passive with respect to the same force. Resolution of these difficulties lies in recognizing that: (a) the fact that a person cares about something is a fact about his will, (b) a person's will need not be under his own voluntary control, and (c) his will may be no less truly his own when it is not by his own voluntary doing that he cares as he does.

Thus volitional necessity may be both self-imposed in virtue of being imposed by the person's own will and, at the same time, imposed involuntarily in virtue of the fact that it is not by his own voluntary act that his will is what it is. Similarly, in such cases, involuntariness does not entail passivity. A person is active when it is by his own will that he does what he does, even when his will is not itself within the scope of his voluntary control. It appears, then, that unless a person cares about certain things regardless of whether or not he chooses to do so, he will not be susceptible to the liberation which volitional necessity can provide.

V

The suggestion that a person may be in some sense liberated through acceding to a power which is not subject to his immediate voluntary control is among the most ancient and persistent themes of our moral and religious tradition. It must surely reflect some quite fundamental structural feature of our lives. This feature remains, however, relatively unexplored. As a consequence, we are unable to give satisfactorily thorough and perspicuous accounts of certain facts which are central to our culture and to our view of ourselves: in particular, that the two human capacities which we prize most highly are those for rationality and for love, and that these capacities are prized not only for their usefulness in enabling us to adapt to our natural and social environments but also because they are supposed to make available to us especially valuable experiences or states of fulfillment and of freedom. The idea that being rational and loving are ways of achieving freedom ought to puzzle us more than it does, given that both require a person *to submit* to something which is beyond his voluntary control and which may be indifferent to his desires.

When we accede to being moved by logic or by love, the feeling with which we do so is not ordinarily one of dispirited impotence. On the contrary, we characteristically experience in both cases – whether we are following reason or following our hearts – a sense of liberation and of enhancement. What accounts for this experience? It appears to have its source in the fact that when a person is responding to a perception of something as rational or as beloved, his relationship to it tends toward *selflessness*. His attention is not merely concentrated upon the object; it is somehow fixed or seized by the object. The object captivates him. He is guided by its characteristics rather than primarily by his own. Quite commonly, he feels that he is overcome – that his own direction of his thoughts and volitions has been superseded. How are we to understand the paradox that a person may be enhanced and liberated through being seized, made captive, and overcome? Why is it that we find ourselves to be most fully realized, and consider that we are at our best, when – through reason or through love – we have lost or escaped from ourselves?[1]

---

1 We are also susceptible to being overcome by beauty and by grandeur; and we encounter similar, though perhaps not identical, experiences when we lose ourselves in the thrill of a moment or in work. These experiences also tend to be liberating. On the other hand, experiences of great fear or pain provide analogues to the selflessness of reason and of love in which the loss of self is not ordinarily construed as fulfilling or as liberating. It seems unlikely that this is merely because these experiences are less

Rationality and love equally entail selflessness. They differ in that the former is also essentially *impersonal*. The substance of this difference between rationality and love is not that what a person loves depends largely upon his own particular characteristics, whereas those characteristics play no role in determining what he considers to be required or permitted by reason. The judgments a person makes concerning rationality are manifestly no less dependent than are any other occurrences in his life upon contingent features of his nature and of his circumstances. What renders these judgments impersonal is that the claims they make are not limited to the person who makes them; rather, it is implicit that anyone who disagrees with the claims must be mistaken. A declaration of love is a personal matter, on the other hand, because the person who makes it does not thereby commit himself to supposing that anyone who fails to love what he does has somehow gone wrong.

Now moral judgments are also impersonal, and in this respect their force differs fundamentally from that of volitional necessity. Even when volitional necessity arises in connection with actions which are required or forbidden by duty, it does not derive from the person's moral convictions as such but from the way in which he cares about certain things. If a mother who is tempted to abandon her child finds that she simply cannot do that, it is probably not because she knows (or even because she cares about) her duty. It is more likely because of how she cares about the child, and about herself as its mother, than because of any recognition on her part that abandoning the child would be morally wrong. Consistency therefore does not require her to suppose that the action which she cannot bring herself to perform must be found to be similarly impossible by every mother whose circumstances are similar to hers.[2]

In the same way, a person who finds that he cannot bring himself to compromise an ideal to which he has been dedicated, despite his anxiety concerning the costs of remaining loyal to it, probably is not being moved most immediately by objective moral considerations even if the ideal in question is of a distinctively moral variety. Suppose that someone's ideal is to be meticulously honest in conducting his business affairs. Everyone is morally obliged, of course, to be honest; but it does not follow that anyone has a duty to pursue honesty as an ideal of his life – i.e., to accord to pursuing it the preemptive attention and concern which

enjoyable than those of love and rationality, but it is unclear what does account for the difference.

2 Although *consistency* does not require her to suppose this, she and others might suppose it anyhow on other grounds. Even if it is not morally obligatory for mothers to care deeply about their children, a mother who does not do so might still be open to criticism – not that her attitude violates a duty but, for instance, that it is "unnatural" or "shameful" and that she lacks important human qualities.

commitment to an ideal entails. A person's discovery that it is volitionally impossible for him to neglect one of his ideals is not to be equated, then, with an acknowledgment on his part of an ethical requirement.

Especially with respect to those we love and with respect to our ideals, we are liable to be bound by necessities which have less to do with our adherence to the principles of morality than with integrity or consistency of a more personal kind. These necessities constrain us from betraying the things we care about most and with which, accordingly, we are most closely identified. In a sense which a strictly ethical analysis cannot make clear, what they keep us from violating are not our duties or our obligations but ourselves.

VI

The formation of a person's will is most fundamentally a matter of his coming to care about certain things, and of his coming to care about some of them more than about others. Although these processes may not be wholly under his voluntary control, it is nonetheless often possible for him to affect them. For that reason, as well as because people are generally interested in knowing what to think of themselves, a person may care about what he cares about. This leads to questions concerning evaluation and justification.

The fact that what a person cares about is a personal matter does not entail that *anything* goes. It may still be possible to distinguish between things that are worth caring about to one degree or another and things that are not. Accordingly, it may be useful to inquire into what makes something worth caring about – that is, what conditions must be satisfied if something is to be suitable or worthy as an ideal or as an object of love – and into how a person is to decide, from among the various things worth caring about, which to care about. Although people may justifiably care about different things, or care differently about the same things, this surely does not mean that their loves and their ideals are entirely unsusceptible to significant criticism of any sort or that no general analytical principles of discrimination can be found.[3]

3 One version of skepticism with regard to these matters is the view that there is really nothing worth caring about. Whatever the merits of this view, it is important not to confuse it with – nor to suppose that it entails – the more radical claim that nothing is of any importance to us. A person who cares about something thereby incurs certain costs, connected with the effort which investing himself requires and with the vulnerability to disappointment and to other losses which it imposes. In virtue of these costs, it is possible for something to be important to a person without being important enough for it to be worth his while to care about it. The view that nothing is worth caring about therefore entails only that nothing is of *sufficient* importance to make caring about it reasonable.

People often do not care about certain things which are quite important to them. They may simply fail to recognize, after all, that those things have that importance. But if there is something that a person does care about, then it follows that it is important to him. This is not because caring somehow involves an infallible judgment concerning the importance of its object. Rather, it is because caring about something *makes* that thing important to the person who cares about it.

It is necessarily the case, of course, that a person who cares about a certain thing is not cold-bloodedly indifferent to it. In other words, what happens to the thing must make a difference to a person who cares about it, and the difference it makes must itself be important to him. This naturally does not mean that he cares about it just because it affects him in important ways. On the contrary, it may well be that he is susceptible to being affected by it or on account of it only in virtue of the fact that he cares about it.

This suggests that it is necessarily important to people what they care about. The fact that a person cares about a certain thing or about some person, or the fact that he does not care about them, makes an important difference to him. It means that he is, or that he is not, susceptible to being affected by various circumstances in ways which he considers important. Thus the question of what to care about (construed as including the question of whether to care about anything) is one which must necessarily be important to him.

It does not quite follow from this that it is necessarily worth a person's while to care about the question. The question may not be sufficiently important to him for that. What does follow, however, is that if *anything* is worth caring about, then it must be worth caring about what to care about. It could hardly be the case both that there is something so important to a person that it is worthwhile for him to care about it, but that it is not worthwhile for him to care about whether or not he cares about that thing.

In any event, there are two distinct (albeit compatible) ways in which something may be important to a person. First, its importance to him may be due to considerations which are altogether independent of whether or not he cares about the thing in question. Second, the thing may become important to him just because he does care about it. Correspondingly, there are two distinct sorts of ground on which a person who thinks it worthwhile to care about a certain thing might attempt to justify his view. He might claim that the thing is independently important to him and that it is worth caring about for this reason. Or he might maintain, without supposing that the thing is antecedently important to him at all, that he is justified in caring about it because caring about it is itself something which is important to him.

People naturally want the things they care about to coincide, up to a point, with those that are independently or antecedently important to them. Thus a person often begins to care about something when he recognizes its capacity to affect him in important ways, ceases to care about it when he discovers that it does not have that capacity, and criticizes himself for caring too much or too little about things whose importance to himself he has misjudged. When the importance of a certain thing to a person is due to the very fact that he cares about it, however, that fact plainly cannot provide a useful measure of the extent to which his caring about the thing is justified.

In such cases, the critical question cannot be whether the object is sufficiently important to the person to warrant his caring about it. It must instead be whether the person is justified in *making* the thing important to him by caring about it. Now the only way to justify doing this is in terms of the importance of the activity of caring as such. It is manifest that the varieties of being concerned or dedicated, and of loving, *are* important to us quite apart from any antecedent capacities for affecting us which what we care about may have. This is not particularly because caring about something makes us susceptible to certain additional gratifications and disappointments. It is primarily because it serves to connect us actively to our lives in ways which are creative of ourselves and which expose us to distinctive possibilities for necessity and for freedom.

It would be a serious mistake to believe that the importance of an object to someone is not fully genuine unless it is independent of his caring about the object. Consider the fact that many of the people we care about most would not affect us in important ways if we did not care about them. This can hardly mean that they are not genuinely important to us. In certain cases, to be sure, it may appear that something does lack real importance to a person despite the fact that he cares about it. But if the importance of the object in such cases is not fully genuine, that is not because it derives from the fact that the person cares about the object.

Suppose, for example, that what a person cares about is avoiding stepping on the cracks in the sidewalk. No doubt he is committing an error of some kind in caring about this. But his error is not that he cares about something which is not really important to him. Rather, his error consists in caring about, and thereby imbuing with genuine importance, something which is not worth caring about. The reason it is not worth caring about seems clear: it is not important to the person to make avoiding the cracks in the sidewalk important to himself. But we need to understand better than we do just why this is so – i.e., what conditions must be satisfied if it is to be important to us to make something important to us which would not otherwise have such importance.

Even when the justification for caring about something rests upon the importance of the caring itself, rather than being derivative from the antecedent importance of its object, the choice of the object is not irrelevant or arbitrary. According to one theological doctrine, divine love is in fact bestowed without regard to the character or antecedent value of its objects. It is God's nature to love, on this view, and He therefore loves everything regardless of any considerations extrinsic to Himself. His love is entirely arbitrary and unmotivated – absolutely sovereign, and in no way conditioned by the worthiness of its objects.[4] Perhaps it is possible only for an omnipotent being – to whom nothing is antecedently important – to love altogether freely and without conditions or restrictions of any kind. In any case, a capacity for wholly unconditioned love is by no means an essential constituent of our finite nature.

What makes it more suitable, then, for a person to make one object rather than another important to himself? It seems that it must be the fact that it is *possible* for him to care about the one and not about the other, or to care about the one in a way which is more important to him than the way in which it is possible for him to care about the other. When a person makes something important to himself, accordingly, the situation resembles an instance of divine *agape* at least in a certain respect. The person does not care about the object because its worthiness commands that he do so. On the other hand, the worthiness of the activity of caring commands that he choose an object which he will be able to care about.

4 Cf. Anders Nygren, *Agape and Eros* (New York, 1969), pp. 75–81, 91–5.

8

What we are morally responsible for

It might have been expected that the freedom of a person's *will* would most naturally be construed as a matter of whether it is up to him what he wills. In fact, it is generally understood as having to do with whether it is up to the person what he *does*. Someone's will is regarded as being free at a given time, in other words, only if at that time it is up to him whether he does one thing or does another instead. When this conception of free will is joined to the supposition that free will is a necessary condition for moral responsibility, the result is the Principle of Alternate Possibilities (PAP): a person is morally responsible for what he has done only if he could have done otherwise.

For those who accept PAP, it is an important question whether people ever *can* do anything other than what they actually do. Incompatibilists maintain that if determinism is true, this is not possible. On the other hand, compatibilists insist that even in a deterministic world a person may have genuine alternatives in the sense PAP requires. In my view, PAP is false.[1] The fact that a person lacks alternatives does preclude his being morally responsible when it alone accounts for his behavior. But a lack of alternatives is not inconsistent with moral responsibility when someone acts as he does for reasons of his own, rather than simply because no other alternative is open to him. It is therefore of no particular significance, so far as ascriptions of moral responsibility are concerned, whether determinism is true or false, or whether it is compatible or incompatible with free will as PAP construes it.

I

The appeal of PAP may owe something to a presumption that it is a corollary of the Kantian thesis that "ought" implies "can."[2] In fact, however, the relation between Kant's doctrine and PAP is not as close as it may seem to be. With respect to any action, Kant's doctrine has to do

1 I argue for this in "Alternate Possibilities and Moral Responsibility," Chapter 1 in this volume.
2 Cf. Robert Cummins, "Could Have Done Otherwise," *The Personalist*. LX, 4 (October 1979): 411–414.

with the agent's ability to perform *that* action. PAP, on the other hand, concerns his ability to do *something else*. Moreover, the Kantian view leaves open the possibility that a person for whom only one course of action is available fulfills an obligation when he pursues that course of action and is morally praiseworthy for doing so. On the other hand, PAP implies that such a person cannot earn any moral credit for what he does. This makes it clear that renouncing PAP does not require denying that "ought" implies "can" and that PAP is not entailed by the Kantian view.

Constructing counterexamples to PAP is not difficult. It is necessary only to conceive circumstances which make it inevitable that a person will perform some action but which do not bring it about that he performs it. Thus let us say that a person decides to take and does take a certain drug, just in order to enjoy the euphoria he expects it to induce. Now suppose further that his taking the drug would have been made to happen in any case, by forces which were in fact inactive but which would have come into play if he had not on his own decided and acted as he did. Let us say that, unknown to himself, the person is addicted to the drug and would therefore have been driven irresistibly to take it if he had not freely gone about doing so. His dormant addiction guarantees that he could have avoided neither deciding to take nor taking the drug, but it plays no role in bringing about his decision or his act. As the actual sequence of events develops, everything happens as if he were not addicted at all. The addiction is clearly irrelevant in this case to the question of whether the person is morally responsible for taking the drug.

The distinctively potent element in this sort of counterexample to PAP is a certain kind of overdetermination, which involves a sequential fail-safe arrangement such that one causally sufficient factor functions exclusively as backup for another. The arrangement ensures that a certain effect will be brought about by one or the other of the two causal factors, but not by both together. Thus the backup factor may contribute nothing whatever to bringing about the effect whose occurrence it guarantees.

II

Peter van Inwagen has argued forcefully that even if counterexamples of this kind – adapting his usage I shall refer to them as "F-style counterexamples" – do require that PAP be abandoned, the compatibilism-incompatibilism dispute retains its significance.[3] In his view the supposition

3 Peter van Inwagen, "Ability and Responsibility," *Philosophical Review*. LXXXVII, 2 (April 1978): 201–24. Hereafter in my text, numbers within parentheses refer to this essay.

that PAP is false does not, as I have claimed, entail the irrelevance to questions concerning moral responsibility of the relationship between determinism and free will. "Even if PAP is false," he says,

it is *nonetheless* true that unless free will and determinism are compatible, determinism and moral responsibility are incompatible. Thus, Frankfurt's arguments do not, even if they are sound, rob the compatibilist-incompatibilist debate of its central place in the old controversy about determinism and moral responsibility. (223)

To support this position van Inwagen formulates three principles, which he regards as "very similar to PAP" but which he believes are unlike it in being immune to objections of the sort by which PAP is undermined (203). He contends that demonstrating this immunity serves to re-establish the relevance of alternate possibilities and, hence, of the compatibilism issue, to the theory of moral responsibility.

Van Inwagen calls his first principle "the Principle of Possible Action":

PPA: A person is morally responsible for failing to perform a given act only if he could have performed that act. (204)

This principle concerns "unperformed acts (things we have left undone)" (203). The second and third principles, which van Inwagen calls "Principles of Possible Prevention," have to do with "the consequences of what we have done (or left undone)" (203):

PPP1: A person is morally responsible for a certain event (particular) only if he could have prevented it. (206)

and

PPP2: A person is morally responsible for a state of affairs only if (that state of affairs obtains and) he could have prevented it from obtaining. (210)

PAP is concerned only with a person's moral responsibility for *what he has done*. Thus the supposition that PAP is false leaves it open that there may be things *other* than items of his own behavior – viz., unperformed acts or events or states of affairs that are consequences of what he has done or left undone – for which a person cannot be morally responsible unless his will is or was free.

Corresponding to each of his three principles van Inwagen provides a version of incompatibilism. According to the first of these, determinism entails that anyone who has failed to perform a given act could not have performed it. The second and third add up to the claim that determinism entails that there are no events or states of affairs – and hence no consequences of what someone has done – such that anyone could have prevented them from occurring or from obtaining. Now van Inwagen is convinced that PPA, PPP1, and PPP2 are true. So his position is that if the versions of incompatibilism that correspond to those principles are also true, then "determinism entails that no one has ever been or could be responsible for any event, state of affairs, or unperformed act" (222).

I believe that, despite van Inwagen's denial, his first principle actually is vulnerable to F-style counterexamples. On the other hand, it may well be that the same strategy does not also work against his other two principles. But if this is so, it is only because PPP1 and PPP2 are irrelevant to the relation between free will and determinism. Their immunity to F-style counterexamples therefore provides no support for the conclusions van Inwagen proposes to draw concerning how the theory of moral responsibility is affected by considerations pertaining to determinism and to free will.

III

In his discussion of PPA van Inwagen does not consider the rather natural suspicion that the principle is simply equivalent to PAP. Instead he proceeds directly to examine a putative counterexample. Since he regards the construction of the example as adapting to the case of unperformed acts the general strategy that makes trouble for PAP, he supposes that the example provides a critical test of whether this strategy is effective against PPA.

In the example, van Inwagen witnesses a crime and considers telephoning the police to report it. Because he does not want to get involved, he decides against calling the police and does nothing. However, unknown to him, the telephone system has in fact collapsed, and every relevant telephone is out of order. Concerning this situation, he poses the following question: "Am I responsible for failing to call the police?" His response is unequivocal and emphatic: "Of course not. I couldn't have called them." Given the circumstances, he says,

I may be responsible for failing to *try* to call the police (that much I *could* have done), or for refraining from calling the police, or for . . . being selfish and cowardly. But I am simply not responsible for failing to call the police. (205)

In van Inwagen's opinion, then, the example leaves PPA altogether unscathed. His conclusion is that "Frankfurt's style of argument cannot be used to refute PPA" (205).

Now being responsible for something may mean, in a certain strong sense of the notion, being *fully* responsible for it, i.e., providing for it *both* a sufficient *and* a necessary condition. A person is fully responsible, then, for all and only those events or states of affairs which come about because of what he does and which would not come about if he did otherwise. The person in van Inwagen's example (hereafter, "P") is not in this sense responsible for his failure to call the police. The fact that he behaved as he did was a sufficient condition for his having failed, but it was not a necessary condition: given the collapse of the telephone system, he would have failed no matter what he had done. Perhaps the reason van Inwagen finds it so obvious that P's inability to do what he failed to do entails that P is not morally responsible for his failure is that he construes moral responsibility as presupposing responsibility in this strong sense.

In my opinion, full responsibility is not a necessary condition for moral responsibility. Thus I believe that P may be morally responsible for failing to call the police even though he could not have avoided the failure. But I do not propose to defend this position here. Instead I shall attempt to establish two other points, which I think are more germane to van Inwagen's ultimate conclusions. The first is that the question of whether moral responsibility presupposes full responsibility has no *moral* interest. The second is that even if moral responsibility does presuppose full responsibility, van Inwagen's putative counterexample to PPA cannot serve his purpose.

IV

Suppose that, as it happens, we do not know whether the telephones were working when P made and acted upon his decision against calling the police. The fact that we lack this information would not stand in the way of our making a competent moral appraisal of P for what he did. At the very most it would make us uncertain just how to *describe* P's failure to act – i.e., just how to *identify* what it is that we are evaluating him *for*. If the telephones were working, it might be more appropriate to refer to his failure to *call* the police; if they were out of order, it might be more appropriate to refer to his failure *to try to call the police.* But both the quality of the moral judgment and its degree – whether P is blameworthy or praiseworthy, and to what extent – will be exactly the same in both cases.

Which of the two failures his moral responsibility is construed as being *for* depends entirely, after all, upon the condition of the telephone system. In no way does it depend upon any act or omission or psychological state or property, whether faulty or meritorious, of his own. The difference between evaluating P for failing to call and evaluating him for failing to try to call can therefore have no *moral* significance. It is pertinent only to a decision concerning whether it would be more suitable to couch in one set of terms or in another what, in either case, remains the same moral estimate.

The point is not that a person's behavior is relevant to moral judgments concerning him only as evidence of his character or of his mental state. To be sure, P's intentions and his other psychological characteristics do remain identical regardless of whether circumstances dictate that he be judged for failing to call the police or for failing to try to call them. But the reason why the moral evaluation of P will be the same in either case is not that he is subject to moral praise or blame exclusively for his psychological characteristics. What a person does is not relevant to moral evaluations of him merely because it is an indicator of his mental state. People merit praise and blame *for* what they do, and not just *on the basis of* what they do.

Notice that P's intentions and the like are not the only things that remain the same whether the telephones are working or out of order. It is also clear that, whatever the condition of the telephone system, P makes or does not make the same bodily movements. Now *this* is what P is morally responsible for: it is for making these movements. He is morally responsible for making them, of course, only under certain conditions – only, for instance, when he makes them with certain intentions or expectations. But if those conditions are satisfied, then what he is morally responsible for is just making the movements themselves.

There are various ways in which a person's movements can be identified or described. Whether it will be more appropriate to describe what P does as calling the police or only as trying to call them will depend heavily upon what consequences his movements have. And the consequences of his movements will in turn depend upon whether the telephones are working. But it is precisely because P is judged simply for the making of his movements that the quality and the degree of his moral responsibility for what he does remain the same in either case. It goes without saying that his movements are unaffected by the consequences to which they lead, however decisively those consequences may affect the terms in which it is appropriate for the movements to be described.[4]

---

4 I am here invoking Donald Davidson's well-known view – developed with compelling lucidity in his essay entitled "Agency" (in Brinkley, Bronaugh, and Marras [eds.], *Agent, Action and Reason* [New York: Oxford, 1971], pp. 3–25) – according to which "we never do more than move our bodies; the rest is up to nature" (23). Adapting and paraphrasing his account (cf. 21) to the case of P, it might be said that after P has moved his hands in the ways one must move them in order to make a telephone call, he has done his work; it only remains for the telephone company to do its.

V

Since P would have failed to call the police no matter what he had done, he is not *fully* responsible for failing to call them. This provides van Inwagen with a reason for his claim that P is not *morally* responsible for the failure. But even if we suppose that moral responsibility requires responsibility in the strong sense, the judgment that PPA is immune to counterexamples would still be unwarranted. This is because the ineffectiveness of van Inwagen's counterexample is due to the particular characteristics of P's failure rather than to the characteristics of all failures as such. Therefore the counterexample does not provide a decisive test of PPA.

Why is P not fully responsible for his failure to call the police? It is because it is not within his power to bring it about that the police telephone rings: regardless of what bodily movements he makes, his movements will not have consequences of the kind that must occur if P is to be correctly describable as having called the police. But there are also failures which, unlike P's, do not depend at all upon the consequences of what a person does. They are failures for which the person's movements themselves, considered wholly apart from their consequences, are both a sufficient and a necessary condition. For example, suppose that as Q is driving he fails to keep his eyes straight ahead because he prefers to examine the interesting scenery to his left; and suppose further that if the scenery had not distracted him something else would have brought it about that he was looking to his left at that time. In these circumstances, Q cannot keep his eyes straight ahead. Is he morally responsible for failing to do so? Of course he is! The fact that he cannot avoid failing has no bearing upon his moral responsibility for the failure, since it plays no role in leading him to fail.

Notice that Q is *fully* responsible for his failure. Failing to keep one's eyes straight ahead is exclusively a matter of what movements a person makes; it is *constituted* by what the person himself does, and what the person does is therefore both a sufficient and a necessary condition for it. It cannot be said, then, that Q's failure would have occurred no matter what he had done – i.e., regardless of what bodily movements he made. If he had not moved his eyes to the left at all he would not have failed. Thus there is not the same reason for denying that Q is morally responsible for his failure as there is for denying that P is morally responsible for having failed to call the police. Even if the assumption that moral responsibility presupposes full responsibility is granted, accordingly, it is possible to find counterexamples that are effective against PPA.

Evaluating PAP and the three principles van Inwagen adduces is a matter of deciding whether a person may be morally responsible for performing or failing to perform an action, or for consequences of what he has done, despite the fact that the action or the failure or the consequences could not have been avoided. Now there are two ways in which a person's action, or his failure to act, or a consequence of what he has done, may be unavoidable. It may be unavoidable in virtue of certain movements which the person makes and which he cannot avoid making; or it may be unavoidable because of events or states of affairs that are bound to occur or to obtain no matter what the person himself does. For want of better terminology, I shall refer to the first type of unavoidability as "personal" and to the second as "impersonal."

Apparently van Inwagen supposes that a person cannot be fully responsible for a failure which he is unable to avoid. This supposition would be correct if unavoidable failures were all like P's failure – i.e., if their unavoidability were always *impersonal*. In fact, however, the unavoidability of some failures is *personal*. Of these it is not true that they will occur no matter what the person in question does. They are unavoidable just because the person, like Q, cannot avoid making the bodily movements by which they are constituted.

VI

It seems to me that there is no inherent difference between performances and failures, in virtue of which PPA might be true even though PAP is false. Nor is PPA immune to counterexamples of the sort to which PAP succumbs. On the other hand, there is a variant of PPA which *does* enjoy immunity to F-style counterexamples. This restricted version of PPA, which I shall call "PPA," refers exclusively to failures whose unavoidability is impersonal. It concerns a person's moral responsibility for failing to bring about some event or state of affairs, when the fact that he does not bring it about is independent of what he himself does – i.e., of the movements he makes. Thus PPA' closely resembles PPP1 and PPP2, since these also concern a person's moral responsibility for events or states of affairs that can occur or obtain regardless of what movements the person himself makes.[5]

5 As I have already pointed out, van Inwagen says that PPP1 and PPP2 have to do with "the consequences of what we have done (or left undone)" (203). This is not explicit in his formulations of the principles. On a rather natural reading of them, in fact, they are vulnerable to any counterexample that is effective against PAP. For, assuming that doing something entails the occurrence of an event and the obtaining of a state of affairs, anything that shows that a person may be morally responsible for what he has done even though he could not have done otherwise also shows that he may be morally

Now it is true by definition that a person cannot be *fully* responsible for something that happens or comes about regardless of his own bodily movements. Whether he can be *morally* responsible for such things depends upon the relationship between moral and full responsibility. Let us suppose that the former presupposes the latter. In that case PPA', PPP1, and PPP2 are immune to F-style counterexamples. But this does not imply, as van Inwagen evidently believes, that there are things for which a person can be morally responsible only if his will is free. Unlike PAP and PPA, three principles in question have nothing at all to do with free will.

The fact that there are events or states of affairs which a person cannot bring about plainly does not in itself mean that the person lacks free will. Given that the freedom of a person's will is essentially a matter of whether it is up to him what he does, it is more a matter of whether it is up to him what bodily movements he makes than of what consequences he can bring about by his movements. Imagine that the equipment malfunction that makes it impossible for P to call the police, despite his freedom to move his body in any way he likes, is due to negligence on the part of the telephone company; and imagine that because of this negligence large numbers of people are unable to do various things. These people may quite properly be resentful. But they will be carrying their resentment too far, and attributing too portentous a role in their lives to the telephone company, if they complain that the company has through its negligence diminished the freedom of their wills.

Just as PPA', PPP1, and PPP2 have nothing to do with the relationship between moral responsibility and free will, neither have they anything to do with the relationship between free will and determinism. Suppose that it is causally undetermined whether the telephones are working. Then it is also undetermined whether P can call the police. But this implies nothing whatever concerning the freedom of P's will.

It has a significant bearing, of course, on the extent of his *power* – i.e., on the effectiveness of what he does. However, in no way does it affect his freedom to move as he likes; nor is it pertinent to the question of whether his movements themselves are undetermined. It is altogether irrelevant, in other words, to the sorts of interests and anxieties by which people have been driven to resist the doctrine that human life is wholly and ineluctably subject to causal determination.

responsible for an event or a state of affairs which he could not have prevented. However, in view of van Inwagen's assurances that PPP1 and PPP2 concern the *consequences* of what people do, I shall construe them as *not* referring to the bodily movements people make or to what those movements necessarily entail.

9

Necessity and desire

I

The language of *need* is used extensively in the representation of our personal and social lives. Its role in political and moral discourse is especially conspicuous and powerful. People commonly attribute needs to themselves and to others in order to support demands, or to establish entitlements, or to influence the ordering of priorities; and we are often inclined to respond to such attributions with a rather special respect and concern. In particular, an assertion that something is *needed* tends to create an impression of an altogether different quality, and to have a substantially greater moral impact, than an assertion that something is *desired*. Claims based upon what a person needs frequently have a distinctive poignancy. They are likely to arouse a more compelling sense of obligation, and to be treated with greater urgency, than claims based merely upon what someone wants.

Care must be taken, however, to avoid exaggerating the inherent superiority of claims grounded in needs over claims grounded in desires. It is surely not the case that the moral force of needs is unconditionally greater than that of desires in the sense that every need, without exception, is properly to be accorded unqualified priority over any desire. There are many occasions when it makes perfectly good sense for a person to sacrifice something he needs, even something he needs very badly, for the sake of something he desires but for which he has no need at all. For example, it might be quite sensible for a seriously ill person to use his limited financial resources for the pleasure cruise he has long wanted to take rather than for the surgery he needs in order to prolong his life. Decisions to enjoy life more at the cost of not taking care of ourselves as well as we might – to enhance the quality of life at the expense of its quantity – are neither uncommon nor always unjustifiable.

Perhaps this is insufficient to show that a claim based upon desire can ever compete successfully on *moral* grounds against a claim supported by need. In fact, however, needs may be no more compelling than desires even so far as strictly moral considerations are concerned. Consider a person who feels like completing a crossword puzzle and who is unable to do so without looking things up. He needs a dictionary, but the moral importance of this need is altogether negligible. It would hardly be difficult to find numerous desires with at least as much moral importance.

But now it seems that if a need may be utterly inconsequential, then attributions of need really have no inherent moral weight after all. This result appears to be decisively confirmed, moreover, by elementary theoretical considerations. Nothing is needed except for the sake of an end for which it is indispensable. The moral importance of meeting or of not meeting a need must therefore be wholly derivative from the importance of the end which gives rise to it. Whatever the importance of attaining the end, it will be exactly that important to meet the need. If the moral significance of the need for a dictionary is negligible, it is just because the goal from which the need derives is of no moral consequence. Thus it seems that the satisfaction of needs cannot be entitled to any systematic moral priority over the gratification of desires. The mere fact that something is needed, considered in isolation from the value of what it is needed for, has no independent justificatory force.

However, we must be as careful to avoid claiming too little for needs as to avoid claiming too much for them. Even apart from other considerations, the view that there is no special moral significance in the fact that a person needs something is difficult to reconcile with the manifest rhetorical potency of certain loosely manipulative uses to which the language of need is often put. These typically involve blurring the distinction between needing something and wanting it, with the obvious intention of attracting for some desire the same degree of moral consideration that tends to be accorded particularly to needs.[1]

---

1   Jean-Paul Sartre and Fidel Castro collaborate in the following conversation to produce an egregious instance:
    "'Man's need is his fundamental right over all others,' said Castro. 'And if they ask you for the moon?' asked Sartre. '. . . it would be because someone needed it,' was Castro's reply." (Quoted by George Lichtheim in *The Concept of Ideology and Other Essays* [New York: 1967], p. 282.)
    Now from the fact that someone asks for something it follows at most, of course, that he wants it. This sort of confusion between what is wanted and what is needed is rather common among Marxists. Thus, although it seems obvious that some commodities may satisfy only desires, Marx himself defines a commodity as "a thing that by its properties satisfies human needs of some sort or another." (*Capital* [Moscow, 1961], vol. I, p. 35.) I shall take it for granted that wanting something does not entail needing it, and vice versa: a person may desire to undergo surgery but not actually need an operation, or need surgery without wanting it. This does not entail, by the way, that the concepts of need and of desire are logically independent. They would be logically independent if, and only if, something could be desired without anything being needed and something could be needed without anything being desired. What the example shows is only that someone may have a need without having a desire *for what he needs*, and that he may have a desire without having a need *for what he wants*.

Maneuvers of this sort would be pointless unless people were widely disposed to accept the proposition that a need for something preempts a desire *for that thing*. This proposition, which I shall call "the Principle of Precedence," attributes to needs only a quite minimal moral superiority over desires. It maintains no more than that when there is a competition between a desire and a need for the same thing, the need starts with a certain moral edge. That is, when A needs something that B wants but does not need, then meeting A's need is *prima facie* morally preferable to satisfying B's desire. If needs do not enjoy at least *this* much precedence over desires, then it must certainly be an error to attribute *any* particular moral significance to them. In any case, the Principle appears to be eminently reasonable. Other things being equal, it seems clearly preferable to allocate a resource to someone who needs it rather than to someone who wants it but who has no need for it at all.

Yet there are exceptions to the Principle of Precedence. Suppose someone undertakes a certain project just on an unreflective whim. The fact that he thereupon needs whatever is indispensable for completing the project has no more justificatory force than a casual or impulsive desire for the same thing would have. The claim of a person who needs a dictionary merely in order to gratify his whim to finish a puzzle is no weightier than the claim of someone who has no specific need for a dictionary but whose desire it is, for no particular reason, to possess one. Giving precedence here to the need would arbitrarily assign greater moral importance to one whim than to another.

The moral significance of a need is not, then, necessarily greater than that of its corresponding desire. Therefore we cannot unequivocally accept the doctrine that it is morally preferable to allocate resources to those who need them rather than to those who only desire them. We must distinguish between the kinds of needs that do merit precedence over the desires that correspond to them, and the kinds of needs that do not.

II

At the heart of the concept of need is the notion that there are things one cannot do without. When something is needed it must therefore always be possible to specify what it is needed *for*, or to explain *what* one cannot do without it. If a person needs surgery in order to survive, then what he cannot do without the surgery is to go on living. All necessities are in this respect conditional: nothing is needed except in virtue of being an indispensable condition for the attainment of a certain end.[2]

2   It appears to be implicit in the concept of need that what something is needed for must be other than itself. That is why it is somewhat dissonant to suggest that life and

In many cases, a person needs something because he actively desires a certain end for the attainment of which that thing is indispensable.[3] Thus the person in my example needs a dictionary because he wants to finish a puzzle. In fact he needs the dictionary *only* because he wants to finish the puzzle; he would not need it except for that desire. But of course a person may need certain things for more than one reason, or in more than one way. When something is needed because there is something else that a person *wants,* then to that extent the need depends upon the person's *will.* I shall refer to needs of this kind as "volitional needs."

Having a volitional need is not necessarily a voluntary matter. This is because a person's will is not invariably under his voluntary control. That is, it may not be up to him whether he has the desire upon which his volitional need depends. Many of a person's desires are indeed voluntary, since they derive simply from his own decisions. Someone typically acquires the desire to see a certain movie, for example, just by making up his mind what movie to see. Desires of this sort are not aroused in us; they are formed or constructed by acts of will that we ourselves perform, often quite apart from any emotional or affective state. However, there are also occasions when what a person wants is not up to him at all, but is rather a matter of feelings or inclinations that arise and persist independently of any choice of his own.

Now suppose that with respect to a certain desire it is up to the person whether or not he has it. Then it is also up to him whether or not he has a volitional need for whatever is indispensable for the satisfaction of that desire. On the other hand, if he has no control over what he wants then he also has no control over whether or not he has volitional needs for those things without which the desire in question cannot be satisfied. I shall refer to volitional needs that depend upon voluntary desires as "free," and to those that depend upon involuntary desires as "constrained."

> happiness are among the things people need. Circumstances may occur in which it actually does serve a special purpose for some person to go on living or to be happy; and in cases of that kind it may be appropriate to say that the person needs to live or to be happy. But we do not suppose that the value of life, or of happiness, derives in general from the value of something else.
>
> 3 Joseph Raz has pointed out to me that a person may want something and yet not need certain things that are indispensable for its attainment, because it is clear that he would be unable to attain it even if he got them. If he recognizes that he cannot satisfy any set of sufficient conditions for the attainment of what he wants, then he does not need to satisfy the necessary conditions. Similar considerations apply if for some reason other than unattainability – e.g., very low priority – the person does not expect or intend even to attempt to satisfy his desire. By speaking of what a person "actively desires," I mean to exclude desires that he has no expectation or intention of trying to satisfy. In what follows I shall assume, without explicitly specifying them as such, that the desires upon which needs are said to depend are in this sense active.

Free volitional needs are not, as such, morally interesting in the sense specified by the Principle of Precedence. In other words, they do not merit priority over the desires corresponding to them. From the fact that a person needs M because it is indispensable for E, which he wants, we cannot conclude that the consideration to which his need for M is entitled is greater than the consideration that would be merited by a mere desire for M. There is no reason to think that his claim for M receives more powerful support from his desire for E than another person's claim for M would receive just from that person's desire for M itself. Why should the latter desire convey a lesser claim, after all, than the former? The fact that one person desires M while another person has a free volitional need for it leaves it entirely open which person's claim for M is better.

If free volitional needs are as such morally unimportant, it is not because the desires from which they derive are uniformly of no consequence. The fact that a desire is voluntary implies nothing whatever concerning how significant it is. A person may decide of his own free will not merely that he wants to finish a crossword puzzle, but also far more portentous matters as well: that he wants to become a musician, that he wants to renounce his obligations and devote himself ruthlessly to the pursuit of his material interests, that he wants to die, and so on. The desires upon which a person's free volitional needs depend may make a very considerable difference to his life.

Other things being equal, the desirability of meeting a free volitional need depends wholly upon how desirable it is to satisfy the pertinent voluntary desire. To whatever extent it is desirable to satisfy someone's desire for a certain end, it will be desirable to the same extent to meet the needs generated by that desire. Thus the desirability of a person's end may justify his claim for what he needs in order to attain it. But insofar as his desire for the end is a voluntary one, the desirability of satisfying it cannot endow his claim with the *distinctive* moral quality which is specific to claims warranted by need.

This is because free volitional needs have too little necessity in them. There are two related considerations here, which illuminate the moral precedence over desires that needs of certain kinds enjoy. In the first place, since the desire from which a free volitional need derives may be for anything whatever, it may be neither important nor necessary for the desire to be satisfied; hence, it cannot be assumed that needs of this kind *need to be met*. Secondly, from the fact that the desire that generates a free volitional need is voluntary, it follows that the person who has such a need does not *need to need* what he needs. In order to be morally interesting, on the other hand, a need must be radically distinct from a desire. It must be what I shall call "categorical" – i.e., characterized by both of the necessities just considered: (1) the need must be one that the person not only wants to meet but needs to meet, and (2) what the person needs must be something that he cannot help needing. I shall discuss these two conditions in turn.

III

The reason free volitional needs do not as such need to be met is that the desires upon which they depend may be for things that are not needed. In such a case the person *wants* his need to be met so that he may enjoy what he desires, but he does not *need* it to be met any more than he needs the desired thing itself. Suppose it should turn out that he cannot meet his free volitional need, and that consequently he cannot have what he wants. Then he may well both be disappointed and have grounds for being resentful. But, given that what he wants is not something he needs, *no harm will have been done.* He will have failed to obtain a benefit of greater or of lesser value, but he will not have been harmed.

It is the linkage to harm that differentiates needs that satisfy the Principle of Precedence, and that are therefore morally interesting, from others. A person's need has moral interest only if it will be a consequence of his failure to meet the need that he incurs or continues to suffer some harm. This condition may be met, of course, even if the person has no desire for the needed object. Insofar as the link to harm does not depend upon a desire, the need is a non-volitional one. Free volitional needs have no inherent moral interest because the mere fact that a person has a certain desire indicates at most that he expects what he desires to be in some way of benefit to him. It does not entail that he will suffer any harm if he does not obtain it.

It is not clear how to distinguish systematically between circumstances in virtue of which a person is harmed and those in virtue of which he merely fails to obtain a benefit; nor is it apparent how to define those special conditions under which someone who fails to obtain a benefit actually does thereby also incur a harm. One way to deal with the latter problem would be to maintain that failing to obtain a benefit is tantamount to incurring a harm just in case the benefit is something the person in question needs. This is plausible, but for obvious reasons not very helpful in the present context. Instead of attempting to formulate a more satisfactory account of the matter, I shall limit myself to three elementary observations pertinent to the relationship between benefits and harms.

First, being harmed has to do with becoming worse off than one was, while failing to obtain a benefit is more a matter of not becoming better off than before. Second, there is sometimes no way to prevent a situation from becoming worse except by making it better. In cases of that kind failure to obtain the pertinent benefit is tantamount to being harmed. Third, the life of a person whose condition is bad becomes worse and worse as long as his condition does not improve, simply because more of a bad thing is worse than less of it. Someone may be harmed, therefore, even when in a certain sense his condition does not deteriorate. This makes it possible to endorse the commonsense judgment that a chronically ill person has a morally relevant need for whatever treatment is essential to the alleviation of his illness. For it implies that even though the state of his health remained very much what it was before, he would not only fail to obtain a valuable benefit if he did not obtain the treatment but would actually be harmed.

These observations suggest why meeting needs merits priority over satisfying desires. It is because making things better is, from a moral point of view, less important (measure for measure) than keeping them from getting worse. We usually expect that when something is entrusted to a person's care, he will make a reasonable effort to protect it from damage or harm; but we do not ordinarily suppose that he has any comparable obligation to enhance its condition. With respect more generally to that part of the world which comes under a person's care – i.e., for which he has responsibility – his obligation to keep it from getting worse is more compelling than his obligation (if any) to improve it. This is why allocating resources to meeting needs takes precedence over allocating them to fulfilling mere desires. The former aims at avoiding harm, while the latter aims only at providing unneeded benefits.

A person's morally interesting needs need to be met, then, because harm will ensue if they are not. But in addition, the link to harm must be of such a nature that whether or not the harm ensues is outside the person's voluntary control. This is the second respect in which free volitional needs have too little necessity in them. Not only do they derive from desires, which means that there may be no harm done even if they fail to be met. But furthermore, the desires from which they derive are voluntary, which means that the person need not have the needs at all.

Suppose it is just in virtue of his own decision concerning what he wants that a person has the desire from which a certain need derives. This hardly puts him in the grip of necessity. The grip in which he is held is merely his own, from which he can free himself as he likes. It is no wonder that needs of this kind do not as such elicit any particular moral concern. Even when the person will in fact suffer some harm if he fails to get the object he needs, this consequence is one which he imposes upon himself and to which he continues to be exposed only as long as he is willing to be exposed to it. He does need the object, since it is indispensable to an end that he desires. But his need for it is his own concoction. The object's indispensability to the end touches him only insofar as he wants it to do so. It does not affect him unless, by his own free choice, he adopts the pertinent desire.

IV

Neither desires nor free volitional needs are inescapably linked to harm. This is why they are morally indistinguishable from each other and why each differs morally from categorical needs. In fact, not only do free volitional needs fail to merit precedence over the desires corresponding to them, but also there is no basis for according them as such any moral interest at all. That is, we cannot even suppose that meeting needs of this sort is inherently desirable or preferable to not meeting them.

Meeting free volitional needs would be inherently desirable only if it were inherently desirable to satisfy desires. Only in that case could the desirability of meeting any given free volitional need be presumed. Now some philosophers do maintain that it is necessarily desirable for a desire to be fulfilled. Thus William James writes, "Take any demand, however slight, which any creature, however weak, may make. Ought it not, for its own sole sake, to be satisfied? . . . Any desire is imperative to the extent of its amount; it *makes* itself valid by the fact that it exists at all."[4] James would of course acknowledge that the desirability of satisfying a desire may be overridden by other considerations. But in his opinion the fact that a person wants something is always a reason in itself for preferring that he have it.

In my view, on the other hand, the mere fact that a person wants something provides no support for a claim that his having it is preferable to his not having it. I do not mean to deny that it is better for some of a person's desires to be satisfied than for none to be satisfied. Perhaps, other things being equal, it is necessarily better that a life include some satisfied desires than that all the desires it includes be unsatisfied. But it does not follow from this that, with respect to each of a person's desires, it is better that he have what he wants than that he not have it. What follows is only that a person's having some of the things he wants is better than his having none of them.

4 William James, "The Moral Philosopher and the Moral Life," in *Essays in Pragmatism by William James*, ed. Alburey Castell (New York, 1948), p. 73.

So far as I know, the only argument available for the position to which James adheres runs more or less as follows. An unsatisfied desire inevitably involves frustration, which is unpleasant. Hence there is always at least the same consideration in favor of satisfying a given desire as there is in favor of minimizing unpleasantness. Now in fact there is a presumption in favor of minimizing unpleasantness. Therefore, there is always a *prima facie* case for satisfying a given desire in preference to not satisfying it. A desire is "imperative to the extent of its amount," as James puts it, because the unpleasantness consequent to frustration will be more or less severe, and thus more or less undesirable, according to how strong the frustrated desire is.

However, the most that can validly be inferred from the premises of this argument is that there is a *prima facie* case against the desirability of any state of affairs in which someone has an unsatisfied desire. The only presumption warranted is, in other words, merely that satisfied desires are preferable to frustrated ones.[5] This differs substantially from a presumption in favor of the satisfaction of desire, because a satisfied desire is not the only possible alternative to a frustrated one. After all, a person also avoids frustration when – through being persuaded or in some other way – he gives up or loses his desire without satisfying it. Some of the methods that may be effective in eliminating a person's desires without satisfying them are, to be sure, quite objectionable. But this is equally true of some of the methods by which desires may be satisfied.

James's thesis undermines the conceptual distance between need and desire by linking desire to harm and thus by implying that wanting something entails needing it. If it were inevitable for a desire that is not satisfied to be frustrated, then a person could not avoid unpleasantness unless he got what he wanted. Now it is plausible to suppose that suffering unpleasantness amounts to being harmed and that everyone wants to avoid it, so that everyone both non-volitionally and volitionally needs whatever is indispensable for avoiding unpleasantness. It is precisely because an object of desire may actually *not* be indispensable for someone's achievement of this goal that wanting something does not entail needing it. Since a desire may be given up or lost, a person may be able to avoid frustration without getting what he wants. Thus the satisfaction of a desire is not necessarily necessary for avoiding harm.

V

With respect to some of the things a person wants, however, it may not be possible for him either to bring himself or to be brought to stop

---

5   Cf. Gary Watson, "Free Agency," *Journal of Philosophy* 72 (1975): 210–11.

wanting them. This is not because the desires in question are especially intense or difficult to control. Even desires that are quite unobtrusive and easily managed may nonetheless be ineradicably persistent. Needs generated by desires of this sort, which must be either satisfied or frustrated, are what I have called "constrained volitional needs." It is clear that they involve more necessity than free volitional needs do. A person whose constrained volitional need is not met will unavoidably, no matter what he voluntarily chooses or does, suffer some harm – viz., frustration. This suffices to make such needs categorical and to warrant gratifying them in preference to gratifying the desires that correspond to them.

All constrained volitional needs satisfy the Principle of Precedence. However, some of them appear worthy only of a rather qualified or equivocal concern. What distinguishes these is not that the harms to which they are linked are relatively minor, for the harms may actually be very severe. Rather, it is that the needs seem somehow to be gratuitous or even perverse. For example, suppose a man is seized by the *idée fixe* that his life will be worthless unless he has a certain sports car; and suppose the frustration of his desire for the car would be so deep that it would indeed ruin his life. The man cannot help wanting the car, and he wants it so badly that he will suffer sustained and crippling misery unless he obtains it. Since there is a link here to substantial harm, which is not under the man's voluntary control, his need for the sports car is both categorical and severe. What is the basis, then, for our uneasiness concerning it? Why are we inclined to be less than wholehearted in acknowledging that the claim it makes is truly legitimate?

Our reaction to the man's need for the car is likely to be the outcome of a variety of considerations. The one to which I want to call particular attention has nothing to do with any judgments concerning the paltriness of his ambition or the shallowness of his character. No doubt our respect for the man is significantly impaired by our feeling that the object of his desire is unworthy of the enormous importance it has for him. But our response to his need is also affected by a feature which that need shares with others whose objects are far more worthy of desire and concern than sports cars: namely, the man's need has less to do with the specific characteristics of its object than with the nature of his desire for that object.

It is not directly because of the car's speed or beauty, or even because of its snob value, that the man will suffer if he does not get it. Presumably, it is in virtue of these characteristics that he wants the car; but they do not account for the fact that he needs it. One might even suggest that what he really needs is not the car as such at all, but the gratification of his desire for it. His need is inescapably linked to harm only in virtue of his desire, and not in virtue of the consequences to him that doing without the car would otherwise entail. If he did not want the sports car as he does, he would in fact have no morally significant need for it. In other words, he has no non-volitional need to which his desire for the car corresponds.

The point may be illuminated by distinguishing needs of this kind from needs due to addiction. The latter commonly have constrained volitional needs associated with them, but they are not themselves essentially volitional. The heroin addict does typically have an involuntary desire for heroin; but it is more likely that this desire arises on account of his need for the drug than that the need derives from the desire. In any event, being addicted to something is not a matter of being unable to avoid wanting it. The characteristic suffering to which heroin addicts are subject is not the pain of frustrated desire. It is a more specific condition, which is caused just by the lack of heroin. It occurs independently of what the addict – who may not know what he is addicted to, or even that there is something to which he is addicted – wants or does not want.

There are two types of situations involving constrained volitional needs. In situations of one type, a person has a non-volitional need as well as a constrained volitional need for a certain object; and he would therefore need the object even if he did not desire it. In situations of the other type, the person's need is exclusively volitional; i.e., he needs a certain object only because he desires it.

Because he has a non-volitional need for heroin, the addict's involuntary desire for the drug serves a useful purpose. It moves him to obtain something that he needs, and that he cannot help needing independently of his desire for it. On the other hand, no such purpose is served by the desire (e.g., for a sports car) upon which a person's constrained volitional need depends, when the person has no non-volitional need corresponding to the desire. In that case, there is no need and no liability to harm apart from the desire. The desire does not respond to or reflect a need; it creates one. Now this creation of a liability to harm in no way enhances either the inherent value of the desired object or its availability. Thus it subjects a person to additional burdens and risks without endowing him with any compensatory benefits. It is in this respect that needs of the kind in question are gratuitous or perverse.

VI

The range and severity of a person's needs are contingent upon what he wants, upon how he wants it, and upon those non-volitional aspects of his situation that determine what will harm him and what will protect him from harm. This means that needs may be generated, altered, or eliminated by changes in the environment and by the natural course of human life. Moreover, needs of each of the three types I have considered may be affected by deliberate or by unintentional human action.

Many social critics maintain that one of the ways in which exploitative societies injure their members is by causing them to incur various needs that the critics characterize as "false" or "inauthentic" or to which they refer in some other manner suggestive of undesirability or defect. One might ask, perhaps, whether it is desirable to have any categorical needs at all. The question hangs upon whether we would be better off if we were not vulnerable to harm or whether it is somehow a good thing for us that we are in this respect less than omnipotent. In any case those who condemn the creation of false or inauthentic needs do not intend to object against any increase whatever in the burden of need which people bear. Their complaint is against increases of a more particular sort. What they consider objectionable in the creation of a false need is not that an additional need has been created, but that the need that has been created is a false one.

I suggest that a criterion that captures at least an important element of what is objectionable in certain needs – needs that it is plausible to consider "false" – may be grounded in the difference between those constrained volitional needs that coincide with non-volitional needs and those that do not. By this criterion a person's need for a certain object is "true" or "authentic" only if the person needs the object regardless of whether or not he wants it. A need is "false" or "inauthentic," on the other hand, if the person needs the object only because he desires it. Volitional needs are true or authentic, in other words, only insofar as they reflect needs that are non-volitional.

This account cuts across the distinction between needs that are natural and needs that are socially imposed. What makes a need false is not that it has causes of a certain kind. Needs may be authentic or true even when they are not only artificial in the sense of being produced by human contrivance, but when the contrivance is malicious or unjust. The falsity of a need is not a matter of its origination in the machinations or in the negligence of the reactionary or the wicked, but of its being gratuitous or perverse in a way that has already been indicated. False needs are those in which there is no necessity except what is created by desire. Their defect is analogous to that of Protagoras' truths, which – according to the representation of his doctrine in the *Theaetetus* – are created wholly out of beliefs. Just as belief cannot correctly be construed as the measure of truth, so desire cannot properly be regarded as the measure of need.

There is a difference between our response to needs that arise exclusively from constrained volition and our response to needs that are not volitional at all. This difference remains even when, as in a case of self-induced addiction, someone's non-volitional need is the result of his own voluntary behavior. The necessities that nature imposes upon a person (even when it is his doing that brings this about) incline us to a more sympathetic and empathic concern than those that derive immediately from the person's own will (even when he has no control over what he wants). Our feeling that it is incumbent upon us to assist a person in need tends to become somewhat attenuated when the need is essentially derivative from that person's desire.

This may be because the hardening of desire into necessity strikes us as an analogue of "bad faith," so that we suspect the person in question of being unable to control his desire only because he does not really want to do so. In that case we do not regard the need as fully constrained and hence we do not construe it as being genuinely categorical. It is possible that there is another reason as well. In seeking to avoid the harm to which a constrained volitional need exposes him, a person is contending not so much against nature as against himself. Perhaps this diminishes our sense of comradeship with him. If he were struggling against nature, which is our common enemy, our instinct to ally ourselves with him would be more compelling.

10

On bullshit

One of the most salient features of our culture is that there is so much bullshit. Everyone knows this. Each of us contributes his share. But we tend to take the situation for granted. Most people are rather confident of their ability to recognize bullshit and to avoid being taken in by it. So the phenomenon has not aroused much deliberate concern, nor attracted much sustained inquiry.

In consequence, we have no clear understanding of what bullshit is, why there is so much of it, or what functions it serves. And we lack a conscientiously developed appreciation of what it means to us. In other words, we have no theory. I propose to begin the development of a theoretical understanding of bullshit, mainly by providing some tentative and exploratory philosophical analysis. I shall not consider the rhetorical uses and misuses of bullshit. My aim is simply to give a rough account of what bullshit is and how it differs from what it is not – or (putting it somewhat differently) to articulate, more or less sketchily, the structure of its concept.

Any suggestion about what conditions are logically both necessary and sufficient for the constitution of bullshit is bound to be somewhat arbitrary. For one thing, the expression *bullshit* is often employed quite loosely – simply as a generic term of abuse, with no very specific literal meaning. For another, the phenomenon itself is so vast and amorphous that no crisp and perspicuous analysis of its concept can avoid being procrustean. Nonetheless it should be possible to say something helpful, even though it is not likely to be decisive. Even the most basic and preliminary questions about bullshit remain, after all, not only un-answered but unasked.

So far as I am aware, very little work has been done on this subject. I have not undertaken a survey of the literature, partly because I do not know how to go about it. To be sure, there is one quite obvious place to look – the *Oxford English Dictionary*. The OED has an entry for *bullshit* in the supplementary volumes, and it also has entries for various perti-nent uses of the word *bull* and for some related terms. I shall consider some of these entries in due course. I have not consulted dictionaries in languages other then English, because I do not know the words for bullshit or bull in any other language.

Another worthwhile source is the title essay in *The Prevalence of Humbug* by Max Black.[1] I am uncertain just how close in meaning the word *humbug* is to the word bullshit. Of course, the words are not freely and fully interchangeable; it is clear that they are used differently. But the difference appears on the whole to have more to do with considerations of gentility, and certain other rhetorical parameters, than with the strictly literal modes of significance that concern me most. It is more polite, as well as less intense, to say "Humbug!" than to say "Bullshit!" For the sake of this discussion, I shall assume that there is no other important difference between the two.

Black suggests a number of synonyms for humbug, including the following: "balderdash," "claptrap," "hokum," "drivel," "buncombe," "imposture," and "quackery." This list of quaint equivalents is not very helpful. But Black also confronts the problem of establishing the nature of humbug more directly, and he offers the following formal definition:

HUMBUG: deceptive misrepresentation, short of lying, especially by pretentious word or deed, of somebody's own thoughts, feelings, or attitudes.[2]

A very similar formulation might plausibly be offered as enunciating the essential characteristics of bullshit. As a preliminary to developing an independent account of those characteristics, I will comment on the various elements of Black's definition.

Deceptive misrepresentation: This may sound pleonastic. No doubt what Black has in mind is that humbug is necessarily designed or intended to deceive, that its misrepresentation is not merely inadvertent. In other words, it is *deliberate* misrepresentation. Now if, as a matter of conceptual necessity, an intention to deceive is an invariable feature of humbug, then the property of being humbug depends at least in part upon the perpetrator's state of mind. It cannot be identical, accordingly, with any properties – either inherent or relational – belonging just to the utterance by which the humbug is perpetrated. In this respect, the property of being humbug is similar to that of being a lie, which is identical neither with the falsity nor with any of the other properties of the statement the liar makes, but which requires that the liar make his statement in a certain state of mind – namely, with an intention to deceive.

It is a further question whether there are any features essential to humbug or to lying that are *not* dependent upon the intentions and

---

1   Max Black, *The Prevalence of Humbug* (Ithaca: Cornell University Press, 1985).
2   Ibid., p. 143.

beliefs of the person responsible for the humbug or the lie, or whether it is, on the contrary, possible for any utterance whatsoever to be — given that the speaker is in a certain state of mind — a vehicle of humbug or of a lie. In some accounts of lying there is no lie unless a false statement is made; in others a person may be lying even if the statement he makes is true, as long as he himself believes that the statement is false and intends by making it to deceive. What about humbug and bullshit? May any utterance at all qualify as humbug or bullshit, given that (so to speak) the utterer's heart is in the right place, or must the utterance have certain characteristics of its own as well?

Short of lying: It must be part of the point of saying that humbug is "short of lying," that while it has some of the distinguishing characteristics of lies, there are others that it lacks. But this cannot be the whole point. After all, every use of language without exception has some, but not all, of the characteristic features of lies — if no other, then at least the feature simply of being a use of language. Yet it would surely be incorrect to describe every use of language as short of lying. Black's phrase evokes the notion of some sort of continuum, on which lying occupies a certain segment while humbug is located exclusively at earlier points. What continuum could this be, along which one encounters humbug only before one encounters lying? Both lying and humbug are modes of misrepresentation. It is not at first glance apparent, however, just how the difference between these varieties of misrepresentation might be construed as a difference in degree.

Especially by pretentious word or deed: There are two points to notice here. First, Black identifies humbug not only as a category of speech but as a category of action as well; it may be accomplished either by words or by deeds. Second, his use of the qualifier "especially" indicates that Black does not regard pretentiousness as an essential or wholly indispensable characteristic of humbug. Undoubtedly, much humbug is pretentious. So far as concerns bullshit, moreover, "pretentious bullshit" is close to being a stock phrase. But I am inclined to think that when bullshit is pretentious, this happens because pretentiousness is its motive rather than a constitutive element of its essence. The fact that a person is behaving pretentiously is not, it seems to me, part of what is required to make his utterance an instance of bullshit. It is often, to be sure, what accounts for his making that utterance. However, it must not be assumed that bullshit always and necessarily has pretentiousness as its motive.

Misrepresentation . . . of somebody's own thoughts, feelings, or attitudes: This provision that the perpetrator of humbug is essentially misrepresenting himself raises some very central issues. To begin with, whenever a person deliberately misrepresents *anything,* he must inevitably misrepresent his own state of mind. It is possible, of course, for a person to misrepresent that alone – for instance, by pretending to have a desire or a feeling which he does not actually have. But suppose that a person, whether by telling a lie or in another way, misrepresents something else. Then he necessarily misrepresents at least two things. He misrepresents whatever he is talking about – i.e., the state of affairs that is the topic or referent of his discourse – and in doing this he cannot avoid misrepresenting his own mind as well. Thus, someone who lies about how much money he has in his pocket both gives an account of the amount of money in his pocket and conveys that he believes this account. If the lie works, then its victim is twice deceived, having one false belief about what is in the liar's pocket and another false belief about what is in the liar's mind.

Now it is unlikely that Black wishes that the referent of humbug is in every instance the state of the speaker's mind. There is no particular reason, after all, why humbug may not be about other things. Black probably means that humbug is not designed primarily to give its audience a false belief about whatever state of affairs may be the topic, but that its primary intention is rather to give its audience a false impression concerning what is going on in the mind of the speaker. Insofar as it is humbug, the creation of this impression is its main purpose and its point.

Understanding Black along these lines suggests a hypothesis to account for his characterization of humbug as "short of lying." If I lie to you about how much money I have, then I do not thereby make an *explicit* assertion concerning my beliefs. Therefore, one might with some plausibility maintain that although in telling the lie I certainly misrepresent what is in my mind, this misrepresentation – as distinct from my misrepresentation of what is in my pocket – is not strictly speaking a lie at all. For I do not come right out with any statement whatever about what is in my mind. Nor does the statement I do affirm – e.g., "I have twenty dollars in my pocket" – imply any statement that attributes a belief to me. On the other hand, it is unquestionable that in so affirming, I provide you with a reasonable basis for making certain judgments about what I believe. In particular, I provide you with a reasonable basis for supposing that I believe there is twenty dollars in my pocket. Since this supposition is by hypothesis false, I do in telling the lie tend to deceive you concerning what is in my mind even though I do not actually tell a lie about that. In this light, it does not seem unnatural or inappropriate to regard me as misrepresenting my own beliefs in a way that is "short of lying."

It is easy to think of familiar situations by which Black's account of humbug appears to be unproblematically confirmed. Consider a Fourth of July orator, who goes on bombastically about "our great and blessed country, whose Founding Fathers under divine guidance created a new beginning for mankind." This is surely humbug. As Black's account suggests, the orator is not lying. He would be lying only if it were his intention to bring about in his audience beliefs which he himself regards as false, concerning such matters as whether our country is great, whether it is blessed, whether the Founders had divine guidance, and whether what they did was in fact to create a new beginning for mankind. But the orator does not really care what his audience thinks about the Founding Fathers, or about the role of the deity in our country's history, or the like. At least, it is not an interest in what anyone thinks about these matters that motivates his speech.

It is clear that what makes Fourth of July oration humbug is not fundamentally that the speaker regards his statements as false. Rather, just as Black's account suggests, the orator intends these statements to convey a certain impression of himself. He is not trying to deceive anyone concerning American history. What he cares about is what people think of *him*. He wants them to think of him as a patriot, as someone who has deep thoughts and feelings about the origins and the mission of our country, who appreciates the importance of religion, who is sensitive to the greatness of our history, whose pride in that history is combined with humility before God, and so on.

Black's account of humbug appears, then, to fit certain paradigms quite snugly. Nonetheless, I do not believe that it adequately or accurately grasps the essential character of bullshit. It is correct to say of bullshit, as he says of humbug, both that it is short of lying and that those who perpetrate it misrepresent themselves in a certain way. But Black's account of these two features is significantly off the mark. I shall next attempt to develop, by considering some biographical material pertaining to Ludwig Wittgenstein, a preliminary but more accurately focused appreciation of just what the central characteristics of bullshit are.

Wittgenstein once said that the following bit of verse by Longfellow could serve him as a motto:[3]

> In the elder days of art
> Builders wrought with greatest care
> Each minute and unseen part,
> For the Gods are everywhere.

The point of these lines is clear. In the old days, craftsmen did not cut corners. They worked carefully, and they took care with every aspect of

3 This is reported by Norman Malcolm, in his "Introduction" to R. Rhees (ed.), *Recollections of Wittgenstein* (Oxford: Oxford University Press, 1984), p. xiii.

their work. Every part of the product was considered, and each was designed and made to be exactly as it should be. These craftsmen did not relax their thoughtful self-discipline even with respect to features of their work which would ordinarily not be visible. Although no one would notice if those features were not quite right, the craftsmen would be bothered by their consciences. So nothing was swept under the rug. Or, one might perhaps also say, there was no bullshit.

It does seem fitting to construe carelessly made, shoddy goods as in some way analogues of bullshit. But in what way? Is the resemblance that bullshit itself is invariably produced in a careless or self-indulgent manner, that it is never finely crafted, that in the making of it there is never the meticulously attentive concern with detail to which Longfellow alludes? Is the bullshitter by his very nature a mindless slob? Is his product necessarily messy or unrefined? The word *shit* does, to be sure, suggest this. Excrement is not designed or crafted at all; it is merely emitted, or dumped. It may have a more or less coherent shape, or it may not, but it is in any case certainly not *wrought*.

The notion of carefully wrought bullshit involves, then, a certain inner strain. Thoughtful attention to detail requires discipline and objectivity. It entails accepting standards and limitations that forbid the indulgence of impulse or whim. It is this selflessness that, in connection with bullshit, strikes us as inapposite. But in fact it is not out of the question at all. The realms of advertising and of public relations, and the nowadays closely related realm of politics, are replete with instances of bullshit so unmitigated that they can serve among the most indisputable and classic paradigms of the concept. And in these realms there are exquisitely sophisticated craftsmen who – with the help of advanced and demanding techniques of market research, of public opinion polling, of psychological testing, and so forth – dedicate themselves tirelessly to getting every word and image they produce exactly right.

Yet there is something more to be said about this. However studiously and conscientiously the bullshitter proceeds, it remains true that he is also trying to get away with something. There is surely in his work, as in the work of the slovenly craftsman, some kind of laxity which resists or eludes the demands of a disinterested and austere discipline. The pertinent mode of laxity cannot be equated, evidently, with simple carelessness or inattention to detail. I shall attempt in due course to locate it more correctly.

Wittgenstein devoted his philosophical energies largely to identifying and combating what he regarded as insidiously disruptive forms of "nonsense." He was apparently like that in his personal life as well. This comes out in an anecdote related by Fania Pascal, who knew him in Cambridge in the 1930s:

I had my tonsils out and was in the Evelyn Nursing Home feeling sorry for myself. Wittgenstein called. I croaked: "I feel just like a dog that has been run over." He was disgusted: "You don't know what a dog that has been run over feels like."[4]

Now who knows what really happened? It seems extraordinary, almost unbelievable, that anyone could object seriously to what Pascal reports herself as having said. That characterization of her feelings – so innocently close to the utterly commonplace "sick as a dog" – is simply not provocative enough to arouse any response as lively or intense as disgust. If Pascal's simile is offensive, then what figurative or allusive uses of language would not be?

So perhaps it did not really happen quite as Pascal says. Perhaps Wittgenstein was trying to make a small joke, and it misfired. He was only pretending to bawl Pascal out, just for the fun of a little hyperbole; and she got the tone and the intention wrong. She thought he was disgusted by her remark, when in fact he was only trying to cheer her up with some playfully exaggerated mock criticism or joshing. In that case the incident is not incredible or bizarre after all.

But if Pascal failed to recognize that Wittgenstein was only teasing, then perhaps the possibility that he was serious was at least not so far out of the question. She knew him, and she knew what to expect from him; she knew how he made her feel. Her way of understanding or of misunderstanding his remark was very likely not altogether discordant, then, with her sense of what he was like. We may fairly suppose that even if her account of the incident is not strictly true to the facts of Wittgenstein's intention, it is sufficiently true to her idea of Wittgenstein to have made sense to her. For the purposes of this discussion, I shall accept Pascal's report at face value, supposing that when it came to the use of allusive or figurative language, Wittgenstein was indeed as preposterous as she makes him out to be.

Then just what is it that the Wittgenstein in her report considers to be objectionable? Let us assume that he is correct about the facts: that is, Pascal really does not know how run-over dogs feel. Even so, when she says what she does, she is plainly not *lying*. She would have been lying if, when she made her statement, she was aware that she actually felt quite good. For however little she knows about the lives of dogs, it must

4   Fania Pascal, "Wittgenstein: A Personal Memoir," in R. Rhees, op. cit., pp. 28–9.

certainly be clear to Pascal that when dogs are run over they do not feel good. So if she herself had in fact been feeling good, it would have been a lie to assert that she felt like a run-over dog.

Pascal's Wittgenstein does not intend to accuse her of lying, but of misrepresentation of another sort. She characterizes her feeling as "the feeling of a run-over dog." She is not really acquainted, however, with the feeling to which this phrase refers. Of course, the phrase is far from being complete nonsense to her; she is hardly speaking gibberish. What she says has an intelligible connotation, which she certainly understands. Moreover, she does know something about the quality of the feeling to which the phrase refers: she knows at least that it is an undesirable and unenjoyable feeling, a *bad* feeling. The trouble with her statement is that it purports to convey something more than simply that she feels bad. Her characterization of her feeling is too specific; it is excessively particular. Hers is not just any bad feeling but, according to her account, the distinctive kind of bad feeling that a dog has when it is run over. To the Wittgenstein in Pascal's story, judging from his response, this is just bullshit.

Now assuming that Wittgenstein does indeed regard Pascal's characterization of how she feels as an instance of bullshit, why does it strike him that way? It does so, I believe, because he perceives what Pascal says as being – roughly speaking, for now – unconnected to a concern with the truth. Her statement is not germane to the enterprise of describing reality. She does not even think she knows, except in the vaguest way, how a run-over dog feels. Her description of her own feeling is, accordingly, something that she is merely making up. She concocts it out of whole cloth; or, if she got it from someone else, she is repeating it quite mindlessly and without any regard for how things really are.

It is for this mindlessness that Pascal's Wittgenstein chides her. What disgusts him is that Pascal is not even concerned whether her statement is correct. There is every likelihood, of course, that she says what she does only in a somewhat clumsy effort to speak colorfully, or to appear vivacious or good-humored; and no doubt Wittgenstein's reaction – as she construes it – is absurdly intolerant. Be this as it may, it seems clear what that reaction is. He reacts as though he perceives her to be speaking about her feeling thoughtlessly, without conscientious attention to the relevant facts. Her statement is not "wrought with greatest care." She makes it without bothering to take into account at all the question of its accuracy.

The point that troubles Wittgenstein is manifestly not that Pascal has made a mistake in her description of how she feels. Nor is it even that she has made a careless mistake. Her laxity, or her lack of care, is not a matter of having permitted an error to slip into her speech on account of some inadvertent or momentarily negligent lapse in the attention she was devoting to getting things right. The point is rather that, so far as Wittgenstein can see, Pascal offers a description of a certain state of affairs without genuinely submitting to the constraints which the endeavor to provide an accurate representation of reality imposes. Her fault is not that she fails to get things right, but that she is not even trying.

This is important to Wittgenstein because, whether justifiably or not, he takes what she says seriously, as a statement purporting to give an informative description of the way she feels. He construes her as engaged in an activity to which the distinction between what is true and what is false is crucial, and yet as taking no interest in whether what she says is true or false. It is in this sense that Pascal's statement is unconnected to a concern with truth: she is not concerned with the truth-value of what she says. That is why she cannot be regarded as lying; for she does not presume that she knows the truth, and therefore she cannot be deliberately promulgating a proposition that she presumes to be false. Her statement is grounded neither in a belief that it is true nor, as a lie must be, in a belief that it is not true. It is just this lack of connection to a concern with truth – this indifference to how things really are – that I regard as of the essence of bullshit.

Now I shall consider (quite selectively) certain items in the *Oxford English Dictionary* that are pertinent to clarifying the nature of bullshit. The *OED* defines a *bull session* as "an informal conversation or discussion, esp. of a group of males." Now as a definition, this seems wrong. For one thing, the dictionary evidently supposes that the use of the term bull in bull session serves primarily just to indicate gender. But even if it were true that the participants in bull sessions are generally or typically males, the assertion that a bull session is essentially nothing more particular than an informal discussion among males would be as far off the mark as the parallel assertion that a hen session is simply an informal conversation among females. It is probably true that the participants in hen sessions must be females. Nonetheless the term *hen session* conveys something more specific than this concerning the particular kind of informal conversation among females to which hen sessions are characteristically devoted. What is distinctive about the sort of informal discussion among males that constitutes a bull session is, it seems to me, something like this: while the discussion may be intense and significant, it is in a certain respect not "for real."

The characteristic topics of a bull session have to do with very personal and emotion-laden aspects of life – for instance, religion, politics, or sex. People are generally reluctant to speak altogether openly about these topics if they expect that they will be taken too seriously. What tends to go on in a bull session is that the participants try out various thoughts and attitudes in order to see how it feels to hear themselves saying such things and in order to discover how others respond, without it being assumed that they are committed to what they say. It is understood by everyone in a bull session that the statements people make do not necessarily reveal what they really believe or how they really feel. The main point is to make possible a high level of candor and an experimental or adventuresome approach to the subjects under discussion. Therefore provision is made for enjoying a certain irresponsibility, so that people will be encouraged to convey what is on their minds without too much anxiety that they will be held to it.

Each of the contributors to a bull session relies, in other words, upon a general recognition that what he expresses or says is not to be understood as being what he means wholeheartedly or believes unequivocally to be true. The purpose of the conversation is not to communicate beliefs. Accordingly, the usual assumptions about the connection between what people say and what they believe are suspended. The statements made in a bull session differ from bullshit in that there is no pretense that this connection is being sustained. They are like bullshit by virtue of the fact that they are in some degree unconstrained by a concern with truth. This resemblance between bull sessions and bullshit is suggested also by the term *shooting the bull*, which refers to the sort of conversation that characterizes bull sessions and in which the term *shooting* is very likely a cleaned-up rendition of *shitting*. The very term bull session is, indeed, quite probably a sanitized version of *bullshit session*.

A similar theme is discernible in a British usage of *bull* in which, according to the *OED*, the term refers to "unnecessary routine tasks or ceremonial; excessive discipline or 'spit-and-polish'; = red-tape." The dictionary provides the following examples of this usage:

"The Squadron . . . felt very bolshie about all that bull that was flying around the station" (I. Gleed, *Arise to Conquer* vi. 51, 1942); "Them turning out the guard for us, us marching past eyes right, all that sort of bull" (A. Baron, *Human Kind* xxiv. 178, 1953); "the drudgery and 'bull' in an MP's life." (*Economist* 8 Feb. 470/471, 1958)

Here the term bull evidently pertains to tasks that are pointless in that they have nothing much to do with the primary intent or justifying purpose of the enterprise which requires them. Spit-and-polish and red tape do not genuinely contribute, it is presumed, to the "real" purposes of military personnel or government officials, even though they are imposed by agencies or agents that purport to be conscientiously devoted to the pursuit of those purposes. Thus the "unnecessary routine tasks or ceremonial" that constitute bull are disconnected from the legitimating motives of the activities upon which they intrude, just as the things people say in bull sessions are disconnected from their settled beliefs, and as bullshit is disconnected from a concern with the truth.

The term bull is also employed, in a rather more widespread and familiar usage, as a somewhat less coarse equivalent of bullshit. In an entry for bull as so used, the *OED* suggests the following as definitive: "trivial, insincere, or untruthful talk or writing; nonsense." Now it does not seem distinctive of bull either that it must be deficient in meaning or that it is necessarily unimportant; so "nonsense" and "trivial," even apart from their vagueness, seem to be on the wrong track. The focus of "insincere, or untruthful" is better, but it needs to be sharpened.[5] The entry at hand also provides the following two definitions:

1914 *Dialect Notes* IV. 162 *Bull*, talk which is not to the purpose; "hot air."
1932 *Times Lit. Supp.* 8 Dec. 933/3 "Bull" is the slang term for a combination of bluff, bravado, "hot air" and what we used to call in the Army "Kidding the troops."

"Not to the purpose" is appropriate, but it is both too broad in scope and too vague. It covers digressions and innocent irrelevancies, which are not invariably instances of bull; furthermore, saying that bull is not to the purpose leaves it uncertain what purpose is meant. The reference in both definitions to "hot air" is more helpful.

When we characterize talk as hot air, we mean that what comes out of the speaker's mouth is only that. It is mere vapor. His speech is empty, without substance or content. His use of language, accordingly, does not contribute to the purpose it purports to serve. No more information is communicated than if the speaker had merely exhaled. There are similarities between hot air and excrement, incidentally, which make *hot air* seem an especially suitable equivalent for *bullshit*. Just as hot air is speech that has been emptied of all informative content, so excrement is matter from which everything nutritive has been removed. Excrement may be regarded as the corpse of nourishment, what remains when the vital elements in food have been exhausted. In this respect, excrement is a representation of death which we ourselves produce and which, indeed, we cannot help producing in the very process of maintaining our lives. Perhaps it is for making death so intimate that we find excrement

---

5 It may be noted that the inclusion of insincerity among its essential conditions would imply that bull cannot be produced inadvertently; for it hardly seems possible to be inadvertently insincere.

so repulsive. In any event, it cannot serve the purposes of sustenance, any more than hot air can serve those of communication.

Now consider these lines from Pound's Canto LXXIV, which the *OED* cites in its entry for bullshit as a verb:

> Hey Snag wots in the bibl'?
> Wot are the books ov the bible?
> Name 'em, don't bullshit ME.[6]

This is a call for the facts. The person addressed is evidently regarded as having in some way claimed to know the Bible, or as having claimed to care about it. The speaker suspects that this is just empty talk, and demands that the claim be supported with facts. He will not accept a mere report; he insists upon seeing the thing itself. In other words, he is calling the bluff. The connection between bullshit and bluff is affirmed explicitly in the definition with which the lines by Pound are associated:

As *v. trans.* and *intr.*, to talk nonsense (to); . . . also, to bluff *one's way through* (something) by talking nonsense.

It does seem that bullshitting involves a kind of bluff. It is closer to bluffing, surely, than to telling a lie. But what is implied concerning its nature by the fact that it is more like the former than it is like the latter? Just what is the relevant difference here between a bluff and a lie?

Lying and bluffing are both modes of misrepresentation or deception. Now the concept most central to the distinctive nature of a lie is that of falsity: the liar is essentially someone who deliberately promulgates a falsehood. Bluffing too is typically devoted to conveying something false. Unlike plain lying, however, it is more especially a matter not of falsity but of fakery. This is what accounts for its nearness to bullshit. For the essence of bullshit is not that it is *false* but that it is *phony*. In order to appreciate this distinction, one must recognize that a fake or a phony need not be in any respect (apart from authenticity itself) inferior to the real thing. What is not genuine need not also be defective in some other way. It may be, after all, an exact copy. What is wrong with a counterfeit is not what it is like, but how it was made. This points to a similar and

---

6 Here is part of the context in which these lines occur: "Les Albigeois, a problem of history, / and the fleet at Salamis made with money lent by the state to the ship-wrights / Tempus tacendi, tempus loquendi. / Never inside the country to raise the standard of living / but always abroad to increase the profits of usurers, / dixit Lenin, / and gun sales lead to more gun sales / they do not clutter the market for gunnery / there is no saturation / Pisa, in the 23rd year of the effort in sight of the tower / and Till was hung yesterday / for murder and rape with trimmings plus Cholkis / plus mythology, thought he was Zeus ram or another one / Hey Snag wots in the bibl'? / wot are the books ov the bible? / Name 'em, don't bullshit ME."

fundamental aspect of the essential nature of bullshit: although it is produced without concern with the truth, it need not be false. The bullshitter is faking things. But this does not mean that he necessarily gets them wrong.

In Eric Ambler's novel *Dirty Story,* a character named Arthur Abdel Simpson recalls advice that he received as a child from his father:

Although I was only seven when my father was killed, I still remember him very well and some of the things he used to say. . . . One of the first things he taught me was, *"Never tell a lie when you can bullshit your way through."*[7]

This presumes not only that there is an important difference between lying and bullshitting, but that the latter is preferable to the former. Now the elder Simpson surely did not consider bullshitting morally superior to lying. Nor is it likely that he regarded lies as invariably less effective than bullshit in accomplishing the purposes for which either of them might be employed. After all, an intelligently crafted lie may do its work with unqualified success. It may be that Simpson thought it easier to get away with bullshitting than with lying. Or perhaps he meant that, although the risk of being caught is about the same in each case, the consequences of being caught are generally less severe for the bullshitter than for the liar. In fact, people do tend to be more tolerant of bullshit than of lies, perhaps because we are less inclined to take the former as a personal affront. We may seek to distance ourselves from bullshit, but we are more likely to turn away from it with an impatient or irritated shrug than with the sense of violation or outrage that lies often inspire. The problem of understanding why our attitude toward bullshit is generally more benign than our attitude toward lying is an important one, which I shall leave as an exercise for the reader.

The pertinent comparison is not, however, between telling a lie and producing some particular instance of bullshit. The elder Simpson identifies the alternative to telling a lie as "bullshitting one's way through." This involves not merely producing one instance of bullshit; it involves a *program* of producing bullshit to whatever extent the circumstances require. This is a key, perhaps, to his preference. Telling a lie is an act with a sharp focus. It is designed to insert a particular falsehood at a specific point in a set or system of beliefs, in order to avoid the consequences of having that point occupied by the truth. This requires a degree of craftsmanship, in which the teller of the lie submits to objective constraints

7   E. Ambler, *Dirty Story* (1967), 1. iii. 25. The citation is provided in the same *OED* entry as the one that included the passage from Pound. The closeness of the relation between bullshitting and bluffing is resonant, it seems to me, in the parallelism of the idioms: "bullshit your way through" and "bluff your way through."

imposed by what he takes to be the truth. The liar is inescapably concerned with truth-values. In order to invent a lie at all, he must think he knows what is true. And in order to invent an effective lie, he must design his falsehood under the guidance of that truth.

On the other hand, a person who undertakes to bullshit his way through has much more freedom. His focus is panoramic rather than particular. He does not limit himself to inserting a certain falsehood at a specific point, and thus he is not constrained by the truths surrounding that point or intersecting it. He is prepared to fake the context as well, so far as need requires. This freedom from the constraints to which the liar must submit does not necessarily mean, of course, that his task is easier than the task of the liar. But the mode of creativity upon which it relies is less analytical and less deliberative than that which is mobilized in lying. It is more expansive and independent, with more spacious opportunities for improvisation, color, and imaginative play. This is less a matter of craft than of art. Hence the familiar notion of the "bullshit artist." My guess is that the recommendation offered by Arthur Simpson's father reflects the fact that he was more strongly drawn to this mode of creativity, regardless of its relative merit or effectiveness, than he was to the more austere and rigorous demands of lying.

What bullshit essentially misrepresents is neither the state of affairs to which it refers nor the beliefs of the speaker concerning that state of affairs. Those are what lies misrepresent, by virtue of being false. Since bullshit need not be false, it differs from lies in its misrepresentational intent. The bullshitter may not deceive us, or even intend to do so, either about the facts or about what he takes the facts to be. What he does necessarily attempt to deceive us about is his enterprise. His only indispensably distinctive characteristic is that in a certain way he misrepresents what he is up to.

This is the crux of the distinction between him and the liar. Both he and the liar represent themselves falsely as endeavoring to communicate the truth. The success of each depends upon deceiving us about that. But the fact about himself that the liar hides is that he is attempting to lead us away from a correct apprehension of reality; we are not to know that he wants us to believe something he supposes to be false. The fact about himself that the bullshitter hides, on the other hand, is that the truth-values of his statements are of no central interest to him; what we are not to understand is that his intention is neither to report the truth nor to conceal it. This does not mean that his speech is anarchically impulsive, but that the motive guiding and controlling it is unconcerned with how the things about which he speaks truly are.

It is impossible for someone to lie unless he thinks he knows the truth.

Producing bullshit requires no such conviction. A person who lies is thereby responding to the truth, and he is to that extent respectful of it. When an honest man speaks, he says only what he believes to be true; and for the liar, it is correspondingly indispensable that he consider his statements to be false. For the bullshitter, however, all these bets are off: he is neither on the side of the true nor on the side of the false. His eye is not on the facts at all, as the eyes of the honest man and of the liar are, except insofar as they may be pertinent to his interest in getting away with what he says. He does not care whether the things he says describe reality correctly. He just picks them out, or makes them up, to suit his purpose.

In his essay, "Lying," St. Augustine distinguishes lies of eight types, which he classifies according to the characteristic intent or justification with which a lie is told. Lies of seven of these types are told only because they are supposed to be indispensable means to some end that is distinct from the sheer creation of false beliefs. It is not their falsity as such, in other words, that attracts the teller to them. Since they are told only on account of their supposed indispensability to a goal other than deception itself, St. Augustine regards them as being told unwillingly: what the person really wants is not to tell the lie but to attain the goal. They are therefore not real lies, in his view, and those who tell them are not in the strictest sense liars. It is only the remaining category that contains what he identifies as "the lie which is told solely for the pleasure of lying and deceiving, that is, the real lie."[8] Lies in this category are not told as means to any end distinct from the propagation of falsehood. They are told simply for their own sakes — i.e., purely out of a love of deception:

There is a distinction between a person who tells a lie and a liar. The former is one who tells a lie unwillingly, while the liar loves to lie and passes his time in the joy of lying. . . . The latter takes delight in lying, rejoicing in the falsehood itself.[9]

What Augustine calls "liars" and "real lies" are both rare and extraordinary. Everyone lies from time to time, but there are very few people to whom it would often (or even ever) occur to lie exclusively from a love of falsity or of deception.

For most people, the fact that a statement is false constitutes in itself a reason, however weak and easily overridden, not to make the statement.

8 "Lying," in *Treatises on Various Subjects,* in R. J. Deferrari (ed.), *Fathers of the Church.* volume 16 (Fathers of the Church: New York, 1952), p. 109. St. Augustine maintains that telling a lie of this type is a less serious sin than telling lies in three of his categories and a more serious sin than telling lies in the other four categories.
9 Ibid., p. 79.

For St. Augustine's pure liar it is, on the contrary, a reason in favor of making it. For the bullshitter it is in itself neither a reason in favor nor a reason against. Both in lying and in telling the truth people are guided by their beliefs concerning the way things are. These guide them as they endeavor either to describe the world correctly or to describe it deceitfully. For this reason, telling lies does not tend to unfit a person for telling the truth in the same way that bullshitting tends to. Through excessive indulgence in the latter activity, which involves making assertions without paying attention to anything except what it suits one to say, a person's normal habit of attending to the ways things are may become attenuated or lost. Someone who lies and someone who tells the truth are playing on opposite sides, so to speak, in the same game. Each responds to the facts as he understands them, although the response of the one is guided by the authority of the truth, while the response of the other defies that authority and refuses to meet its demands. The bullshitter ignores these demands altogether. He does not reject the authority of the truth, as the liar does, and oppose himself to it. He pays no attention to it at all. By virtue of this, bullshit is a greater enemy of the truth than lies are.

One who is concerned to report or to conceal the facts assumes that there are indeed facts that are in some way both determinate and knowable. His interest in telling the truth or in lying presupposes that there is a difference between getting things wrong and getting them right, and that it is at least occasionally possible to tell the difference. Someone who ceases to believe in the possibility of identifying certain statements as true and others as false can have only two alternatives. The first is to desist both from efforts to tell the truth and from efforts to deceive. This would mean refraining from making any assertion whatever about the facts. The second alternative is to continue making assertions that purport to describe the way things are but that cannot be anything except bullshit.

Why is there so much bullshit? Of course it is impossible to be sure that there is relatively more of it nowadays than at other times. There is more communication of all kinds in our time than ever before, but the proportion that is bullshit may not have increased. Without assuming that the incidence of bullshit is actually greater now, I will mention a few considerations that help to account for the fact that it is currently so great.

Bullshit is unavoidable whenever circumstances require someone to talk without knowing what he is talking about. Thus the production of bullshit is stimulated whenever a person's obligations or opportunities to speak about some topic are more extensive than his knowledge of the facts that are relevant to that topic. This discrepancy is common in public life, where people are frequently impelled – whether by their own propensities or by the demands of others – to speak extensively about matters of which they are to some degree ignorant. Closely related instances arise from the widespread conviction that it is the responsibility of a citizen in a democracy to have opinions about everything, or at least everything that pertains to the conduct of his country's affairs. The lack of any significant connection between a person's opinions and his apprehension of reality will be even more severe, needless to say, for someone who believes it his responsibility, as a conscientious moral agent, to evaluate events and conditions in all parts of the world.

The contemporary proliferation of bullshit also has deeper sources, in various forms of skepticism which deny that we can have any reliable access to an objective reality and which therefore reject the possibility of knowing how things truly are. These "anti-realist" doctrines undermine confidence in the value of disinterested efforts to determine what is true and what is false, and even in the intelligibility of the notion of objective inquiry. One response to this loss of confidence has been a retreat from the discipline required by dedication to the ideal of *correctness* to a quite different sort of discipline, which is imposed by pursuit of an alternative ideal of *sincerity*. Rather than seeking primarily to arrive at accurate representations of a common world, the individual turns toward trying to provide honest representations of himself. Convinced that reality has no inherent nature, which he might hope to identify as the truth about things, he devotes himself to being true to his own nature. It is as though he decides that since it makes no sense to try to be true to the facts, he must therefore try instead to be true to himself.

But it is preposterous to imagine that we ourselves are determinate, and hence susceptible both to correct and to incorrect descriptions, while supposing that the ascription of determinacy to anything else has been exposed as a mistake. As conscious beings, we exist only in response to other things, and we cannot know ourselves at all without knowing them. Moreover, there is nothing in theory, and certainly nothing in experience, to support the extraordinary judgment that it is the truth about himself that is the easiest for a person to know. Facts about ourselves are not peculiarly solid and resistant to skeptical dissolution. Our natures are, indeed, elusively insubstantial – notoriously less stable and less inherent than the natures of other things. And insofar as this is the case, sincerity itself is bullshit.

I I

Equality as a moral ideal

First Man: "How are your children?"
Second Man: "Compared to what?"

I

Economic egalitarianism is, as I shall construe it, the doctrine that it is desirable for everyone to have the same amounts of income and of wealth (for short, "money").[1] Hardly anyone would deny that there are situations in which it makes sense to tolerate deviations from this standard. It goes without saying, after all, that preventing or correcting such deviations may involve costs which – whether measured in economic terms or in terms of non-economic considerations – are by any reasonable measure unacceptable. Nonetheless, many people believe that economic equality has considerable moral value in itself. For this reason they often urge that efforts to approach the egalitarian ideal should be accorded – with all due consideration for the possible effects of such efforts in obstructing or in conducing to the achievement of other goods – a significant priority.[2]

In my opinion, this is a mistake. Economic equality is not as such of particular moral importance. With respect to the distribution of economic assets, what *is* important from the point of view of morality is not that everyone should have *the same* but that each should have *enough*. If everyone had enough, it would be of no moral consequence whether

---

1 This version of economic egalitarianism (for short, simply "egalitarianism") might also be formulated as the doctrine that there should be no inequalities in the *distribution* of money. The two formulations are not unambiguously equivalent, because the term "distribution" is equivocal. It may refer either to a pattern of possession or to an activity of allocation, and there are significant differences in the criteria for evaluating distributions in the two senses. Thus it is quite possible to maintain consistently both that it is acceptable for people to have unequal amounts of money, and that it is objectionable to allocate money unequally.

2 Thus, Thomas Nagel writes: "The defense of economic equality on the ground that it is needed to protect political, legal and social equality [is not] a defense of equality *per se* – equality in the possession of benefits in general. Yet the latter is a further moral idea of great importance. Its validity would provide an independent reason to favor economic equality as a good in its own right." ("Equality," in T. Nagel, *Mortal Questions* [Cambridge: Cambridge University Press, 1979], p. 107.)

some had more than others. I shall refer to this alternative to egalitarianism – namely, that what is morally important with respect to money is for everyone to have enough – as "the doctrine of sufficiency."[3]

The fact that economic equality is not in its own right a morally compelling social ideal is in no way, of course, a reason for regarding it as undesirable. My claim that equality in itself lacks moral importance does not entail that equality is to be avoided. Indeed, there may well be good reasons for governments or for individuals to deal with problems of economic distribution in accordance with an egalitarian standard, and to be concerned more with attempting to increase the extent to which people are economically equal than with efforts to regulate directly the extent to which the amounts of money people have are enough. Even if equality is not as such morally important, a commitment to an egalitarian social policy may be indispensable to promoting the enjoyment of significant goods besides equality, or to avoiding their impairment. Moreover, it might turn out that the most feasible approach to the achievement of sufficiency would be by the pursuit of equality.

But despite the fact that an egalitarian distribution would not necessarily be objectionable, the error of believing that there are powerful moral reasons for caring about equality is far from innocuous. In fact, this belief tends to do significant harm. It is often argued as an objection to egalitarianism that there is a dangerous conflict between equality and liberty: if people are left to themselves inequalities of income and wealth inevitably arise, and therefore an egalitarian distribution of money can be achieved and maintained only at the cost of repression. Whatever may be the merit of this argument concerning the relationship between equality and liberty, economic egalitarianism engenders another conflict which is of even more fundamental moral significance.

To the extent that people are preoccupied with equality for its own sake, their readiness to be satisfied with any particular level of income or wealth is guided not by their own interests and needs but just by the magnitude of the economic benefits that are at the disposal of others. In this way egalitarianism distracts people from measuring the requirements

3   I focus attention here on the standard of equality in the distribution of money chiefly in order to facilitate my discussion of the standard of sufficiency. Many egalitarians, of course, consider economic equality to be morally less important than equality in certain other matters: for instance, welfare, opportunity, respect, need satisfaction. In fact, some of what I have to say about economic egalitarianism and sufficiency applies as well to these other benefits. But I shall not attempt in this essay to define the scope of its applicability; nor shall I attempt to relate my views to other recent criticism of egalitarianism (e.g., Larry S. Temkin, "Inequality," *Philosophy and Public Affairs*, vol. 15, no. 2 [Spring, 1986], pp. 99–121; Robert E. Goodin, "Epiphenomenal Egalitarianism," *Social Research*, vol. 52, no. 1 [Spring, 1985], pp. 99–117).

to which their individual natures and their personal circumstances give rise. It encourages them instead to insist upon a level of economic support that is determined by a calculation in which the particular features of their own lives are irrelevant. How sizeable the economic assets of others are has nothing much to do, after all, with what kind of person someone is. A concern for economic equality, construed as desirable in itself, tends to divert a person's attention away from endeavoring to discover – within his experience of himself and of his life – what he himself really cares about and what will actually satisfy him, although this is the most basic and the most decisive task upon which an intelligent selection of economic goals depends. Exaggerating the moral importance of economic equality is harmful, in other words, because it is alienating.[4]

To be sure, the circumstances of others may reveal interesting possibilities and provide data for useful judgments concerning what is normal or typical. Someone who is attempting to reach a confident and realistic appreciation of what to seek for himself may well find this helpful. It is not only in suggestive and preliminary ways like these, moreover, that the situations of other people may be pertinent to someone's efforts to decide what economic demands it is reasonable or important for him to make. The amount of money he needs may depend in a more direct way on the amounts others have. Money may bring power or prestige or other competitive advantages. A determination of how much money would be enough cannot intelligently be made by someone who is concerned with such things except on the basis of an estimate of the resources available to those with whose competition it may be necessary for him to contend. What is important from this point of view, however, is not the comparison of levels of affluence as such. The measurement of inequality is important only as it pertains contingently to other interests.

The mistaken belief that economic equality is important in itself leads people to detach the problem of formulating their economic ambitions from the problem of understanding what is most fundamentally significant to them. It influences them to take too seriously, as though it were a matter of great moral concern, a question that is inherently rather insignificant and not directly to the point: viz., how their economic status compares with the economic status of others. In this way the doctrine of

4   It might be argued (as some of the editors of *Ethics* have suggested to me) that pursuing equality as an important social ideal would not be so alienating as pursuing it as a personal goal. It is indeed possible that individuals devoted to the former pursuit would be less immediately or less intensely preoccupied with their own economic circumstances than those devoted to the latter. But they would hardly regard the achievement of economic equality as important for the society unless they had the false and alienating conviction that it was important for individuals to enjoy economic equality.

equality contributes to the moral disorientation and shallowness of our time.

The prevalence of egalitarian thought is harmful in another respect as well. It not only tends to divert attention from considerations of greater moral importance than equality. It also diverts attention from the difficult but quite fundamental philosophical problems of understanding just what these considerations are and of elaborating, in appropriately comprehensive and perspicuous detail, a conceptual apparatus which would facilitate their exploration. Calculating the size of an equal share is plainly much easier than determining how much a person needs in order to have enough. In addition, the very concept of having an equal share is itself considerably more patent and accessible than the concept of having enough. It is far from self-evident, needless to say, precisely what the doctrine of sufficiency means and what applying it entails. But this is hardly a good reason for neglecting the doctrine or for adopting an incorrect doctrine in preference to it. Among my primary purposes in this essay is to suggest the importance of systematic inquiry into the analytical and theoretical issues raised by the concept of having enough, whose importance egalitarianism has masked.[5]

II

There are a number of ways of attempting to establish the thesis that economic equality is important. Sometimes it is urged that the prevalence of fraternal relationships among the members of a society is a desirable goal and that equality is indispensable to it.[6] Or it may be maintained that inequalities in the distribution of economic benefits are to be avoided because they lead invariably to undesirable discrepancies of other kinds — for example, in social status, in political influence, or in the abilities of people to make effective use of their various oppor-

---

5   I shall address some of these issues in section VII below.
6   In the Sterling Memorial Library at Yale University (8.5 million volumes) there are
     1,159 entries in the card catalogue under the subject heading "liberty," and there are
     326 under "equality." Under "fraternity" there are none. This is because the catalogue
     refers to the social ideal in question as "brotherliness." Under that heading there are
     four entries! Why does fraternity (or brotherliness) have so much less salience than
     liberty and equality? Perhaps the explanation is that, in virtue of our fundamental
     commitment to individualism, the political ideals to which we are most deeply and
     actively attracted have to do with what we suppose to be the rights of individuals; and
     no one claims a right to fraternity. It is also possible that liberty and equality get more
     attention in certain quarters because, unlike fraternity, they are considered to be sus-
     ceptible to more or less formal treatment. In any event, the fact is that there has been
     very little serious investigation into just what fraternity is, what it entails, or why it
     should be regarded as especially desirable.

tunities and entitlements. In both of these arguments, economic equality is endorsed because of its supposed importance in creating or preserving certain non-economic conditions. Such considerations may well provide convincing reasons for recommending equality as a desirable social good, or even for preferring egalitarianism as a policy over the alternatives to it. But both arguments construe equality as valuable derivatively, in virtue of its contingent connections to other things. In neither argument is there an attribution to equality of any unequivocally inherent moral value.

A rather different kind of argument for economic equality, which comes closer to construing the value of equality as independent of contingencies, is based upon the principle of diminishing marginal utility. According to this argument, equality is desirable because an egalitarian distribution of economic assets maximizes their aggregate utility.[7] The argument presupposes: (a) for each individual the utility of money invariably diminishes at the margin; and (b) with respect to money, or with respect to the things money can buy, the utility functions of all individuals are the same.[8] In other words, the utility provided by or derivable from an nth dollar is the same for everyone, and it is less than the utility for anyone of dollar $(n - 1)$. Unless (b) were true, a rich man might obtain greater utility than a poor man from an extra dollar. In that case an egalitarian distribution of economic goods would not maximize aggregate utility even if (a) were true. But given both (a) and (b), it follows that a marginal dollar always brings less utility to a rich person than to one who is less rich. And this entails that total utility must increase when inequality is reduced by giving a dollar to someone poorer than the person from whom it is taken.

In fact, however, both (a) and (b) are false. Suppose it is conceded, for

---

7   Nagel, in *Mortal Questions,* endorses this argument as establishing the moral importance of economic equality. Other formulations and discussions of the argument may be found in: Kenneth Arrow, "A Utilitarian Approach to the Concept of Equality in Public Expenditures," *Quarterly Journal of Economics* 85 (1971); Walter Blum and Harry Kalven, *The Uneasy Case for Progressive Taxation* (Chicago: University of Chicago Press, 1966); Abba Lerner, *The Economics of Control* (New York: Macmillan, 1944); Paul Samuelson, *Economics* (New York: McGraw-Hill, 1973), and "A. P. Lerner at Sixty," in Robert C. Merton (ed.), *Collected Scientific Papers of Paul A. Samuelson,* volume iii (Cambridge, Mass.: MIT Press, 1972).

8   Thus, Arrow ("A Utilitarian Approach," p. 409) says: "In the utilitarian discussion of income distribution, equality of income is derived from the maximization conditions if it is further assumed that individuals have the same utility functions, each with diminishing marginal utility." And Samuelson (*Economics,* p. 164 fn.) offers the following formulation: "If each extra dollar brings less and less satisfaction to a man, and if the rich and poor are alike in their capacity to enjoy satisfaction, a dollar taxed away from a millionaire and given to a median-income person is supposed to add more to total utility than it subtracts."

the sake of the argument, that the maximization of aggregate utility is in its own right a morally important social goal. Even so, it cannot legitimately be inferred that an egalitarian distribution of money must therefore have similar moral importance. For in virtue of the falsity of (a) and (b), the argument linking economic equality to the maximization of aggregate utility is unsound.

So far as concerns (b), it is evident that the utility functions for money of different individuals are not even approximately alike. Some people suffer from physical, mental, or emotional weaknesses or incapacities that limit the satisfactions they are able to obtain. Moreover, even apart from the effects of specific disabilities, some people simply enjoy things more than other people do. Everyone knows that there are, at any given level of expenditure, large differences in the quantities of utility that different spenders derive.

So far as concerns (a), there are good reasons against expecting any consistent diminution in the marginal utility of money. The fact that the marginal utilities of certain goods do indeed tend to diminish is not a principle of reason. It is a psychological generalization, which is accounted for by such considerations as that people often tend after a time to become satiated with what they have been consuming and that the senses characteristically lose their freshness after repetitive stimulation.[9] It is common knowledge that experiences of many kinds become increasingly routine and unrewarding as they are repeated.

It is questionable, however, whether this provides any reason at all for expecting a diminution in the marginal utility of *money* − that is, of anything that functions as a generic instrument of exchange. Even if the utility of everything money can buy were inevitably to diminish at the margin, the utility of money itself might nonetheless exhibit a different pattern. It is quite possible that money would be exempt from the phenomenon of unrelenting marginal decline because of its limitlessly protean versatility. As Blum and Kalven explain:

In . . . analysing the question whether money has a declining utility it is . . . important to put to one side all analogies to the observation that particular commodities have a declining utility to their users. There is no need here to enter into the debate whether it is useful or necessary, in economic theory, to assume that commodities have a declining utility. Money is infinitely versatile. And even

9 "With successive new units of [a] good, your total utility will grow at a slower and slower rate because of a fundamental tendency for your psychological ability to appreciate more of the good to become less keen. This fact, that the increments in total utility fall off, economists describe as follows: as the amount consumed of a good increases, the *marginal utility* of the good (or the extra utility added by its last unit) tends to decrease" (Samuelson, *Economics,* p. 431).

if all the things money can buy are subject to a law of diminishing utility, it does not follow that money itself is.[10]

From the supposition that a person tends to lose more and more interest in what he is consuming as his consumption of it increases, it plainly cannot be inferred that he must also tend to lose interest in consumption itself or in the money that makes consumption possible. For there may always remain for him, no matter how tired he has become of what he has been doing, untried goods to be bought and fresh new pleasures to be enjoyed.

There are in any event many things of which people do not from the very outset immediately begin to tire. From certain goods, they actually derive more utility after sustained consumption than they derive at first. This is the situation whenever appreciating or enjoying or otherwise benefitting from something depends upon repeated trials, which serve as a kind of "warming up" process: for instance, when relatively little significant gratification is obtained from the item or experience in question until the individual has acquired a special taste for it, or has become addicted to it, or has begun in some other way to relate or respond to it profitably. The capacity for obtaining gratification is then smaller at earlier points in the sequence of consumption than at later points. In such cases marginal utility does not decline; it increases. Perhaps it is true of everything, without exception, that a person will ultimately lose interest in it. But even if in every utility curve there is a point at which the curve begins a steady and irreversible decline, it cannot be assumed that every segment of the curve has a downward slope.[11]

III

When marginal utility diminishes, it does not do so on account of any deficiency in the marginal unit. It diminishes in virtue of the position of that unit as the latest in a sequence. The same is true when marginal utility increases: the marginal unit provides greater utility than its prede-

---

10 Blum and Kalven, pp. 57–8.
11 People tend to think that it is generally more important to avoid a certain degree of harm than to acquire a benefit of comparable magnitude. It may be that this is in part because they assume that utility diminishes at the margin; for in that case the additional benefit would have less utility than the corresponding loss. However, it should be noted that the tendency to place a lower value on acquiring benefits than on avoiding harms is sometimes reversed: when people are so miserable that they regard themselves as "having nothing to lose," they may well place a higher value on improving things than on preventing them from becoming (to a comparable extent) even worse. In that case, what is diminishing at the margin is not the utility of benefits but the disutility of harms.

cessors in virtue of the effect which the acquisition or consumption of those predecessors has brought about. Now when the sequence consists of units of money, what corresponds to the process of warming up – at least, in one pertinent and important feature – is *saving*. Accumulating money entails, as warming up does, generating a capacity to derive at some subsequent point in a sequence gratifications that cannot be derived earlier.

The fact that it may at times be especially worthwhile for a person to save money rather than to spend each dollar as it comes along is due in part to the incidence of what may be thought of as *utility thresholds*. Consider an item with the following characteristics: it is non-fungible, it is the source of a fresh and otherwise unobtainable type of satisfaction, and it is too expensive to be acquired except by saving up for it. The utility of the dollar that finally completes a program of saving up for such an item may be greater than the utility of any dollar saved earlier in the program. That will be the case when the utility provided by the item is greater than the sum of the utilities that could be derived if the money saved were either spent as it came in or divided into parts and used to purchase other things. In a situation of this kind, the final dollar saved permits the crossing of a utility threshold.[12]

It is sometimes argued that, for anyone who is rational in the sense that he seeks to maximize the utility generated by his expenditures, the marginal utility of money must necessarily diminish. Abba Lerner presents this argument as follows:

The principle of diminishing marginal utility of income can be derived from the assumption that consumers spend their income in the way that maximizes the satisfaction they can derive from the good obtained. With a given income, all the things bought give a greater satisfaction for the money spent on them than any of the other things that could have been bought in their place but were not bought

12 In virtue of these thresholds a marginal or incremental dollar may have conspicuously greater utility than dollars that do not enable a threshold to be crossed. Thus, a person who uses his spare money during a certain period for some inconsequential improvement in his routine pattern of consumption – perhaps a slightly better quality of meat for dinner every night – may derive much less additional utility in this way than by saving up the extra money for a few weeks and going to see some marvelous play or opera. The threshold effect is particularly integral to the experience of collectors, who characteristically derive greater satisfaction from obtaining the item that finally completes a collection – whichever item it happens to be – than from obtaining any of the other items in the collection. Obtaining the final item entails crossing a utility threshold: A complete collection of twenty different items, each of which when considered individually has the same utility, is likely to have greater utility for a collector than an incomplete collection that is of the same size but that includes duplicates. The completeness of the collection itself possesses utility, in addition to the utility provided individually by the items of which the collection is comprised.

for this very reason. From this it follows that if income were greater the additional things that would be bought with the increment of income would be things that are rejected when income is smaller because they give less satisfaction; and if income were greater still, even less satisfactory things would be bought. The greater the income the less satisfactory are the additional things that can be bought with equal increases of income. That is all that is meant by the principle of the diminishing marginal utility of income.[13]

Lerner invokes here a comparison between the utility of $G(n)$ − the goods which the rational consumer actually buys with his income of n dollars − and "the other things that could have been bought in their place but were not." Given that he prefers to buy $G(n)$ rather than the other things, which by hypothesis cost no more, the rational consumer must regard $G(n)$ as offering greater satisfaction than the others can provide. From this Lerner infers that with an additional n dollars the consumer would be able to purchase only things with less utility than $G(n)$; and he concludes that, in general, "the greater the income the less satisfactory are the additional things that can be bought with equal increases of income." This conclusion, he maintains, is tantamount to the principle of the diminishing marginal utility of income.

It seems apparent that Lerner's attempt to derive the principle in this way fails. One reason is that the amount of satisfaction a person can derive from a certain good may vary considerably according to whether or not he also possesses certain other goods. The satisfaction obtainable from a certain expenditure may therefore be greater if some other expenditure has already been made. Suppose that the cost of a serving of popcorn is the same as the cost of enough butter to make it delectable; and suppose that some rational consumer who adores buttered popcorn gets very little satisfaction from unbuttered popcorn, but that he nonetheless prefers it to butter alone. He will buy the popcorn in preference to the butter, accordingly, if he must buy one and cannot buy both. Suppose now that this person's income increases so that he can buy the butter too. Then he can have something he enjoys enormously: his incremental income makes it possible for him not merely to buy butter in addition to popcorn, but to enjoy buttered popcorn. The satisfaction he will derive by combining the popcorn and the butter may well be considerably greater than the sum of the satisfactions he can derive from the two goods taken separately. Here, again, is a threshold effect.

In a case of this sort, what the rational consumer buys with his incremental income is a good − $G(i)$ − which, when his income was smaller, he had rejected in favor of $G(n)$ because having it alone would have been

13   Lerner, pp. 26–7.

less satisfying than having only $G(n)$. Despite this, however, it is not true that the utility of the income he uses to buy $G(i)$ is less than the utility of the income he used to buy $G(n)$. When there is an opportunity to create a combination which is (like buttered popcorn) synergistic in the sense that adding one good to another increases the utility of each, the marginal utility of income may not decline even though the sequence of marginal items – taking each of these items by itself – does exhibit a pattern of declining utilities.

Lerner's argument is flawed in virtue of another consideration as well. Since he speaks of "the *additional* things that can be bought with equal increases of income," he evidently presumes that a rational consumer uses his first n dollars to purchase a certain good and that he uses any incremental income beyond that to buy something else. This leads Lerner to suppose that what the consumer buys when his income is increased by i dollars (where i is equal to or less than n) must be something which he could have bought and which he chose not to buy when his income was only n dollars. But this supposition is unwarranted. With an income of $(n + i)$ dollars the consumer need not use his money to purchase both $G(n)$ and $G(i)$. He might use it to buy something which costs more than either of these goods – something which was too expensive to be available to him at all before his income increased. The point is that if a rational consumer with an income of n dollars defers purchasing a certain good until his income increases, this does not necessarily mean that he "rejected" purchasing it when his income was smaller. The good in question may have been out of his reach at that time because it cost more than n dollars. His reason for postponing the purchase may have had nothing to do with comparative expectations of satisfaction or with preferences or priorities at all.

There are two possibilities to consider. Suppose on the one hand that, instead of purchasing $G(n)$ when his income is n dollars, the rational consumer saves that money until he can add an additional i dollars to it and then purchases $G(n + i)$. In this case it is quite evident that his deferral of the purchase of $G(n + i)$ does not mean that he values it less than $G(n)$. On the other hand, suppose that the rational consumer declines to save up for $G(n + i)$ and that he spends all the money he has on $G(n)$. In this case too it would be a mistake to construe his behavior as indicating a preference for $G(n)$ over $G(n + i)$. For the explanation of his refusal to save for $G(n + i)$ may be merely that he regards doing so as pointless because he believes that he cannot reasonably expect to save enough to make a timely purchase of it.

The utility of $G(n + i)$ may not only be greater than the utility either of $G(n)$ or of $G(i)$. It may also be greater than the sum of their utilities.

That is, in acquiring $G(n + i)$ the consumer may cross a utility threshold. The utility of the increment i to his income is then actually greater than the utility of the n dollars to which it is added, even though i equals or is less than n. In such a case, the income of the rational consumer does not exhibit diminishing marginal utility.

IV

The preceding discussion has established that an egalitarian distribution may fail to maximize aggregate utility. It can also easily be shown that, in virtue of the incidence of utility thresholds, there are conditions under which an egalitarian distribution actually minimizes aggregate utility.[14] Thus suppose that there is enough of a certain resource (e.g., food or medicine) to enable some but not all members of a population to survive. Let us say that the size of the population is ten, that a person needs at least five units of the resource in question to live, and that forty units are available. If any members of this population are to survive, some must have more than others. An equal distribution, which gives each person four units, leads to the worst possible outcome: viz., everyone dies. Surely in this case it would be morally grotesque to insist upon equality! Nor would it be reasonable to maintain that, under the conditions specified, it is justifiable for some to be better off only when this is in the interests of the worst off. If the available resources are used to save eight people, the justification for doing this is manifestly not that it somehow benefits the two members of the population who are left to die.

An egalitarian distribution will almost certainly produce a net loss of aggregate utility whenever it entails that fewer individuals than otherwise will have, with respect to some necessity, enough to sustain life – in other words, whenever it requires a larger number of individuals to be below the threshold of survival. Of course, a loss of utility may also occur even when the circumstances involve a threshold that does not separate life and death. Allocating resources equally will reduce aggregate utility whenever it requires a number of individuals to be kept below *any* utility threshold without ensuring a compensating move above some threshold by a suitable number of others.

Under conditions of scarcity, then, an egalitarian distribution may be morally unacceptable. Another response to scarcity is to distribute the available resources in such a way that as many people as possible have enough, or, in other words, to maximize the incidence of sufficiency.

---

14   Conditions of these kinds are discussed in Nicholas Rescher, *Distributive Justice* (Indianapolis: Bobbs Merrill, 1966), pp. 28–30.

This alternative is especially compelling when the amount of a scarce resource that constitutes enough coincides with the amount that is indispensable for avoiding some catastrophic harm — as in the example just considered, where falling below the threshold of enough food or enough medicine means death. But now suppose that there are available, in this example, not just forty units of the vital resource but forty-one. Then maximizing the incidence of sufficiency by providing enough for each of eight people leaves one unit unallocated. What should be done with this extra unit?

It has been shown above that it is a mistake to maintain that *where some people have less than enough, no one should have more than anyone else.* When resources are scarce, so that it is impossible for everyone to have enough, an egalitarian distribution may lead to disaster. Now there is another claim that might be made here, which may appear to be quite plausible, but which is also mistaken: *where some people have less than enough, no one should have more than enough.* If this claim were correct, then — in the example at hand — the extra unit should go to one of the two people who have nothing. But one additional unit of the resource in question will not improve the condition of a person who has none. By hypothesis, that person will die even with the additional unit. What he needs is not one unit, but five.[15] It cannot be taken for granted that a person who has a certain amount of a vital resource is necessarily better off than a person who has a lesser amount, for the larger amount may still be too small to serve any useful purpose. Having the larger amount may even make a person worse off. Thus it is conceivable that while a dose of five units of some medication is therapeutic, a dose of one unit is not better than none but actually toxic. And while a person with one unit of food may live a bit longer than someone with no food whatever, perhaps it is worse to prolong the process of starvation for a short time than to terminate quickly the agony of starving to death.

The claim that no one should have more than enough while anyone has less than enough derives its plausibility, in part, from a presumption that is itself plausible but that is nonetheless false: to wit, giving resources to people who have less of them than enough necessarily means giving resources to people who need them and, therefore, making those people better off. It is indeed reasonable to assign a higher priority to improving the condition of those who are in need than to improving the condition

15 It might be correct to say that he does need one unit if there is a chance that he will get four more, since in that case the one unit can be regarded as potentially an integral constituent of the total of five that puts him across the threshold of survival. But if there is no possibility that he will acquire five, then acquiring the one does not contribute to the satisfaction of any need.

of those who are not in need. But giving additional resources to people who have less than enough of those resources, and who are accordingly in need, may not actually improve the condition of these people at all. Those below a utility threshold are not necessarily benefitted by additional resources that move them closer to the threshold. What is crucial for them is to attain the threshold. Merely moving closer to it may either fail to help them or be disadvantageous.

By no means do I wish to suggest, of course, that it is never or only rarely beneficial for those below a utility threshold to move closer to it. Certainly it may be beneficial, either because it increases the likelihood that the threshold will ultimately be attained or because, quite apart from the significance of the threshold, additional resources provide important increments of utility. After all, a collector may enjoy expanding his collection even if he knows that he has no chance of ever completing it. My point is only that additional resources do not necessarily benefit those who have less than enough. The additions may be too little to make any difference. It may be morally quite acceptable, accordingly, for some to have more than enough of a certain resource even while others have less than enough of it.

V

Quite often, advocacy of egalitarianism is based less upon an argument than upon a purported moral intuition: economic inequality, considered as such, just seems wrong. It strikes many people as unmistakably apparent that, taken simply in itself, the enjoyment by some of greater economic benefits than are enjoyed by others is morally offensive. I suspect, however, that in many cases those who profess to have this intuition concerning manifestations of inequality are actually responding not to the inequality but to another feature of the situations they are confronting. What I believe they find intuitively to be morally objectionable, in the types of situations characteristically cited as instances of economic inequality, is not the fact that some of the individuals in those situations have *less* money than others but the fact that those with less have *too little*.

When we consider people who are substantially worse off than ourselves, we do very commonly find that we are morally disturbed by their circumstances. What directly touches us in cases of this kind, however, is not a quantitative discrepancy but a qualitative condition – not the fact that the economic resources of those who are worse off are *smaller in magnitude* than ours, but the different fact that these people are so *poor*. Mere differences in the amounts of money people have are not in themselves distressing. We tend to be quite unmoved, after all, by inequalities between the well-to-do and the rich; our awareness that the former are substantially worse off than the latter does not disturb us morally at all. And if we believe of some person that his life is richly fulfilling, that he himself is genuinely content with his economic situation, and that he suffers no resentments or sorrows which more money could assuage, we are not ordinarily much interested – from a moral point of view – in the question of how the amount of money he has compares with the amounts possessed by others. Economic discrepancies in cases of these sorts do not impress us in the least as matters of significant moral concern. The fact that some people have much less than others is morally undisturbing when it is clear that they have plenty.

It seems clear that egalitarianism and the doctrine of sufficiency are logically independent: considerations that support the one cannot be presumed to provide support also for the other. Yet proponents of egalitarianism frequently suppose that they have offered grounds for their position when in fact what they have offered is pertinent as support only for the doctrine of sufficiency. Thus they often, in attempting to gain acceptance for egalitarianism, call attention to disparities between the conditions of life characteristic of the rich and those characteristic of the poor. Now it is undeniable that contemplating such disparities does often elicit a conviction that it would be morally desirable to redistribute the available resources so as to improve the circumstances of the poor. And, of course, that would bring about a greater degree of economic equality. But the indisputability of the moral appeal of improving the condition of the poor by allocating to them resources taken from those who are well off does not even tend to show that egalitarianism is, as a moral ideal, similarly indisputable. To show of poverty that it is compellingly undesirable does nothing whatsoever to show the same of inequality. For what makes someone poor in the morally relevant sense – in which poverty is understood as a condition from which we naturally recoil – is not that his economic assets are simply of lesser magnitude than those of others.

A typical example of this confusion is provided by Ronald Dworkin. Dworkin characterizes the ideal of economic equality as requiring that "no citizen has less than an equal share of the community's resources just in order that others may have more of what he lacks."[16] But in support of his claim that the United States now falls short of this ideal, he refers to circumstances that are not primarily evidence of inequality but of poverty:

16 Ronald Dworkin, "Why Liberals Should Care about Equality," in his *A Matter of Principle* (Cambridge, Mass.: Harvard University Press, 1985), p. 206. Numbers within parentheses in this paragraph and the next refer to pages of this essay.

It is, I think, apparent that the United States falls far short now [of the ideal of equality]. A substantial minority of Americans are chronically unemployed or earn wages below any realistic "poverty line" or are handicapped in various ways or burdened with special needs; and most of these people would do the work necessary to earn a decent living if they had the opportunity and capacity. (208)

What mainly concerns Dworkin — what he actually considers to be morally important — is manifestly not that our society permits a situation in which a substantial minority of Americans have *smaller shares* than others of the resources which he apparently presumes should be available for all. His concern is, rather, that the members of this minority *do not earn decent livings.*

The force of Dworkin's complaint does not derive from the allegation that our society fails to provide some individuals with as much as others, but from a quite different allegation: viz., our society fails to provide each individual with "the opportunity to develop and lead a life he can regard as valuable both to himself and to [the community]" (211). Dworkin is dismayed most fundamentally, not by evidence that the United States permits economic inequality, but by evidence that it fails to ensure that everyone has enough to lead "a life of choice and value" (212) — in other words, that it fails to fulfill for all the ideal of sufficiency. What bothers him most immediately is not that certain quantitative relationships are widespread but that certain qualitative conditions prevail. He cares principally about the value of people's lives, but he mistakenly represents himself as caring principally about the relative magnitudes of their economic assets.

My suggestion that situations involving inequality are morally disturbing only to the extent that they violate the ideal of sufficiency is confirmed, it seems to me, by familiar discrepancies between the principles egalitarians profess and the way in which they commonly conduct their own lives. My point here is not that some egalitarians hypocritically accept high incomes and special opportunities for which, according to the moral theories they profess, there is no justification. It is that many egalitarians (including many academic proponents of the doctrine) are not truly concerned whether they are as well off economically as other people are. They believe that they themselves have roughly enough money for what is important to them, and they are therefore not terribly preoccupied with the fact that some people are considerably richer than they. Indeed, many egalitarians would consider it rather shabby or even reprehensible to care, with respect to their own lives, about economic comparisons of that sort. And, notwithstanding the implications of the doctrines to which they urge adherence, they would be appalled if their children grew up with such preoccupations.

VI

The fundamental error of egalitarianism lies in supposing that it is moral-ly important whether one person has less than another regardless of how much either of them has. This error is due in part to the false assumption that someone who is economically worse off has more important un-satisfied needs than someone who is better off. In fact the morally signifi-cant needs of both individuals may be fully satisfied or equally un-satisfied. Whether one person has more money than another is a wholly extrinsic matter. It has to do with a relationship between the respective economic assets of the two people, which is not only independent of the amounts of their assets and of the amounts of satisfaction they can derive from them, but which is also independent of the attitudes of these people toward those levels of assets and of satisfaction. The economic com-parison implies nothing concerning whether either of the people com-pared has any morally important unsatisfied needs at all, nor concerning whether either is content with what he has.

This defect in egalitarianism appears plainly in Thomas Nagel's devel-opment of the doctrine. According to Nagel:

The essential feature of an egalitarian priority system is that it counts improve-ments to the welfare of the worse off as more urgent than improvements to the welfare of the better off . . . . What makes a system egalitarian is the priority it gives to the claims of those . . . at the bottom. . . . Each individual with a more urgent claim has priority . . . over each individual with a less urgent claim.[17]

And in discussing Rawls's Difference Principle, which he endorses, Nagel says the Difference Principle "establishes an order of priority among needs and gives preference to the most urgent."[18] But the prefer-ence actually assigned by the Difference Principle is not in favor of those whose needs are most urgent; it is in favor of those who are identified as worst off. It is a mere assumption, which Nagel makes without providing any grounds for it whatever, that the worst off individuals have urgent needs. In most societies the people who are economically at the bottom are indeed extremely poor; and they do, as a matter of fact, have urgent needs. But this relationship between low economic status and urgent need is wholly contingent. It can be established only on the basis of empirical data. There is no necessary conceptual connection between a person's relative economic position and whether he has needs of any degree of urgency.[19]

17 Nagel, p. 118.
18 Ibid., p. 117.
19 What I oppose is the claim that when it comes to justifying attempts to improve the
   circumstances of those who are economically worst off, a good reason for making the

It is possible for those who are worse off not to have more urgent needs or claims than those who are better off, because it is possible for them to have no urgent needs or claims at all. The notion of "urgency" has to do with what is *important*. Trivial needs or interests, which have no significant bearing upon the quality of a person's life or upon his readiness to be content with it, cannot properly be construed as being urgent to any degree whatever or as supporting the sort of morally demanding claims to which genuine urgency gives rise. From the fact that a person is at the bottom of some economic order, moreover, it cannot even be inferred that he has *any* unsatisfied needs or claims. After all, it is possible for conditions at the bottom to be quite good; the fact that they are the worst does not in itself entail that they are bad, or that they are in any way incompatible with richly fulfilling and enjoyable lives.

Nagel maintains that what underlies the appeal of equality is an "ideal of acceptability to each individual."[20] On his account, this ideal entails that a reasonable person should consider deviations from equality to be acceptable only if they are in his interest in the sense that he would be worse off without them. But a reasonable person might well regard an unequal distribution as entirely acceptable even though he did not presume that any other distribution would benefit him less. For he might believe that the unequal distribution provided him with quite enough; and he might reasonably be unequivocally content with that, with no concern for the possibility that some other arrangement would provide him with more. It is gratuitous to assume that every reasonable person must be seeking to maximize the benefits he can obtain, in a sense requiring that he be endlessly interested in or open to improving his life. A certain deviation from equality might not be *in* someone's interest, because it might be that he would in fact be better off without it. But as long as it does not *conflict* with his interest, by obstructing his opportunity to lead the sort of life that it is important for him to lead, the deviation from equality may be quite acceptable. To be wholly satisfied with a certain state of affairs, a reasonable person need not suppose that there is no other available state of affairs in which he would be better off.[21]

Nagel illustrates his thesis concerning the moral appeal of equality by

attempt is that it is morally important for people to be as equal as possible with respect to money. The only morally compelling reason for trying to make the worse off better off is, in my judgment, that their lives are in some degree bad lives. The fact that some people have more than enough money suggests a way in which it might be arranged for those who have less than enough to get more, but it is not in itself a good reason for redistribution.

20   Nagel, p. 123.
21   For further discussion, see section VII below.

considering a family with two children, one of whom is "normal and quite happy" while the other "suffers from a painful handicap."[22] If this family were to move to the city the handicapped child would benefit from medical and educational opportunities that are unavailable in the suburbs, but the healthy child would have less fun. If the family were to move to the suburbs, on the other hand, the handicapped child would be deprived but the healthy child would enjoy himself more. Nagel stipulates that the gain to the healthy child in moving to the suburbs would be greater than the gain to the handicapped child in moving to the city: in the city the healthy child would find life positively disagreeable, while the handicapped child would not become happy "but only less miserable."

Given these considerations, the egalitarian decision is to move to the city; for "it is more urgent to benefit the [handicapped] child even though the benefit we can give him is less than the benefit we can give the [healthy] child." Nagel explains that this judgment concerning the greater urgency of benefitting the handicapped child "depends on the worse off position of the [handicapped] child. An improvement in his situation is more important than an equal or somewhat greater improvement in the situation of the [normal] child." But it seems to me that Nagel's analysis of this matter is flawed by an error similar to the one that I attributed above to Dworkin. The fact that it is preferable to help the handicapped child is not due, as Nagel asserts, to the fact that this child is worse off than the other. It is due to the fact that this child, and not the other, suffers from a painful handicap. The handicapped child's claim is important because his condition is *bad* – significantly undesirable – and not merely because he is *less well off* than his sibling.

This does not imply, of course, that Nagel's evaluation of what the family should do is wrong. Rejecting egalitarianism certainly does not mean maintaining that it is always mandatory simply to maximize benefits, and that therefore the family should move to the suburbs because the normal child would gain more from that than the handicapped child would gain from a move to the city. However, the most cogent basis for Nagel's judgment in favor of the handicapped child has nothing to do with the alleged urgency of providing people with as much as others. It pertains rather to the urgency of the needs of people who do not have enough.[23]

22 Quotations from Nagel's discussion of this illustration are from his *Mortal Questions*. pp. 123–4.
23 The issue of equality or sufficiency that Nagel's illustration raises does not, of course, concern the distribution of *money*.

VII

What does it mean, in the present context, for a person to have enough? One thing it might mean is that any more would be too much: a larger amount would make the person's life unpleasant, or it would be harmful or in some other way unwelcome. This is often what people have in mind when they say such things as "I've had enough!" or "Enough of that!" The idea conveyed by statements like these is that *a limit has been reached,* beyond which it is not desirable to proceed. On the other hand, the assertion that a person has enough may entail only that *a certain require-ment or standard has been met,* with no implication that a larger quantity would be bad. This is often what a person intends when he says some-thing like "That should be enough." Statements such as this one charac-terize the indicated amount as sufficient while leaving open the pos-sibility that a larger amount might also be acceptable.

In the doctrine of sufficiency the use of the notion of "enough" per-tains to *meeting a standard* rather than to *reaching a limit.* To say that a person has enough money means that he is content, or that it is reason-able for him to be content, with having no more money than he has. And to say this is, in turn, to say something like the following: the person does not (or cannot reasonably) regard whatever (if anything) is unsatisfying or distressing about his life as due to his having too little money. In other words, if a person is (or ought reasonably to be) content with the amount of money he has, then insofar as he is or has reason to be unhappy with the way his life is going, he does not (or cannot reasonably) suppose that more money would – either as a sufficient or as a necessary condition – enable him to become (or to have reason to be) significantly less unhappy with it.[24]

It is essential to understand that having enough money differs from merely having enough to get along, or enough to make life marginally tolerable. People are not generally content with living on the brink. The point of the doctrine of sufficiency is not that the only morally important distributional consideration with respect to money is whether people have enough to avoid economic misery. A person who might naturally and appropriately be said to have just barely enough does not, by the standard invoked in the doctrine of sufficiency, have enough at all.

There are two distinct kinds of circumstances in which the amount of money a person has is enough – that is, in which more money will not

24 Within the limits of my discussion it makes no difference which view is taken concern-ing the very important question of whether what counts is *the attitude a person actually has* or *the attitude it would be reasonable for him to have.* For the sake of brevity, I shall henceforth omit referring to the latter alternative.

enable him to become significantly less unhappy. On the one hand, it may be that the person is suffering no substantial distress or dissatisfaction with his life. On the other hand, it may be that although the person is unhappy about how his life is going, the difficulties that account for his unhappiness would not be alleviated by more money. Circumstances of this second kind obtain when what is wrong with the person's life has to do with non-economic goods such as love, a sense that life is meaningful, satisfaction with one's own character, and so on. These are goods that money cannot buy; moreover, they are goods for which none of the things money can buy are even approximately adequate substitutes. Sometimes, to be sure, non-economic goods are obtainable or enjoyable only (or more easily) by someone who has a certain amount of money. But the person who is distressed with his life while content with his economic situation may already have that much money.

It is possible that someone who is content with the amount of money he has might also be content with an even larger amount of money. Since having enough money does not mean being at a limit beyond which more money would necessarily be undesirable, it would be a mistake to assume that for a person who already has enough the marginal utility of money must be either negative or zero. Although this person is by hypothesis not distressed about his life in virtue of any lack of things which more money would enable him to obtain, nonetheless it remains possible that he would enjoy having some of those things. They would not make him less unhappy, nor would they in any way alter his attitude toward his life or the degree of his contentment with it, but they might bring him pleasure. If that is so, then his life would in this respect be better with more money than without it. The marginal utility for him of money would accordingly remain positive.

To say that a person is content with the amount of money he has does not entail, then, that there would be no point whatever in his having more. Thus someone with enough money might be quite *willing* to accept incremental economic benefits. He might in fact be *pleased* to receive them. Indeed, from the supposition that a person is content with the amount of money he has it cannot even be inferred that he would not *prefer* to have more. And it is even possible that he would actually be prepared to *sacrifice* certain things that he values (for instance, a certain amount of leisure) for the sake of more money.

But how can all this be compatible with saying that the person is content with what he has? What *does* contentment with a given amount of money preclude, if it does not preclude being willing or being pleased or preferring to have more money or even being ready to make sacrifices for more? It precludes his having an *active interest* in getting more. A contented person regards having more money as *inessential* to his being satisfied with his life. The fact that he is content is quite consistent with his recognizing that his economic circumstances could be improved and that his life might as a consequence become better than it is. But this possibility is not important to him. He is simply not much interested in being better off, so far as money goes, than he is. His attention and interest are not vividly engaged by the benefits which would be available to him if he had more money. He is just not very responsive to their appeal. They do not arouse in him any particularly eager or restless concern, although he acknowledges that he would enjoy additional benefits if they were provided to him.

In any event, let us suppose that the level of satisfaction that his present economic circumstances enable him to attain is high enough to meet his expectations of life. This is not fundamentally a matter of how much utility or satisfaction his various activities and experiences provide. Rather, it is most decisively a matter of his attitude toward being provided with that much. The satisfying experiences a person has are one thing. Whether he is satisfied that his life includes just those satisfactions is another. Although it is possible that other feasible circumstances would provide him with greater amounts of satisfaction, it may be that he is wholly satisfied with the amounts of satisfaction that he now enjoys. Even if he knows that he could obtain a greater quantity of satisfaction overall, he does not experience the uneasiness or the ambition that would incline him to seek it. Some people feel that their lives are good enough, and it is not important to them whether their lives are as good as possible.

The fact that a person lacks an active interest in getting something does not mean, of course, that he prefers not to have it. This is why the contented person may without any incoherence accept or welcome improvements in his situation and why he may even be prepared to incur minor costs in order to improve it. The fact that he is contented means only that the possibility of improving his situation is not *important* to him. It only implies, in other words, that he does not resent his circumstances, that he is not anxious or determined to improve them, and that he does not go out of his way or take any significant initiatives to make them better.

It may seem that there can be no reasonable basis for accepting less satisfaction when one could have more, that therefore rationality itself entails maximizing, and hence that a person who refuses to maximize the quantity of satisfaction in his life is not being rational. Such a person cannot, of course, offer it as his reason for declining to pursue greater satisfaction that the costs of this pursuit are too high; for if that were his reason then, clearly, he would be attempting to maximize satisfaction after all. But what other good reason could he possibly have for passing up an opportunity for more satisfaction? In fact, he may have a very good reason for this: namely, *that he is satisfied with the amount of satisfaction he already has.* Being satisfied with the way things are is unmistakably an excellent reason for having no great interest in changing them. A person who is indeed satisfied with his life as it is can hardly be criticized, accordingly, on the grounds that he has no good reason for declining to make it better.

He might still be open to criticism on the grounds that he *should not* be satisfied — that it is somehow unreasonable, or unseemly, or in some other mode wrong for him to be satisfied with less satisfaction than he could have. On what basis, however, could *this* criticism be justified? Is there some decisive reason for insisting that a person ought to be so hard to satisfy? Suppose that a man deeply and happily loves a woman who is altogether worthy. We do not ordinarily criticize the man in such a case just because we think he might have done even better. Moreover, our sense that it would be inappropriate to criticize him for that reason need not be due simply to a belief that holding out for a more desirable or worthier woman might end up costing him more than it would be worth. Rather, it may reflect our recognition that the desire to be happy or content or satisfied with life is a desire for a satisfactory amount of satisfaction, and is not inherently tantamount to a desire that the quantity of satisfaction be maximized.

Being satisfied with a certain state of affairs is not equivalent to preferring it to all others. If a person is faced with a choice between less and more of something desirable, then no doubt it would be irrational for him to prefer less to more. But a person may be satisfied without having made any such comparisons at all. Nor is it necessarily irrational or unreasonable for a person to omit or to decline to make comparisons between his own state of affairs and possible alternatives. This is not only because making comparisons may be too costly. It is also because if someone is satisfied with the way things are, he may have no motive to consider how else they might be.[25]

Contentment may be a function of excessive dullness or diffidence. The fact that a person is free both of resentment and of ambition may be due to his having a slavish character or to his vitality being muffled by a kind of negligent lassitude. It is possible for someone to be content merely, as it were, by default. But a person who is content with resources providing less utility than he could have may be neither irresponsible nor

25 Cf. the sensible adage: "If it's not broken, don't fix it."

indolent nor deficient in imagination. On the contrary, his decision to be content with those resources – in other words, to adopt an attitude of willing acceptance toward the fact that he has just that much – may be based upon a conscientiously intelligent and penetrating evaluation of the circumstances of his life.

It is not essential for such an evaluation to include an *extrinsic* comparison of the person's circumstances with alternatives to which he might plausibly aspire, as it would have to do if contentment were reasonable only when based upon a judgment that the enjoyment of possible benefits has been maximized. If someone is less interested in whether his circumstances enable him to live as well as possible than in whether they enable him to live satisfyingly, he may appropriately devote his evaluation entirely to an *intrinsic* appraisal of his life. Then he may recognize that his circumstances lead him to be neither resentful nor regretful nor drawn to change and that, on the basis of his understanding of himself and of what is important to him, he accedes approvingly to his actual readiness to be content with the way things are. The situation in that case is not so much that he rejects the possibility of improving his circumstances because he thinks there is nothing genuinely to be gained by attempting to improve them. It is rather that this possibility, however feasible it may be, fails as a matter of fact to excite his active attention or to command from him any lively interest.[26]

APPENDIX

Economic egalitarianism is a drily formalistic doctrine. The amounts of money its adherents want for themselves and for others are calculated without regard to anyone's personal characteristics or circumstances. In this formality egalitarians resemble people who desire to be as rich as possible but who have no idea what they would do with their riches. In neither case are the individual's ambitions, so far as money is concerned, limited or measured according to an understanding of the goals that he intends his money to serve or of the importance of these goals to him.

The desire for unlimited wealth is fetichistic, insofar as it reflects with respect to a *means* an attitude – namely, desiring something for its own

---

26 People often adjust their desires to their circumstances. There is a danger that sheer discouragement, or an interest in avoiding frustration and conflict, may lead them to settle for too little. It surely cannot be presumed that someone's life is genuinely fulfilling, or that it is reasonable for the person to be satisfied with it, simply because he does not complain. On the other hand, it also cannot be presumed that when a person has accommodated his desires to his circumstances, this is itself evidence that something has gone wrong.

sake – that is appropriate only with respect to an *end*. It seems to me that
the attitude taken by John Rawls toward what he refers to as "primary
goods" ("rights and liberties, opportunities and powers, income and
wealth")[27] tends toward fetishism in this sense. The primary goods are
"all purpose means," Rawls explains, which people need no matter what
other things they want: "Plans differ, since individual abilities, circumstances, and wants differ . . . ; but whatever one's system of ends, primary goods are a necessary means." (93) Despite the fact that he identifies the primary goods not as ends but as means, Rawls considers it
rational for a person to want as much of them as possible. Thus, he says:

> Regardless of what an individual's rational plans are in detail, it is assumed that
> there are various things which he would prefer more of rather than less. . . .
> While the persons in the original position do not know their conception of the
> good, they do know, I assume, that they prefer more rather than less primary
> goods. (92–3)

The assumption that it must always be better to have more of the primary
goods rather than less implies that the marginal utility of an additional
quantity of a primary good is invariably greater than its cost. It implies, in
other words, that the incremental advantage to an individual of possessing a larger quantity of primary goods is never outweighed by corresponding incremental liabilities, incapacities, or burdens.

But this seems quite implausible. Apart from any other consideration,
possessing more of a primary good may well require of a responsible
individual that he spend more time and effort in managing it and in
making decisions concerning its use. These activities are for many people
intrinsically unappealing; and they also characteristically involve both a
certain amount of anxiety and a degree of distraction from other pur-
suits. Surely it must not be taken simply for granted that incremental
costs of these kinds can never be greater than whatever increased benefits a corresponding additional amount of some primary good would provide.

Individuals in the original position are behind a veil of ignorance. They
do not know their own conceptions of the good or their own life plans.
Thus it may seem rational for them to choose to possess primary goods in
unlimited quantities: since they do not know what to prepare for, perhaps it would be best for them to be prepared for anything. Even in the
original position, however, it is possible for people to appreciate that at
some point the cost of additional primary goods might exceed the bene-

27 *A Theory of Justice* (Cambridge, Mass.: Harvard University Press, 1971), p. 92. Numbers within parentheses in this Appendix refer to pages of this book.

fits those goods provide. It is true that an individual behind the veil of ignorance cannot know at just what point he would find that an addition to his supply of primary goods costs more than it is worth. But his ignorance of the exact location of that point hardly warrants his acting as though no such point exists at all. Yet that is precisely how he does act if he chooses that the quantity of primary goods he possesses be unlimited.

Rawls acknowledges that additional quantities of primary goods may be, for some individuals, more expensive than they are worth. In his view, however, this does not invalidate the supposition that it is rational for everyone in the original position to want as much of these goods as they can get. Here is how he explains the matter:

> I postulate that they [i.e., the persons in the original position] assume that they would prefer more primary social goods rather than less. Of course, it may turn out, once the veil of ignorance is removed, that some of them for religious or other reasons may not, in fact, want more of these goods. But from the stand-point of the original position, it is rational for the parties to suppose that they do want a larger share, since in any case they are not compelled to accept more if they do not wish to, nor does a person suffer from a greater liberty. (142–3)

I do not find this argument convincing. It neglects the fact that dispensing with or refusing to accept primary goods that have been made available is itself an action that may entail significant costs. Burdensome calculations and deliberations may be required in order for a person to determine whether an increment of some primary good is worth having; and making decisions of this sort may involve responsibilities and risks in virtue of which the person experiences considerable anxiety. What is the basis, moreover, for the claim that no one suffers from a greater liberty? Under a variety of circumstances, it would seem, people may reasonably prefer to have fewer alternatives from which to choose rather than more. Surely liberty, like all other things, has its costs. It is an error to suppose that a person's life is invariably improved, or that it cannot be made worse, when his options are increased.[28]

---

28 For pertinent discussion of this issue, cf. Gerald Dworkin, "Is More Choice Better than Less?" in P. French, T. Uehling, and H. Wettstein (eds.), *Midwest Studies in Philosophy* VII (Minneapolis, 1982).

12

Identification and wholeheartedness

I

The phrase "the mind-body problem" is so crisp, and its role in philosophical discourse is so well established, that to oppose its use would simply be foolish. Nonetheless, the usage *is* rather anachronistic. The familiar problem to which the phrase refers concerns the relationship between a creature's body and the fact that the creature is conscious. A more appropriate name would be, accordingly, "the consciousness-body problem." For it is no longer plausible to equate the realm of conscious phenomena – as Descartes did – with the realm of mind. This is not only because psychoanalysis has made the notion of unconscious feelings and thoughts compelling. Other leading psychological theories have also found it useful to construe the distinction between the mental and the nonmental as being far broader than that between situations in which consciousness is present and those in which it is not.

For example, both William James and Jean Piaget are inclined to regard mentality as a feature of all living things. James takes the presence of mentality to be essentially a matter of intelligent or goal-directed behavior, which he opposes to behavior that is only mechanical:

The pursuance of future ends and the choice of means for their attainment are the mark and criterion of the presence of mentality in a phenomenon. We all use this test to discriminate between an intelligent and a mechanical performance.[1]

Piaget similarly, but with even greater emphasis, construes the difference between the mental and the nonmental in terms of purposefulness:

There is no sort of boundary between the living and the mental or between the biological and the psychological. [Psychology] is not the science of consciousness only but of behavior in general . . . of conduct. [Psychology begins] when the organism behaves with regard to external situations and solves problems.[2]

1   William James, *The Principles of Psychology I* (Cambridge, Mass.: Harvard University Press, 1983), p. 21.
2   J.-C. Brinquier, *Conversations with Piaget* (Chicago: University of Chicago Press, 1980), pp. 3, 4.

Powerful currents of thought, then, lead away from the supposition that being conscious is essential to mentality. The psychoanalytic expansion of the mind to include unconscious phenomena does not itself actually require, of course, that mentality be attributed to creatures who are entirely *incapable* of consciousness. On the other hand, the conceptions of James and Piaget do entail that mentality characterizes the lives of vast numbers of creatures – not only animals but plants as well – which enjoy no conscious experience at all.[3]

Now what is this *consciousness*, which is distinct from mentality and which we generally suppose to be peculiar to human beings and to the members of certain relatively advanced animal species? Anthony Kenny offers the following view:

> I think that consciousness . . . is a matter of having certain sorts of ability. To be conscious is, for instance, to see and hear. Whether somebody can see or hear is a matter of whether he can discriminate between certain things, and whether he can discriminate between certain things is something that we can test both in simple everyday ways and in complicated experimental ways.[4]

Kenny's suggestion is that to be conscious is to be able to discriminate. But what is it to discriminate? It would seem that discriminating between two things is in the most fundamental sense a matter of being affected differently by the one than by the other. If my state remains exactly the same regardless of whether a certain feature is present in my environment or absent from it, then I am not discriminating between the presence and the absence of that feature. If my state does differ according to the presence or absence of the feature, then that is a mode of discriminating between its presence and its absence. To discriminate sounds, colors, levels of temperature, and the like just means – in its most general sense – to respond differentially to them.

It does seem indisputable that discrimination is central to consciousness: Seeing necessarily involves responding to differences in color; hearing, to differences in sound; and so on. By no means, however, does this effectively grasp what we ordinarily think of as consciousness. The usual way of identifying the state of being conscious is by contrasting it to unconsciousness, and one way of being unconscious is to be asleep. But even while they are asleep, animals respond to visual, auditory, tactile, and other stimuli. Otherwise it would be difficult to wake them up. To be sure, the range of responses when they are sleeping is narrower than when they are awake. But they do not while asleep entirely lack the

---

3 Piaget himself cites the behavior of sunflowers as indicative of mentality.
4 Anthony Kenny et al., *The Nature of Mind* (Edinburgh: University Press, 1972), p. 43.

ability to discriminate, and Kenny cannot therefore regard them as being at that time altogether unconscious.

Now it might well be acceptable to consider sleep as consistent with a certain level of consciousness – lower than that of wakefulness but above zero. In the view Kenny proposes, however, it is not only sleeping animals that are conscious – so is everything else in the world. After all, there is no entity that is not susceptible to being differentially affected by something. If the notion of consciousness is understood as having merely the very general and primitive sense allotted to it by Kenny's account, then a piece of metal is conscious of the ambient temperature to the extent that it becomes hotter and colder, or expands and contracts, as that temperature changes. Consciousness so construed is a state to which the contrasting state is clearly not unconsciousness, understanding unconsciousness to be what we ordinarily attribute to those who are deeply asleep or anesthetized or in a coma. Rather, the state to which consciousness in this sense contrasts is causal isolation.

Consciousness in the everyday sense cannot be exclusively a matter of discrimination, then, since all sorts of discriminating responses may occur (so to speak) in the dark. One might perhaps avoid this difficulty by saying that consciousness is the ability to discriminate *consciously,* but that would not be helpful. In any event, I wish to consider another feature, distinct from discrimination, which is essential to ordinary consciousness: *reflexivity.* Being conscious necessarily involves not merely differentiating responses to stimuli, but an awareness of those responses. When I am awake on a hot day, the heat raises the temperature of my skin; it also raises the surface temperature of a piece of metal. Both the metal and I respond to the heat, and in this sense each of us is aware of it. But I am also aware of my response, while the metal is not. The increase in the temperature of my skin is itself something which I discriminate, and this is essential to the mode of being conscious that consists in feeling warm.

Of course the fact that a creature responds to its own responses does not entail that it is conscious. It goes without saying that the second response may be no more conscious than the first. Thus, adding reflexivity to discrimination does not provide an explanation of how consciousness arises or of how it and unconsciousness differ. Nonetheless, being conscious in the everyday sense does (unlike unconsciousness) entail reflexivity: It necessarily involves a secondary awareness of a primary response. An instance of exclusively primary and unreflexive consciousness would not be an instance of what we ordinarily think of as consciousness at all. For what would it be like to be conscious of something without being aware of this consciousness? It would mean having an experience with no awareness whatever of its occurrence. This would be, precisely, a case of unconscious experience. It appears, then, that being conscious is identical with being self-conscious. Consciousness *is* self-consciousness.[5]

The claim that waking consciousness is self-consciousness does not mean that consciousness is invariably dual in the sense that every instance of it involves both a primary awareness and another instance of consciousness which is somehow distinct and separable from the first and which has the first as its object. That would threaten an intolerably infinite proliferation of instances of consciousness. Rather, the self-consciousness in question is a sort of *immanent reflexivity* by virtue of which every instance of being conscious grasps not only that of which it is an awareness but also the awareness of it. It is like a source of light which, in addition to illuminating whatever other things fall within its scope, renders itself visible as well.

II

There is a baffling problem about what consciousness is *for*. It is equally baffling, moreover, that the function of consciousness should remain so baffling. It seems extraordinary that despite the pervasiveness and familiarity of consciousness in our lives, we are uncertain in what way (if at all) it is actually indispensable to us.[6] Be this as it may, the importance of *reflexivity* to those in whose lives it occurs is readily apparent. A creature's sensitivity to its own condition — whether it is by way of the inwardness or immanent reflexivity of waking consciousness or by way of a less dazzling variety of secondary responsiveness — is essential for purposeful behavior.

5   What I am here referring to as "self-consciousness" is neither consciousness of a self – a subject or ego – nor consciousness that there is awareness. Both require rational capacities beyond what would seem to be necessary for consciousness itself to occur. The reflexivity in question is merely consciousness's awareness of itself. To hear a sound consciously, rather than to respond to it unconsciously, involves being aware of hearing it or being aware of the sound as heard.

6   Thus, the Nobel laureate physiologist John Eccles says: "I would like to [ask] as a neurophysiologist, why do we have to be conscious at all? We can, in principle, explain all our input-output performances in terms of activity of neuronal circuits; and, consequently, consciousness seems to be absolutely unnecessary. I don't believe this story, of course; but at the same time I do not know the logical answer to it. In attempting to answer the question, why do we have to be conscious? it surely cannot be claimed as self-evident that consciousness is a necessary requisite for such performances as logical argument or reasoning, or even for initiative and creative activities." (In J. Eccles [ed.], *Brain and Conscious Experience* [New York: Springer-Verlag, 1964].) Perhaps, despite Eccles's reluctance to admit it, the inwardness of human life is an ontological absurdity – something which takes itself enormously seriously but actually has no important role to play.

The metal does not change in any purposeful way when it becomes hot; on the other hand, under certain conditions a sunflower turns toward the light. Both the metal and the sunflower respond to what goes on around them. Each is affected by, and hence discriminates, environmental stimuli. But the sunflower, unlike the metal, makes second-order as well as primary discriminations. This contributes essentially to its capacity for purposeful change. The metal lacks this capacity, since it is insensitive to its own responses – which is to say that it is altogether unresponsive or indifferent to what happens to it. A creature engaged in secondary responsiveness is monitoring its own condition; to that extent the creature is in a position, or at least is closer to being in a position, to do something about its condition.

Thus reflexivity has a point, just as action itself does, in virtue of the riskiness of existence. It enables a creature, among other things, to respond to the circumstance that its interests are being adversely affected. This makes reflexivity an indispensable condition for behavior that is directed purposefully to avoiding or to ameliorating circumstances of this kind, in which there is a conflict between the interests of a creature and forces that are endangering or undermining them.

There is also another sort of reflexivity or self-consciousness, which appears similarly to be intelligible as being fundamentally a response to conflict and risk. It is a salient characteristic of human beings, one which affects our lives in deep and innumerable ways, that we care about what we are. This is closely connected both as cause and as effect to our enormous preoccupation with what other people think of us. We are ceaselessly alert to the danger that there may be discrepancies between what we wish to be (or what we wish to seem to be) and how we actually appear to others and to ourselves.

We are particularly concerned with our own motives. It matters greatly to us whether the desires by which we are moved to act as we do motivate us because we want them to be effective in moving us or whether they move us regardless of ourselves or even despite ourselves. In the latter cases we are moved to act as we do without wanting wholeheartedly to be motivated as we are. Our hearts are at best divided, and they may even not be in what we are doing at all.

This means, moreover, that we are to some degree passive with respect to the action we perform. For in virtue of the fact that we do not unequivocally endorse or support our own motive, it can appropriately be said that what we want – namely, the object of our motivating desire, and the desire itself – is in a certain ordinary sense not something we *really* want. So while it may be that we perform our action on account of the motivating force of our own desire, it is nonetheless also true that we are being moved to act by something other than what we really want. In that case we are in a way passive with respect to what moves us, as we always are when we are moved by a force that is not fully our own.

It is possible for a human being to be at times, and perhaps even always, indifferent to his own motives – to take no evaluative attitude toward the desires that incline him to act. If there is a conflict between those desires, he does not care which of them proves to be the more effective. In other words, the individual does not participate in the conflict. Therefore, the outcome of the conflict can be neither a victory for him nor a defeat. Since he exercises no authority, by the endorsement or concurrence of which certain of his desires might acquire particular legitimacy, or might come to be specially constitutive of himself, the actions engendered by the flow and clash of his feelings and desires are quite wanton.

III

Now what conceptualization of this range of phenomena fits its contours in the most authentic and perspicuous way? My own preference has been for a model that involves levels of reflexivity or self-consciousness. According to this schema, there are at the lowest level first-order desires to perform one or another action. Whichever of these first-order desires actually leads to action is, by virtue of that effectiveness, designated the will of the individual whose desire it is. In addition, people characteristically have second-order desires concerning what first-order desires they want, and they have second-order volitions concerning which first-order desire they want to be their will. There may also be desires and volitions of higher orders.

This makes it natural to distinguish two ways in which the volitional aspects of a person's life may be radically divided or incoherent. In the first place, there may be a conflict between how someone wants to be motivated and the desire by which he is in fact most powerfully moved. An example of this sort of inner conflict is provided by the situation of a person who wants to refrain from smoking – that is, who wants the desire to refrain from smoking to be what effectively motivates his behavior – but whose desire for a cigarette proves to be so strong that it becomes his will despite the fact that he prefers not to act upon it and even struggles against it. Here there is a lack of coherence or harmony between the person's higher-order volition or preference concerning which of his desires he wants to be most effective and the first-order desire that actually is the most effective in moving him when he acts. Since the desire that prevails is one on which he would prefer not to act, the outcome of the division within him is that he is unable to do what he really wants to do. His will is not under his own control. It is not the will he wants, but one that is imposed on him by a force with which he does not identify and which is in that sense external to him.

Another sort of inner division occurs when there is a lack of coherence within the realm of the person's higher-order volitions themselves. This does not concern the relation between volitions and will. It is a matter not of volitional strength but of whether the highest-order preferences concerning some volitional issue are *wholehearted*. It has to do with the possibility that there is no unequivocal answer to the question of what the person really wants, even though his desires do form a complex and extensive hierarchical structure. There might be no unequivocal answer, because the person is *ambivalent* with respect to the object he comes closest to really wanting: In other words, because, with respect to that object, he is drawn not only toward it but away from it too. Or there might be no unequivocal answer because the person's preferences concerning what he wants are not fully integrated, so that there is some *inconsistency* or *conflict* (perhaps not yet manifest) among them.

Incoherence of the first kind (the kind that afflicts the smoker) might be characterized as being *between* what the person really wants and other desires — like the rejected but nonetheless inescapably preemptive desire to smoke — that are *external* to the volitional complex with which the person identifies and by which he wants his behavior to be determined. The second kind of incoherence is *within* this volitional complex. In the absence of wholeheartedness, the person is not merely in conflict with forces "outside" him; rather, he himself is divided.

One advantage of this model is that it provides a convenient way of explaining how, as in the case of the reluctant smoker, passivity or impaired autonomy may be due to the force of what is in some basically literal sense the individual's own desires. The model also lends itself in fairly obvious ways to the articulation and explication of a variety of useful concepts pertaining to structural features of the mind (e.g., weakness of the will, ego-ideal, and so on). But the model's central notion of a hierarchy of desires seems not to be entirely adequate to its purpose. For it appears to be impossible to explain, using the resources of this notion alone, in what way an individual with second-order desires or volitions may be less wanton with respect to *them* than a wholly unreflective creature is with respect to its first-order desires.[7]

7   The notion of reflexivity seems to me much more fundamental and indispensable, in dealing with the phenomena at hand, than that of a hierarchy. On the other hand, it is not clear to me that adequate provision can be made for reflexivity without resorting to the notion of a hierarchical ordering. While articulating volitional life in terms of a

Someone does what he *really wants* to do only when he acts in accordance with a pertinent higher-order volition. But this condition could not be sufficient unless the higher-order volition were *itself* one by which the person *really wanted* to be determined. Now it is pretty clear that this requirement cannot be satisfied simply by introducing *another* desire or volition at the next higher level. That would lead to a regress which it would be quite arbitrary to terminate at any particular point. The difficulty bears on both types of volitional incoherence I have distinguished. A characterization of either type of incoherence requires construing some of a person's desires as integral to him in a way in which others are not. Yet it is not obvious what account to give of the distinction between volitional elements that are integrated into a person and those that remain in some relevant sense external to him.

The mere fact that one desire occupies a higher level than another in the hierarchy seems plainly insufficient to endow it with greater authority or with any constitutive legitimacy. In other words, the assignment of desires to different hierarchical levels does not by itself provide an explanation of what it is for someone to be *identified* with one of his own desires rather than with another. It does not make clear why it should be appropriate to construe a person as *participating* in conflicts within himself between second-order volitions and first-order desires, and hence as vulnerable to being defeated by his own desires, when a *wanton* is not to be construed as a genuine participant in (or as having any interest in the outcomes of) conflicts within himself between desires all of which are of the first order. Gary Watson has formulated the issue succinctly: "Since second-order volitions are themselves simply desires, to add them to the context of conflict is just to increase the number of contenders; it is not to give a special place to any of those in contention."[8] It appears that the hierarchical model cannot as such cope with this difficulty. It merely enables us to describe an inner conflict as being between desires of different orders. But this alone is hardly adequate to determine – with respect to that conflict – where (if anywhere) the person himself stands.[9]

I tried some time ago to deal with this problem, in the following passage:

> hierarchy of desires does seem a bit contrived, the alternatives – such as the one proposed by Gary Watson in "Free Agency" (*Journal of Philosophy*, 1975) – strike me as worse: more obscure, no less fanciful, and (I suspect) requiring a resort to hierarchy in the end themselves.

8 Watson, p. 218.
9 The problem of explaining identification is not, of course, peculiar to the hierarchical model. It must be dealt with by any account of the structure of volition. Accordingly, it is not a fault of the hierarchical model that it requires an explanation of identification.

When a person identifies himself *decisively* with one of his first-order desires, this commitment "resounds" throughout the potentially endless array of higher orders. . . . The fact that his second-order volition to be moved by this desire is a decisive one means that there is no room for questions concerning the pertinence of volitions of higher orders. . . . The decisiveness of the commitment he has made means that he has decided that no further questions about his second-order volition, at any higher order, remain to be asked.[10]

The trouble with what I wrote in this passage is that the notions I invoked – namely, "identification," "decisive commitment," "resounding" – are terribly obscure. Therefore, the passage left it quite unclear just how the maneuver of avoiding an interminable regress by making a decisive commitment can escape being unacceptably arbitrary. Thus, Watson says:

We wanted to know what prevents wantonness with regard to one's higher-order volitions. What gives these volitions any special relation to "oneself"? It is unhelpful to answer that one makes a "decisive commitment," where this just means that an interminable ascent to higher orders is not going to be permitted. This *is* arbitrary.[11]

Now in fact Watson is in error here. As I shall attempt to explain, making a decisive commitment does not consist merely in an arbitrary *refusal* to permit an interminable ascent to higher orders.

IV

Consider a situation somewhat analogous to that of a person who is uncertain whether to identify himself with one or with another of his own desires, but which is rather more straightforward: the situation of someone attempting to solve a problem in arithmetic. Having performed a calculation, this person may perform another in order to check his answer. The second calculation may be just the same as the first, or it may be equivalent to it in the sense that it follows a procedure which is different from the first but which must yield the same result. In any case, suppose the first calculation is confirmed by the second. It is possible that both calculations are faulty, so the person may check again. This sequence of calculations can be extended indefinitely. Moreover, there is nothing about the position of any particular item in the sequence that gives it definitive authority. A mistake can be made at any point, and the same mistake may be repeated any number of times. So what is to

10   "Freedom of the Will and the Concept of a Person," Chapter 2 in this volume.
11   Watson, p. 218.

distinguish a calculation with which the person can reasonably terminate the sequence? How does the person avoid being irresponsible or arbitrary when he ends at some particular point a sequence that he might extend further?

One way in which a sequence of calculations might end is that the person conducting it simply quits, negligently permitting the result of his last calculation to serve as his answer. Perhaps he just loses interest in the problem, or perhaps he is diverted from further inquiry by some compelling distraction. In cases like these, his behavior resembles that of a wanton: He allows a certain result to stand without evaluating its suitability or considering the desirability of allowing it to be his answer. He does not *choose* a result, nor does he *endorse* one. He acts as though it is a matter of complete indifference to him whether there is in fact adequate support for the acceptability of his answer.

On the other hand, a sequence of calculations might end because the person conducting it *decides for some reason* to adopt a certain result. It may be that he is unequivocally confident that this result is correct, and therefore believes that there is no use for further inquiry. Or perhaps he believes that even though there is some likelihood that the result is not correct, the cost to him of further inquiry – in time or in effort or in lost opportunities – is greater than the value to him of reducing the likelihood of error. In either event there may be a "decisive" identification on his part. In a sense that I shall endeavor to explain, such an identification resounds through an unlimited sequence of possible further reconsiderations of his decision.

Suppose the person is confident that he knows the correct answer. He then expects to get that answer each time he accurately performs a suitable calculation. In this respect, the future is transparent to him, and his decision that a certain answer is correct resounds endlessly in just this sense: It enables him to anticipate the outcomes of an indefinite number of possible further calculations. Now suppose he is not entirely confident which answer is correct, but is convinced that it would nonetheless be most reasonable for him to adopt a certain answer as his own. Then he cannot with full confidence expect this answer to be confirmed by further inquiry; he acknowledges that accurate calculation might produce a different result. But if he has made a genuinely unreserved commitment to the view that adopting the answer is his most reasonable alternative, he can anticipate that *this* view will be endlessly confirmed by accurate reviews of it.

The fact that a commitment resounds endlessly *is* simply the fact that the commitment is *decisive.* For a commitment is decisive if and only if it is made without reservation, and making a commitment without reservation means that the person who makes it does so in the belief that no further accurate inquiry would require him to change his mind. It is therefore pointless to pursue the inquiry any further. This is, precisely, the resonance effect.[12]

Now what leads people to form desires of higher orders is similar to what leads them to go over their arithmetic. Someone checks his calculations because he thinks he may have done them wrong. It may be that there is a conflict between the answer he has obtained and a different answer which, for one reason or another, he believes may be correct; or perhaps he has merely a more generalized suspicion, to the effect that he may have made some kind of error. Similarly, a person may be led to reflect on his own desires either because they conflict with each other or because a more general lack of confidence moves him to consider whether to be satisfied with his motives as they are.

Both in the case of desires and in the case of arithmetic a person can without arbitrariness terminate a potentially endless sequence of evaluations when he finds that there is no disturbing conflict, either between results already obtained or between a result already obtained and one he might reasonably expect to obtain if the sequence were to continue. Terminating the sequence at that point – the point at which there is no conflict or doubt – is not arbitrary. For the only reason to continue the sequence would be to cope with an actual conflict or with the possibility that a conflict might occur. Given that the person does not have this reason to continue, it is hardly arbitrary for him to stop.

Perhaps it will be suggested that there remains an element of arbitrariness here, in the judgment that no pertinent conflict can be found: This judgment is also subject to error, after all, and it would be possible to reassess it endlessly without any of the reassessments being inherently definitive or final. Whatever the merit of this point, however, it does not imply a deficiency specific to the principle that a person is justified in terminating a sequence of calculations or reflections when he sees no conflict to be avoided or resolved. For the point is quite general. It is *always* possible, in the deployment of any principle whatever, to make a mistaken or unwarranted judgment that the conditions for applying the principle correctly have been satisfied. It should go without saying that no criterion or standard can guarantee that it will be wielded accurately and without arbitrariness.

---

12 I am here agreeing with the suggestion concerning the relation between resonance and decisive commitment made by Jon Elster in his *Ulysses and the Sirens: Studies in Rationality and Irrationality* (Cambridge: Cambridge University Press, 1979), p. 111, n. 135. My own treatment of these matters owes much to Descartes's discussion of clear and distinct perception.

V

The etymological meaning of the verb "to decide" is "to cut off." This is apt, since it is characteristically by a decision (though, of course, not necessarily or even most frequently in that way) that a sequence of desires or preferences of increasingly higher orders is terminated. When the decision is made without reservation, the commitment it entails is decisive. Then the person no longer holds himself apart from the desire to which he has committed himself. It is no longer unsettled or uncertain whether the object of that desire — that is, what he wants — is what he really wants: The decision determines what the person really wants by making the desire on which he decides fully his own. To this extent the person, in making a decision by which he identifies with a desire, *constitutes himself*. The pertinent desire is no longer in any way external to him. It is not a desire that he "has" merely as a subject in whose history it happens to occur, as a person may "have" an involuntary spasm that happens to occur in the history of his body. It comes to be a desire that is incorporated into him by virtue of the fact that he has it *by his own will*.

This does not mean that it is through the exercise of the will that the desire originates; the desire may well preexist the decision made concerning it. But even if the person is not responsible for the fact that the desire *occurs,* there is an important sense in which he takes responsibility for the fact of having the desire — the fact that the desire is in the fullest sense his, that it constitutes what he really wants — when he identifies himself with it. Through his action in deciding, he is responsible for the fact that the desire has become his own in a way in which it was not unequivocally his own before.

There are two quite different sorts of conflicts between desires. In conflicts of the one sort, desires compete for priority or position in a preferential order; the issue is which desire to satisfy *first*. In conflicts of the other sort, the issue is whether a desire should be given *any* place in the order of preference at all — that is, whether it is to be endorsed as a legitimate candidate for satisfaction or whether it is to be rejected as entitled to no priority whatsoever. When a conflict of the first kind is resolved, the competing desires are *integrated* into a single ordering, within which each occupies a specific position. Resolving a conflict of the second kind involves a radical *separation* of the competing desires, one of which is not merely assigned a relatively less favored position but extruded entirely as an outlaw. It is these acts of ordering and of rejection — integration and separation — that create a self out of the raw materials of inner life. They define the intrapsychic constraints and boundaries with respect to which a person's autonomy may be threatened even by his own desires.[13]

Aristotle maintained that behavior is voluntary only when its moving principle is inside the agent. This cannot be correct if "inside" is construed in its literal sense: The movements of an epileptic seizure are not voluntary, but their moving principle or cause is spatially internal to the agent. The location of a moving principle with respect to the agent's body is plainly less relevant than its "location" with respect to the agent's volition. What counts, even with respect to a moving principle that operates as an element of his psychic life, is whether or not the agent has constituted himself to include it. On the one hand, the principle may be internal, in the sense pertinent to whether the behavior to which it leads is voluntary, by virtue of the fact that the person has joined himself to what moves him by a commitment through which he takes responsibility for it. On the other hand, the moving principle of his behavior may remain external to the person in the pertinent sense because he has not made it part of himself.

This suggests another respect in which Aristotle's theory is unsatisfactory. He maintains that a person may be responsible for his own character on account of having taken (or having failed to take) measures that affect what his habitual dispositions are. In other words, a person acquires responsibility for his own character, according to Aristotle, by acting in ways that are causally instrumental in bringing it about that he has the particular set of dispositions of which his character is constituted. I think that Aristotle's treatment of this subject is significantly out of focus because of his preoccupation with causal origins and causal responsibility. The fundamental responsibility of an agent with respect to his own character is not a matter of whether it is as the effect of his own actions that the agent *has* certain dispositions to feel and to behave in various ways. That bears only on the question of whether the person is responsible for having these *characteristics*. The question of whether the person is responsible for his own *character* has to do with whether he has *taken responsibility for* his characteristics. It concerns whether the dispositions at issue, regardless of whether their *existence* is due to the person's own initiative and causal agency or not, are characteristics with which he

---

13 The determining conditions that are pertinent here are exclusively *structural* arrangements. I mention this, although I shall not pursue the point, since it bears on the familiar issue of whether *historical* considerations – especially causal stories – have any essential relevance to questions concerning whether a person's actions are autonomous.

identifies and which he thus by his own will incorporates into himself as constitutive of what he is.

When someone identifies himself with one rather than with another of his own desires, the result is not necessarily to eliminate the conflict between those desires, or even to reduce its severity, but to alter its nature. Suppose that a person with two conflicting desires identifies with one rather than with the other. This *might* cause the other – the desire with which the person does not identify – to become substantially weaker than it was, or to disappear altogether. But it need not. Quite possibly, the conflict between the two desires will remain as virulent as before. What the person's commitment to the one eliminates is not the conflict between it and the other. It eliminates the conflict *within the person* as to which of these desires he prefers to be his motive. The conflict between the *desires* is in this way transformed into a conflict between *one* of them and the *person* who has identified himself with its rival. That person is no longer uncertain which side he is on, in the conflict between the two desires, and the persistence of this conflict need not subvert or diminish the wholeheartedness of his commitment to the desire with which he identifies.

VI

Since it is most conspicuously by making a decision that a person identifies with some element of his psychic life, deciding plays an important role in the formation and maintenance of the self. It is difficult to articulate what the act of deciding consists in – to make fully clear just what we do when we perform it. But while the nature of deciding is aggravatingly elusive, at least it is apparent that making a decision is something that we do *to ourselves*. In this respect it differs fundamentally from making a choice, the immediate object of which is not the chooser but whatever it is that he chooses. This difference between deciding and choosing accounts for the fact that deciding to make a certain choice is not the same as actually making it (after all, the time or occasion for doing that may not yet have arrived), whereas deciding to make a particular decision (that is, deciding to decide things a certain way) cannot be distinguished from making the decision itself.

In some languages, the reflexivity of deciding – the fact that it is an action done to oneself – is indicated in the form of the pertinent verb. Thus, the French verb is *se décider*. The closest parallel among English synonyms for "to decide" is the phrase "to make up one's mind," in which there is an explicit representation of the reflexive character of deciding. Now what are we to make of the rather protean metaphor this phrase invokes? Is making up one's mind like "making up a story," or is it like "making up a bed"? Is it like "making up one's face," or is it rather like "making up a list of things to do"? Or is it, perhaps, more like "making up after a quarrel"? What is the difference, in these various instances, between what is made up and what is not? And which of these differences corresponds most closely to the difference between a mind that is made up and one that is undecided?

The use of cosmetics pertains to a contrast between what a person looks like naturally and how the person may contrive to appear. A similar contrast is implicit in the idea of making up a story, which resembles making up a face in that the outcome is in both cases something artificial or fictitious; it does not simply exhibit the way things really are. One difference between using makeup and making up a story is, of course, that there is a face before it is made up – something to which being made up happens. This has no ready analogue in the case of a story, which is not transformed by being made up, but which comes into existence only as it is contrived. In this respect making up a face more closely resembles making up a bed. As for making up a list, it plainly has nothing to do with the fictitious or the contrived; it is more a matter of establishing certain relationships among the items listed, or of recording relationships among them that already exist.

What appears to be fundamentally common to all occurrences of the notion of making something up is not the contrast between fiction and reality or between the natural and the artificial, but the theme of creating an orderly arrangement. It seems to me that in this light the closest analogue to a situation in which someone makes up his mind is, rather surprisingly perhaps, a situation in which two people make up their differences. People who do that after a quarrel pass from a condition of conflict and hostility to a more harmonious and well-ordered relationship. Of course, people do not always make up when their quarrel ends; sometimes their hostility continues even after the conflict that was its original cause has been resolved. Moreover, people who have been quarreling may restore harmony between themselves even though their disagreement continues. Making up concerns healing a relationship disrupted by conflict, and it has nothing directly or necessarily to do with whether or not the conflict has ended.

Construed on this analogy, the making of a decision appears to differ from the self-reparative activities of the body, which in some other ways it resembles. When the body heals itself, it *eliminates* conflicts in which one physical process (say, infection) interferes with others and undermines the homeostasis, or equilibrium, in which health consists. A person who makes up his mind also seeks thereby to overcome or to supersede a condition of inner division and to make himself into an integrated whole. But he may accomplish this without actually eliminating the desires that conflict with those on which he has decided, as long as he dissociates himself from them.

A person may fail to integrate himself when he makes up his mind, of course, since the conflict or hesitancy with which he is contending may continue despite his decision. All a decision does is to create an intention; it does not guarantee that the intention will be carried out. This is not simply because the person can always change his mind. Apart from inconstancy of that sort, it may be that energies tending toward action inconsistent with the intention remain untamed and undispersed, however decisively the person believes his mind has been made up. The conflict the decision was supposed to supersede may continue despite the person's conviction that he has resolved it. In that case the decision, no matter how apparently conscientious and sincere, is not wholehearted: Whether the person is aware of it or not, he has other intentions, intentions incompatible with the one the decision established and to which he is also committed. This may become evident when the chips are down and the person acts in a way ostensibly precluded by the intention on which he thought he had settled.

VII

But why are we interested in making up our minds at all? It might seem that the point of deciding is to provide for the performance of an action that would otherwise not be performed. Suppose I make up my mind to show anger more openly the next time I am gratuitously insulted by an arrogant functionary. This might be thought of as establishing a connection, which did not previously exist, between insulting behavior of a certain kind and the sort of response on which I have now decided – a connection such that the response will ensue if the provocation occurs. In fact, however, people often decide to do things which – whether they realize it or not – they would do in any case. The connection between the provocation and the response, which the decision appears to establish, may already exist: I would have shown my anger openly even if I had not previously formed the intention to do so. The point of making up one's mind is not, accordingly, to ensure a certain action.

Nor is it to ensure that one will act well. That is the function of deliberation, which is designed to increase the likelihood that decisions will be good ones. Hobbes suggests that the word "deliberation" connotes an activity in which freedom is lost.[14] It is, after all, *de-liberation*. This may seem paradoxical, since we customarily regard deliberation as paradigmatically connected to the exercise of autonomy. The difficulty disappears when we recognize that the liberty with which deliberation interferes is not that of the autonomous agent but that of someone who blindly follows impulse – in other words, of the wanton. A person who is deliberating about what to do is seeking an alternative to "doing what comes naturally." His aim is to replace the liberty of anarchic impulsive behavior with the autonomy of being under his own control.

One thing a deliberate decision accomplishes, when it creates an intention, is to establish a constraint by which other preferences and decisions are to be guided. A person who decides what to believe provides himself with a criterion for other beliefs; namely, they must be coherent with the belief on which he has decided. And a person who makes a decision concerning what to do similarly adopts a rule for coordinating his activities to facilitate his eventual implementation of the decision he has made. It might be said, then, that a function of decision is to integrate the person both dynamically and statically. Dynamically insofar as it provides – in the way I have just mentioned – for coherence and unity of purpose over time; statically insofar as it establishes – in the way discussed earlier – a reflexive or hierarchical structure by which the person's identity may be in part constituted.

In both respects, the intent is at least partly to resolve conflict or to avoid it. This is not achieved by eliminating one or more of the conflicting elements so that those remaining are harmonious, but by endorsing or identifying with certain elements which are then authoritative for the self. Of course, this authority may be resisted and even defeated by outlaw forces – desires or motives by which the person does not want to be effectively moved, but which are too strong and insistent to be constrained. It may also turn out that there is conflict within the authority itself – that the person has identified himself inconsistently. This is the issue of *wholeheartedness*.

Wholeheartedness, as I am using the term, does not consist in a feeling of enthusiasm, or of certainty, concerning a commitment. Nor is it likely to be readily apparent whether a decision which a person intends to be wholehearted is actually so. We do not know our hearts well enough to be confident whether our intention that nothing should interfere with a decision we make is one we ourselves will want carried out when – perhaps recognizing that the point of no return has been reached – we

---

14 *Leviathan*, Part I, Chapter 6: "And it is called *deliberation* because it is a putting an end to the *liberty* we had of doing, or omitting, according to our own appetite, or aversion."

come to understand more completely what carrying it out would require us to do or to sacrifice doing.

In making up his mind a person establishes preferences concerning the resolution of conflicts among his desires or beliefs. Someone who makes a decision thereby performs an action, but the performance is not of a simple act that merely implements a first-order desire. It essentially involves reflexivity, including desires and volitions of a higher order. Thus, creatures who are incapable of this volitional reflexivity necessarily lack the capacity to make up their minds. They may desire and think and act, but they cannot decide. Insofar as we construe the making of decisions as the characteristic function of the faculty of volition, we must regard such creatures as lacking this faculty.

In "Freedom of the Will and the Concept of a Person" (Chapter 2 of this volume) I asserted that being wanton does not preclude deliberation. My thought then was that although a creature might be wanton with respect to goals, he might nonetheless engage in calculation or reasoning about technical questions concerning how to get what he wantonly desires. But reasoning involves making decisions concerning what to think, which appear no less incompatible with thoroughgoing wantonness than deciding what one wants to do. Making a decision does seem different from figuring out how to implement it, but it is unclear that the latter activity can be accomplished without making up one's mind in ways structurally quite similar to those entailed in the former.

We are accustomed to thinking of our species as distinguished particularly by virtue of the faculty of reason. We tend to suppose that volition or will is a more primitive or cruder faculty, which we share with creatures of lesser psychic complexity. But this seems dubious not only because of the reflexivity that volition itself requires but also to the extent that reasoning requires making up one's mind. For to that extent the deliberate use of reason necessarily has a hierarchical structure, requiring higher-order elements that are unavailable to a genuine wanton. In this respect, then, reason depends on will.

13

Rationality and the unthinkable

I

With respect to actions of whatever sort, circumstances are conceivable in which an action of just that sort would have greater utility than any available alternative. This means that if utilitarianism is correct, anything might at some point be morally imperative. There are people who make a similar point about atheism. If God does not exist, they say, anything goes. A person may do or be whatever he likes.

These observations concerning atheism and utilitarianism are not the same, but they are closely related. Each suggests that the doctrine to which it pertains makes it impossible to believe that there are absolute moral limits. Atheism is supposed to have the consequence that nothing is forbidden: If there is no God, *everything is permitted.* Utilitarianism is supposed to imply, correspondingly, that *anything may be required.* On the assumption that these characterizations of the two doctrines are correct, adherents of neither doctrine acknowledge any unconditional moral constraints. Utilitarians and atheists agree, in other words, that *nothing can be ruled out in advance.*

We are accustomed to taking it for granted that enlargements of our freedom enrich us. They do so, however, only up to a point. If the restrictions upon the choices that a person can make are loosened too far, he may become disoriented and uncertain about what and how to choose. Extensive proliferation of his options may weaken his grasp of his own identity. When he confronts the task of evaluating and ranking a large number of additional alternatives, his previously established appreciation of what his interests and priorities are may well become less decisive. His confidence in his own preferences – confidence developed when the possibilities open to him were fewer and more familiar – may be undermined. That is, there may be a disturbance of his clarity and confidence as to who he is.

Now suppose that the field of alternatives from which a person may select is not merely extended; suppose that its boundaries are wiped out entirely. In other words, suppose that now every possible course of action is available and eligible for choice, including those courses of action that would affect the person's preferences themselves. Since he can in that case even alter his own will, it seems that he has to confront the choices he must make without any specific volitional character that is definitively his. The person's will, we are supposing, is whatever he chooses it to be. Therefore, it is nothing until he has decided what will to choose.

But how, then, is he to make any choice at all? What preferences and priorities are to guide him in choosing, when his own preferences and priorities are among the very things he must choose. It appears that he is left with so little volitional substance that no choice he makes can be regarded as originating in a nature that is genuinely his. With respect to a person whose will has no fixed determinate character, it seems that the notion of autonomy or of self-direction cannot find a grip. A person like that is so vacant of identifiable tendencies and constraints that he will be unable to deliberate or to make conscientious decisions. He may possibly remain capable of some hollow semblance of choice. If he does, however, it will only be by virtue of a vestigial susceptibility to inchoate volitional spasms. And movements of his will of that sort are inherently so arbitrary as to be wholly devoid of authentically personal significance.[1]

Of course, no one alleges that adherents of utilitarianism are also doomed to such paralyzing volitional emptiness. What *is* sometimes maintained is that utilitarians cannot make substantive moral commitments. They are unable, it is alleged, to sustain meaningful conceptions of personal integrity. The claim is that this is because a utilitarian must be willing to alter his principles, his priorities, and all other elements of his character, as well as to modify his behavior, whenever doing so would have more utility than doing otherwise. As Rawls puts it:

Members of a utilitarian well-ordered society . . . have no determinate conception of the good to which they are committed, but regard the various desires and capacities of the self as features to be adjusted in the quest [for the greatest utility].[2]

This appears to entail that a utilitarian cannot really commit himself to conduct of any specific type or to any particular set of moral ideals. It

---

1 For quite some time, many of those who have been widely admired as among the most enlightened and humane thinkers have neglected the incipient conflict or tension between freedom and identity. They have exhibited a steady tendency *both* to urge the general expansion of opportunity and choice *and* to place a high value on individuality. It should be no surprise, then, that things have been going wrong.

2 John Rawls, "Social Unity and Primary Goods," in Amartya Sen and Bernard Williams (eds.), *Utilitarianism and Beyond* (Cambridge: Cambridge University Press, 1982), p. 180.

seems, therefore, that he can form no stable conception of his own moral identity.

For utilitarianism, the only rational good is well-being. Now the degree of a person's well-being is a function not only of his external circumstances but also of his personal characteristics. Thus it is rational for a utilitarian to modify any of his personal characteristics, including his commitments to particular values, whenever that would increase well-being. According to Rawls, this gives rise to a conception of the self or person as having no inherent character:

> [Utilitarianism] defines persons as what we may call "bare persons." Such persons are ready to consider any new convictions and aims, and even to abandon attachments and loyalties, when doing this promises a life with greater overall satisfaction, or well-being. . . . The notion of a bare person . . . represents the dissolution of the person as leading a life expressive of character and of devotion to specific final ends and adopted (or affirmed) values which define the distinctive points of view associated with different (and incommensurable) conceptions of the good.[3]

The trouble with utilitarianism, in this view, is that it mandates too much flexibility. In the account of people that it gives, which is oddly and disturbingly impersonal, moral integrity is a notion for which there seems to be no room. This is because a utilitarian must not regard any aspect of his volitional nature as properly exempt from being deliberately changed. On the contrary, he must be prepared to alter himself in any way that will increase well-being. Thus he cannot commit himself to respecting as inviolable any limits that might serve at once to anchor his judgment and to specify the requirements of his integrity.

It is possible to argue, then, that atheists and utilitarians, in their efforts to decide what to do or what to be, have too little to fall back on in the way of securely grounded personal values or other stable guides to choice. They lack what Rawls refers to as "antecedent moral structure."[4] Their doctrines prohibit them (so, at least, the arguments go) from thinking of themselves as having fixed volitional limits. In both cases an excess of freedom gives rise to a diminution, or even to a dissolution, of the reality of the self.

---

3 Ibid., pp. 180–1. The notion of a "bare person" resembles the old theological idea of the soul: something that is identical in all men, that is unaffected by experience, that we cannot identify with anything in ourselves of which we are conscious, but that nonetheless provides each of us somehow with his essential nature and his ultimate value.
4 Ibid., p. 182.

II

It seems to me, however, that Rawls is mistaken when he claims that utilitarians can have "no determinate conception of the good to which they are committed." His argument for this claim is that since a utilitarian must include his own personal values among the "desires and capacities of the self . . . to be adjusted" whenever that would increase well-being, he can never be fully or unreservedly committed to those values. But this appears to overlook an important point. Even though someone is in principle ready to adjust his values whenever that would increase well-being, he may nonetheless be legitimately and fully convinced that in fact there are certain kinds of adjustments by which he would never actually be able to increase it. In other words, a person might have good reason to be confident that circumstances that would require him to make certain adjustments in his own desires and capacities will never come about. The fact that circumstances of a certain kind are conceivable surely does not entail that no one has evidence sufficient to justify denying that they will occur.

There is no reason why a utilitarian with a specific set of personal values should not make to them a commitment that is just as wholehearted as his expectation that he will never encounter circumstances in which maintaining those values would require him to sacrifice well-being. If his expectation concerning this is unqualified, his commitment also need not be equivocal or at all reserved. Without jeopardizing his integrity in any way, someone who is committed to a principle of conduct may acknowledge that circumstances are conceivable in which it would be reasonable for him to violate the principle and in which he would indeed violate it. For if he is fully convinced that none of those circumstances will occur, he will be equally convinced that his principle will never require him to perform actions that his commitment forbids. Hence, there will be no need for him to regard actions of that kind as having any place whatever in his repertoire of conduct.

Of course he may be wrong. In that case, contrary to his expectation, he will at some point encounter a situation in which the only way he can sustain his adherence to utilitarianism is by violating his commitment to other values. But this does not mean that he cannot reasonably make unequivocal commitments both to utilitarianism and to his other values. The possibility that one's expectations are wrong means only that there is a risk in basing a wholehearted commitment on them. It does not imply that taking the risk is either impossible or unjustified. Thus utilitarianism does not preclude personal commitments to refrain from (or to engage in) specific types of conduct. Even though conduct of those types would under certain conditions maximize utility (or fail to maximize it) and hence be obligatory (or forbidden), it may be *unquestionable* that those conditions will never arise.

A parallel point can be made concerning atheism. Even if the atheist believes that everything is allowable, there may be certain things that he simply cannot bring himself to do. Those things can be ruled out as possible courses of action for him. Although he might be able to pursue them quite successfully if he chose, and despite his understanding that pursuing them is *permitted,* they are not among his genuine options. They have no place in his repertoire of conduct because, as we may say, for him they are *unthinkable.*

III

What does it mean to say that an action is for a certain person unthinkable? What kind of disability or impediment is at work when the explanation of someone's failure to perform an action is that he cannot bring himself to perform it? Sometimes people are unable to do things because the circumstances are not right or because they lack the necessary power or skill. No one can leave a room whose exits are securely blocked, or render himself invisible, or play the piano when he does not know how or when there is no piano for him to play. Sometimes, however, a person may be incapable of performing a certain action even though, so far as considerations of these kinds go, he is in a perfectly good position to perform it. It may be, further, that he thinks he should perform the action, and that he has a desire to perform it. If he is nevertheless unable to act because he finds the action unthinkable, then what keeps him from acting is a volitional matter. He cannot perform the action because *he cannot will to perform it.*

Someone who has decided to perform a certain action may discover, when the chips are down, that he just cannot go through with it. In that case it is unclear whether, strictly speaking, he did truly make a decision after all. No doubt he made up his *mind,* but doing that manifestly failed to shape his *will.* It is, of course, possible to insist that, nonetheless, a decision was in fact made. But since no effective volitional commitment was actually accomplished, insisting that a decision was made would require conceding that the "decision" was no more than a merely verbal or intellectual event. Perhaps it would be best to say, concerning situations that are problematic in this respect, that no *effective* decision was made.

Of a person who cannot bring himself to perform an action, then, it can also be said that he cannot make an effective decision to perform it.

The difficulty for him is that he cannot organize himself volitionally in the necessary way. In attempting to do so, he runs up against the limits of his will. This is shown by the fact that he is unable to perform the action even when all the nonvolitional conditions for his performing it (for instance, opportunity and power) are satisfied. It may be that he would be able to perform the action easily if only he had the will. But he cannot will to perform the action. For him, willing to perform it is unthinkable.[5]

The category of the unthinkable is not essentially a moral category. To be sure, an inability to bring oneself to act may sometimes derive from considerations that are distinctively moral. It is reported that some military officers refused to carry out the procedures for launching nuclear weapons when they believed that the orders they had received to do so were not part of a test or a drill and that executing the procedures would bring about an actual nuclear strike. These officers had volunteered for their assignments; they had presumably thought themselves willing to obey orders like those they disobeyed. At the critical moment, as it turned out, they could not bring themselves to act. They discovered that participating in the initiation of a nuclear assault was for them unthinkable. No doubt this was on account of moral inhibitions. On the other hand, the considerations on account of which something is unthinkable may be entirely self-regarding and without any moral significance at all. Someone may be unable to bring himself to perform an action because he would be severely maimed by it, or because it is intolerably injurious to his pride, or because it is too disgusting.

Being unable to bring oneself to perform an action is not the same as simply being overwhelmingly averse to performing it. Of course, the person who cannot bring himself to act does have an aversion by which his conduct is constrained. In addition, the aversion has his endorsement; and it constrains his conduct so effectively precisely *because* of this.[6] The person's endorsement of his aversion is what distinguishes situations in which someone finds an action unthinkable from those in which an inability to act is due to addiction or to some other type of irresistible impulse. It is true, no doubt, that a person who is constrained by an irresistible impulse might also endorse that impulse. But it is not because the impulse in such a case has his endorsement that it effectively con-

---

5 There is a difference between wanting to perform an action and willing to perform it. Someone who *wills* to perform an action will at least try to perform it. But having a desire or wanting to perform a certain action may not lead a person to any action the motive of which is to fulfill that desire. In such a case, the person's desire is not his will.

6 The nature and structure of this endorsement need to be elaborated, but I shall not pursue the matter here.

strains his conduct. His endorsement of the impulse is not what makes the impulse irresistible.

In Chapter 59 of *The Eustace Diamonds,* Anthony Trollope describes a man who cannot bring himself to carry out a course of conduct on which he had freely and deliberately resolved. Lord Fawn is a high government official and a peer of the realm. He has invited Andy Gowran, a low-born and uncultivated estate-steward, to give him an eyewitness account of an incident in which Fawn's fiancée (Lizzie Eustace) was reported to have embraced another man (her cousin Frank Greystock). Now Gowran, in the course of giving this account, winks at Fawn. Thereupon, Fawn finds it impossible to continue the interview:

It was dreadful to Lord Fawn that the man should wink his eye at him. He did not quite understand what Andy had last said, but he did understand that some accusation as to indecent familiarity with her cousin was intended to be brought by this Scotch steward against the woman to whom he had engaged himself. Every feeling of his nature revolted against the task before him, and he found that on trial it became absolutely impracticable. He could not bring himself to inquire minutely as to poor Lizzie's flirting down among the rocks. He was weak, and foolish, and in many respects ignorant, but he was a gentleman. As he got nearer to the point which it had been intended that he should reach, the more he hated Andy Gowran, and the more he hated himself for having submitted to such contact. He paused a moment, and then he declared that the conversation was at an end.

For Lord Fawn, it is unthinkable to share a matter of such intimate concern with a person so inferior to himself in breeding and class. He had thought it would be a good idea to discover from Gowran just what Lizzie Eustace had been up to with Frank Greystock, and he had made up his mind to do that. But in the event, "every feeling of his nature revolted." He found that he simply could not do it.

It is not against his *will* that Lord Fawn's feelings revolt. The feelings that make it "absolutely impracticable" for him to continue his interview with Gowran are not opposed to his will. What they revolt against is his attempt to shape his will in a certain way. It is Fawn's judgment that the best thing for him to do would be to speak with Gowran about Lizzie, and he tries to carry out that course of action. At bottom, however, he is unwilling for his will to be shaped in that way.

A person's will may be overpowered and violated by forces, such as those of anxiety or addiction, that are generated within him but that are nonetheless not in the fullest sense his own. They are forces with which he does not identify, whose influence he struggles to resist. When they dominate, he is dominated by them; he is not in control of himself. Now when someone finds that an action is for him unthinkable, what he discovers is not that he is unable to maintain control over himself. That would entail the passage of control to forces that are not truly his own. But in a case like Fawn's, the forces that revolt and establish control – namely, "every feeling of his nature" – are not opposed to the agent. They are in the most authentic sense his own forces, which are not only within him in a simple, literal way but are also integral to his nature. Although they prevent him from performing an action that he had thought he wanted to perform, they do so only by virtue of the fact that he does not really want to perform it. His inability to go through with the action reveals it as one that he is unwilling to will.

A person who asserts that he finds an action unthinkable means that there are no circumstances in which he would be willing to perform it. This may reflect a paucity of imagination on his part. Perhaps there really are possible circumstances that he has failed to consider or to appreciate, in which he would perform the action quite willingly. Be this as it may, his assertion that the action is for him unthinkable does not require him to maintain that there could be no circumstances in which it would be his best alternative. Nor does it require him to deny that there might be circumstances in which it would be reasonable for him to perform the action. After all, it is quite possible for someone to anticipate realistically that he would be unable to bring himself to pursue a certain course of action even if he were to recognize it as the best. It may be clear to him that there are matters with respect to which he is incapable of acting rationally.

IV

There is a familiar way of construing the notion of *rationality* that despite its importance, is often neglected by philosophers. Among those who neglect it, Hume is conspicuous. He insists that a desire or preference is contrary to reason only if it is based on a false judgment either about what exists or about some causal relationship. This narrowly restricted way of understanding rationality leads Hume to make some startling claims:

Where a passion is neither founded on false suppositions, nor chooses means insufficient for the end, the understanding can neither justify nor condemn it. 'Tis not contrary to reason to prefer the destruction of the whole world to the scratching of my finger. 'Tis not contrary to reason to choose my total ruin, to prevent the least uneasiness of an Indian or person wholly unknown to me. 'Tis as little contrary to reason to prefer even my own acknowledged lesser good to my greater, and have a more ardent affection for the former than the latter. . . .

In short, a passion must be accompanied with some false judgment, in order to its being unreasonable; and even then 'tis not the passion, properly speaking, which is unreasonable, but the judgment.[7]

Preferences such as those Hume describes here may be quite independent of any factual error. Thus the faculty of reason or understanding can neither justify them nor condemn them if, as he maintains, that faculty is concerned exclusively with distinguishing between true and false judgments of fact. In this sense the preferences, no matter how outrageous or bizarre they may be, are not unreasonable.

There is a well-established and valuable usage, however, according to which the passions and preferences to which Hume refers are emphatically not reasonable. Consider what we should say of someone who really did care more about injury to his finger than about the destruction of the whole world. We would say that *he must be crazy*. In other words, we would attribute to him a defect of reason. Moreover, this attribution of irrationality would be justified. Whatever Hume says, to regard the destruction of the whole world as less important than a scratched finger is not a rational option. It is *lunatic*.

There must be some way other than Hume's, then, of understanding what it is to be contrary to reason. Otherwise we could not properly use terms like "lunatic" or "crazy" or "irrational" to characterize the preferences at issue, unless we used those terms very loosely as vehicles of merely generic abuse. It seems to me that when we say that someone with a preference of this kind must be crazy, we do not intend merely to express a general and unfocused disapproval. We intend specifically to charge the person with a kind of irrationality. Of course, this does not mean that we would not also charge him with being wicked. But what is wrong with him cannot be conveyed accurately in terms that pertain simply to his moral character. It would be egregiously insufficient to say that his trouble is that his moral character is poor, and this would be insufficient even if we increased the intensity of the statement by saying that he is *extraordinarily* wicked or that his moral character is *extremely* poor. We cannot satisfactorily construe his wickedness as an exclusively moral fault.

Immorality is not, as such, abnormal. In many instances, it is only too easily recognizable as deriving in quite an ordinary way from human nature. But the immorality in the example under consideration is of a special order. It does not fall within the range of what we understand to be normal; rather, it strikes us as unnatural or even monstrous. That is

---

7   *A Treatise of Human Nature*, edited by L. A. Selby-Bigge (Oxford: Oxford University Press, 1888), Bk. II, Part III, section III, p. 416.

why the notions of irrationality and insanity seem germane. Rationality belongs distinctively to the essential nature of a human being. If we regard a judgment or a choice as opposed to human nature – that is, if it strikes us as unnatural or inhuman – we are inclined to think of it as therefore involving a defect of reason.[8]

But what do all these epithets actually mean? What is the specific character of the irrationality to which they allude? Hume attributes "irrationality" only when a belief is inconsistent either with itself or with the facts. Someone who prefers his finger to the world may very well not be irrational in this sense. His defect is volitional, rather than epistemic or cognitive. He is abnormal not on account of what he believes but on account of what he is able to bring himself to do. The reason we consider him irrational is that he fails to find certain conduct unthinkable.

Of course, what warrants the attribution of irrationality cannot be merely that the person is capable of conduct *we* happen to find unthinkable. Most of us do not, simply by virtue of the fact that we would be unable to bring ourselves to perform a certain action, presume that this inability of ours is a reliable mark or general requirement of sanity. It goes without saying that someone who is capable of doing what we happen to find unthinkable may be quite free of any defect. It may well be our own incapacity, after all, that is abnormal. Or it may be that there is no abnormality either in being able or in being unable to bring oneself to perform the action in question. Perhaps both the ability and the inability depend on beliefs, commitments, or personal idiosyncrasies – having to do with matters of taste, politics, religion, love, or the like – with respect to which it is natural and in no way pathological for people to be diverse.

To be sure, we do sometimes take what we find unthinkable as defining a criterion of normality. The unthinkability seems to us to be not merely personal but to have for some reason a more general import. Even in those cases, however, we are likely to acknowledge that the scope of the criterion is limited. We know that preferences or types of conduct that are irrational in one cultural locale may often be entirely rational in another. Consider, for example, this report:

One of the last of the Fratellini family of clowns, an old man, made a television address in Paris a few years ago in which he [offered an explanation] for the dearth of good young circus clowns. "When I was a child, my father, bless him, broke my legs, so that I would walk comically, as a clown should," the old man

---

8 The terms "insane," "unnatural," and "irrational" are convergent. The insane are irrational, and irrationality is unnatural for a creature to whose nature reason is essential.

said. . . . "Now there are people who would take a poor view of that sort of thing."9

What is unthinkable for some people may be for others not only perfectly reasonable but exquisitely correct.

Moreover, what is unthinkable for a person may vary from one time to another. The necessities of the will are not necessarily or always permanent. They are subject to change, according to changes in the contingent circumstances from which they derive. It is even possible for a person to desire that the limits of his will should be different from what they are, and to attempt deliberately to alter them. Suppose that an action (for instance, eating human flesh) disgusts him so deeply that he cannot bring himself to perform it. But now suppose that he finds himself in circumstances that lead him to recognize both that this inability is inimical to his interests (perhaps there is nothing but people available for him to eat) and that he has no overriding reason for wishing to retain it (it was never a matter of considered principle, but only of a gut reaction). Then he might take steps to alter his volitional capacities so as to become capable of doing what he now finds unthinkable.

Needless to say, it would be out of the question for him to change himself in any such way by a sheer act of will. He could not alter his will just by making up his mind that what has been for him unthinkable is so no longer. That might be possible if the task were merely to overcome a powerful inhibition; an inhibition may sometimes be overcome by a strenuous effort of will alone. But a will limited by genuine necessity would hardly be susceptible to alteration by that sort of effort. On the other hand, it is surely open to someone for whom an action is unthinkable to try by other means, less direct than the exercise of willpower alone, to alter his own will in such a way that the action becomes thinkable for him. The fact that a person cannot bring himself to perform an action does not entail that he cannot bring himself to act with the intention of changing that fact. Nor does it entail that he cannot succeed in carrying out this intention.

In certain cases, however, acting with an intention to make the unthinkable thinkable is itself something that the person cannot bring himself to do. It may not only be unthinkable for him to perform a certain action; it may also be unthinkable for him to form an effective intention to become willing to perform it. The very idea of changing himself in that way is one he could not bring himself to endorse. Then the unthinkability of the action is so decisive that it constitutes for him a limit not only on

9 A. J. Liebling, *Between Meals* (New York: Simon and Schuster, 1962), p. 149.

what he can do but also on what he can be. It is a genuine necessity of his volitional nature. Of course, it might change, since it is a logically contingent matter and is therefore susceptible to being affected by causal forces. But the person himself cannot deliberately change it. Thus, at least in part, it defines what he must be. In this sense it is a constitutive element of his nature or essence as the person he is.

There is for triangles an alternative to being isosceles. Being isosceles is therefore an inessential or accidental characteristic of a triangle. On the other hand, it is an essential characteristic of any triangle that its interior angles equal 180 degrees. There is no alternative for a triangle but to have this characteristic; under no circumstances will a triangle have interior angles that equal more than or fewer than 180 degrees. Under no circumstances, similarly, will a person will to do what is for him unthinkable. As the set of its essential characteristics specifies the limits of what a triangle can be, so does the set of actions that are unthinkable for a person specify the limits of what the person can will to do. It defines his essence as a volitional creature. There are individuals who are prepared to do *anything,* if the consequences are sufficiently desirable – that is, if the price is right. What they will to do is therefore never determined exclusively by their own nature but is always a function of their circumstances. This means that as far as their wills are concerned, they have only accidental characteristics. And to the extent that a person is a volitional entity, such an individual is a person with no essential nature at all.

V

It is widely assumed that a person is acting under the guidance of reason, and that he is in control of himself, only when what he does accords with his judgment concerning what to do. If his judgment is overwhelmed or superseded by his feelings, he is presumed to have lost his rational self-control. According to this way of looking at things, Lord Fawn loses his self-control and ceases to be guided by reason when he finds that he cannot bring himself to continue his conversation with Andy Gowran. Suppose we say that being guided by reason is a matter of acting in accordance with one's judgment. Then Fawn is not under the guidance of reason when his judgment concerning the best course of action is swept aside by the revolt of his feelings. Moreover, to the extent that we are inclined to identify a person with what he thinks, we will not regard Fawn as being in control of himself when he is controlled instead by what he feels.

It seems to me, however, that this way of looking at things is wrong. It is a fundamental error to regard every surge of emotion against judgment as an uprising of the irrational. To be sure, there is a rather trivial sense in which feelings are inherently nonrational: They do not pertain to the faculty of reason, because they are not essentially discursive. In a more substantial sense, feelings may accord better with reason than judgment does. A person's judgment may itself be radically contrary to reason. Therefore, the fact that his judgment guides his conduct hardly means in itself that he is acting rationally. Indeed, it may well be that a failure of his will to accord with his judgment is precisely what saves him from irrationality. There is – not only among philosophers but also in the law, and even in common sense – an unfortunate tendency to suppose that when someone's will is so powerfully constrained by his emotions that he cannot help acting in a certain way, his condition is in this respect pathological. In fact, however, it may be just the opposite.

Suppose that an individual has only two options: He can incur a minor injury to his finger or he can bring about the destruction of the world. Is it a necessary condition of sanity that, so far as the influence of his emotions goes, he must be no less capable of pursuing the latter alternative than of pursuing the former? Does the emotional balance implied by mental health require that he possess an equal capacity to choose either one of the two courses of action? Must the conduct of a psychologically sound person depend exclusively on his judgment concerning which of the two alternatives is preferable? Surely not. Someone who made up his mind to sacrifice the world in order to spare his finger would thereby give a convincing indication of severe mental disorder. But the indication would be considerably more grave if he not only made this judgment but also showed that he was capable of actually carrying it out. In that case, he would without question be altogether out of his mind.

On the other hand, suppose that someone made up his mind to let the world be destroyed for the sake of his finger, but that he could not go through with this intention because an overpowering surge of emotion prevented him despite himself from doing so. Suppose that his feelings revolted against his judgment, in other words, and that they constrained him from doing what he had deliberately made up his mind to do. The emergence into view of his incapacity to perform the action in question would substantially, or at least to some degree, *vindicate* his sanity. It would show that the irrationality displayed in his horrendous judgment did not, after all, go very deep.

Unthinkability is a mode of necessity with which the will sometimes binds itself and limits choice. This limitation may be an affirmation and revelation of fundamental sanity. There are certain things that no thoroughly rational individual would ever consider doing. But if a person did somehow *consider* doing them, and even go so far as to *make up his mind* to do them, a basically sane person could not actually bring himself to *do* them. Sanity consists partly in being subject to just such incapacities.

It is often mistakenly supposed that irresistible inclinations and insurmountable inhibitions are invariably symptoms or constituents of mental or emotional disorder. Sometimes they are in fact manifestations of a person's fundamental rationality – a rationality so deeply rooted that it cannot be rendered impotent by mere transient conviction or intent. This fundamental rationality may at times protect the person, by mobilizing his emotions, from succumbing to the influence of radical disturbances of his judgment.

The will of a rational agent need not be, then, empty or devoid of substantial character. It is not necessarily altogether formal and contentless, having no inherent proclivities of its own. If a person's will were a completely featureless instrument, with no capacity other than to transmute his judgment about what to do into an effective expression of his active powers, then he would closely resemble the "bare person" to which Rawls says utilitarianism reduces the agent of rational choice. In fact, however, it is precisely in the particular content or specific character of his will – which may salubriously lead him to act against his judgment – that the rationality of a person may in part reside.

There is a mode of rationality that pertains to the will itself. Like the mode of rationality that is articulated in the necessary truths of logic, it has to do with the inviolability of certain limits. Logical necessities define what it is impossible for us to conceive. The necessities of the will concern what we are unable to bring ourselves to do.